D0351026

FREE TO ACT

FREE TO ACT
An Integrated Approach to Acting

Mira Felner
Hunter College
The City University of New York

HOLT, RINEHART AND
WINSTON, INC.
Fort Worth   Chicago
San Francisco   Philadelphia
Montreal   Toronto   London
Sydney   Tokyo

Publisher:	Charlyce Jones Owen
Acquisitions Editor:	Janet Wilhite
Project Editor:	Michael D. Hinshaw
Production Manager:	Kathy Ferguson
Art & Design Supervisor:	Guy Jacobs
Text Designer:	Caliber Design Planning, Inc.

Library of Congress Cataloging-in-Publication Data

Felner, Mira, date.
    Free to act : an integrated approach to acting / Mira Felner.
        p.   cm.
    Bibliography: p.
    Includes index.
    ISBN 0-03-013237-1
    1. Acting.   I. Title.
PN2061.F44   1989
792′.028—dc20   89-11034
                                                                    CIP

ISBN: 0-03-013237-1

Address editorial correspondence to: 301 Commerce Street, Suite 3700, Fort Worth, TX 76102

Address orders to: 6277 Sea Harbor Drive, Orlando, FL 32887
                            1-800-782-4479, or 1-800-433-0001 (in Florida)

Printed in the United States of America

0 1 2 3   118   9 8 7 6 5 4 3 2 1

Holt, Rinehart and Winston, Inc.
The Dryden Press
Saunders College Publishing

FOR JOSHUA
who loves the audience

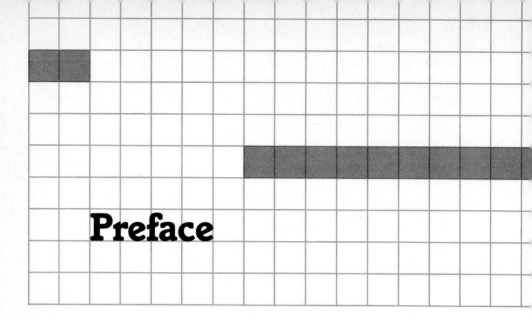

Preface

The freedom to act is born in the union of feeling, thought, and action. This book presents an integrated approach to acting that links understanding with experiential knowledge. Its system of progressively developed exercises enables students to relate physical, psychological, and analytic techniques. The principles presented in the text are not offered as dogma, but as a guide toward discovering a personal and organic creative process.

The departure point for the book is the importance of a strong physical technique for the actor. Although action and intention are underscored, purposeful action is not inherently theatrical if physical energy is blocked and the body dynamic is flaccid and unfocused. The directed use of physical energy serves as the basis for psychological technique. The work on text emphasizes discovering the action inherent in a play and provides a bridge between analysis and stage energy.

The book is designed for a one-year sequence of course work that acquaints students with the fundamentals of acting. One-semester courses may use the material selectively. Mastery of these techniques, of course, requires years of intensive study, and the text may complement more advanced classes as well. Questions of style are inappropriate for beginning work and are not directly addressed

The book is divided into four sections designed to provide a carefully developed system of training. Part I—**Preparing the Body to Act**—frees the body and voice to permit the effective expression of thoughts and feelings. It emphasizes the dynamic use of focused physical energy. Part II—**Internalizing the Dramatic Situation**—teaches the use of that energy to give physical life to the elements of the dramatic situation. The fundamentals of the Stanislavski system are introduced and each concept is explored through exercises. Part III—**Understanding the Script**—establishes a basic understanding of dramatic structure as it informs an actor's choice of action. The guide to scene analysis enables the actor to draw maximum physical energy from dramatic content. Part IV—**The Integrated Process**—explores characterization and the rehearsal process. Its goal is to provide the actor with a working integrated technique.

Although each chapter builds developmentally, the book is designed to be flexible enough to serve a variety of instructional situations. The linear development required of a text does not necessarily reflect the way an actor learns. Physical technique is integrated over a period of time during which the actor is also learning the analytic and psychological base of the work. Because actors develop physical, emotional, and intellectual skills simultaneously, an instructor can easily draw from each section of the text as needed. In a class that emphasizes scene study, the first chapters in Parts I, II, and III could be assigned concurrently. A student would be readying the body while learning the process of action and intention and developing analytic tools for scene study. Teachers who work improvisationally before beginning scene study may prefer to use the book sequentially. Where voice and movement classes are part of the curriculum, Part I can help the actor find the bridge between physical technique and scene work. The material in Part IV integrates earlier skills and requires technical readiness. The text can accommodate various approaches; however, within each chapter, the technical development is progressive and the material is best studied in the order presented.

Each chapter contains a logical system of technical and theoretical information immediately followed by illustrative exercises that relate each new concept to a physical experience. Many of the exercises are original, others are variations on ones I was taught, some are borrowed from colleagues. Feel free to experiment with these. I agree with Bobby Lewis that exercises are meant to be "handed down." Exercises are followed by questions that guide the students toward an understanding of the experience they are exploring. Voice and movement exercises are straightforward in their presentation so that instructors who have not been trained in these areas can easily use and assess them. A constant lookout for inhibiting tension and improper respiration can aid students in this work. Observe all warnings carefully and avoid any risk of injury. The use of an acting journal to record responses facilitates the assimilation of the technical lessons into an integrated process.

Two chapters are devoted to the development of a character, unusual in a beginning acting text. This is based on the conviction that unless characterization is broached early in the training, students fall into the comfortable pattern of personalizing a scene and playing themselves in every role. This becomes a limiting approach to dramatic material and leads to confusion as to who is on the line in the dramatic situation—the actor or the character. Characterization is an important arena for **integrated technique**—the unifying concept of this book.

The final chapter on rehearsal guides students through the process of preparing a scene for acting class. It integrates the techniques of earlier lessons into a workable and practical approach to scene study. Checklists are offered to help beginning actors keep track of the many elements that need to be included as they work. A glossary that contains technical terms is included. These terms appear in bold italics the first time they are used in the text for cross reference. A bibliography is provided for those who wish to pursue further study.

The goal of this book is to provide the student-actor with an understanding and experience of the complex process through which an actor is formed. It dispels the myth that actors are born not taught. While there is no doubt that talent, intuition, and instinct are vital, they enhance technique, they do not replace it. Good actors work to develop their skills over a lifetime. This book strives to make the actor's work intelligible, without detracting from its magic.

Acknowledgments

No book on acting can be written in isolation. The many exercises and ideas developed in this text were inspired by my teachers and evolved through my students. To both I am indebted. The influence of Kristin Linklater, with whom I studied many years ago, is particularly evident in the chapter on voice. Several of my students made extraordinary contributions to the work—Diana Schmitt, who worked as my acting partner to refine many of the exercises; Margit Edwards and Art Duquette, who posed for the solo photographs; and my students from 1987 to 1988, who tested the exercises and posed for the group photos. A special thank you to Ashley Shepherd for her careful reading of the manuscript and comments from the student's perspective.

I am grateful to my colleagues at Hunter College—Edwin Wilson, Patricia Sternberg, and Marvin Seiger for their interest and encouragement; Ruth Ramsey for sharing her knowledge of articulation and phonetics; Gregory Cole for thoughts on voice and movement; and Michael Posnick for his ever-inspirational dialogue. To Polina Klimovitskaya, thank you for your presence as editor, sounding board, questioner, technical authority, and caring friend.

I am appreciative of all the help I received from my editor at Holt, Rinehart and Winston, Karen Dubno, who made me say more with less.

Thanks are also due Robert Corrigan for his comments and concern. My gratitude to Viking Penguin Inc. for permission to reprint excerpts from plays, to Patrick Sciarrata and Joanna Sherman of the Bond Street Theatre Coalition, and to Jim Moore for his ability to make marathon exercise photo sessions enjoyable. I would like to acknowledge the contribution of Peter Cunningham, whose production photographs enhance this book, and the role of the following colleagues, whose comments helped during the final drafts: Robert Barton, University of Oregon; Betty Bernhard, Pomona College (California); Gladys Crane, University of Wyoming; Murray Hudson, Ashland College (Ohio); Bill Kester, San Jose City College (California); Bill Kuhlke, University of Kansas; Tom Mitchell, University of Illinois; Jack McCullough, Trenton State University (New Jersey); Henry McDaniel, Freed Hardeman College (Tennessee); Robert McDonald, University of Connecticut; Norman Myers, Bowling Green State University (Kentucky); Pauline Peotter, Portland State University (Oregon); Stephen Rudnicki, State University of New York at Old Westbury; and Tom Whitaker, Indiana State University—many thanks.

Thanks to my son Joshua for understanding my commitment and forgiving those maternal lapses. The greatest debt is owed my husband Richard for his generous willingness to discuss ideas, edit copy, and serve as an exercise guinea pig. Thank you both for the love and support that makes all things possible.

New York City
November 1988   *M.F.*

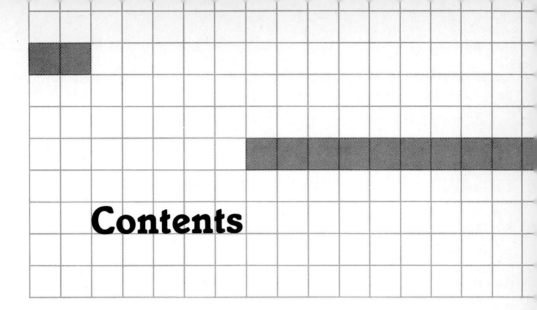

Contents

PART III   Understanding the Script   155

10 The Elements of Dramatic Analysis   157

11 The Scene as Microcosm of the Play   172

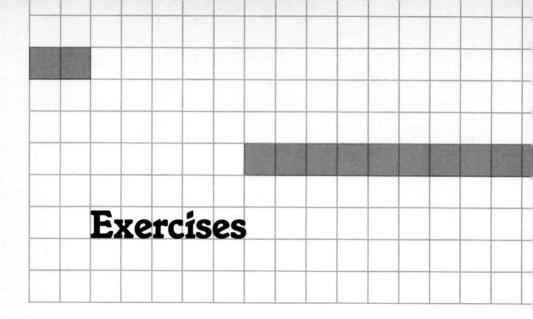

Exercises

FREE TO ACT

Introduction

Behind whatever is dramatic lies the movement of the soul outward toward forms of action, the movement from perception toward patterns of desire, and the passionate struggle to and from the deed or event in which it can manifest its nature.

Stark Young, *The Theatre*

We are about to explore the process through which an actor meets the technical demands of the stage—honing the body, voice, intellect, and emotions into a potent tool of expression. The magic and power of the theatrical experience lie in the actor's ability to integrate creative energy.

The relationship between mind and feeling, action and emotion, body and intellect is the subject of this book. Too often we see these ideas as polarities. In fact, they are part of a dynamic series of reciprocal relationships that inform the actor's creative choices. You will discover that it is impossible to isolate your physical, emotional, and mental processes. They each trigger responsive action in the others. Thoughts and feelings reside in the body, so our work will emphasize the release of physical blocks as the key to opening an actor's creative potential.

Because a responsive and expressive body is the basis of acting technique, Part I develops your physical skills and awareness. Part II guides you in using this new-found physical energy to give life to the drama. Since you must make strong action choices according to the logic of your character and play, Part III focuses on script analysis as a source of action. The concluding section works to integrate earlier lessons through work on characterization and the rehearsal process.

The Nature of the Dramatic Situation

Action is at the very heart of the dramatic situation. It is the word we use to describe both dramatic structure and its portrayal on stage. The very words *actor* and *performer* reflect the idea of actively doing something. It is not possible to be a passive actor. The two terms are mutually contradictory. If you are not in action, you are preparing for action or responding to action. Complete passivity is antitheatrical. The word *theatre* comes from the Greek word *teatron*, which means "seeing place," and you, the actor, must provide the audience with something to actively watch.

Much of good acting depends on making interesting and creative action choices. Because every decision you make must enable you to act effectively within the dramatic situation, it is crucial to understand how the elements of the drama interact to produce good theatre. The better able you are to analyze your scenes and plays, the more informed your artistic judgment. Understanding brings confidence, and confidence fosters the freedom to create.

Your life on stage is always prescribed by the dramatic situation. Most plays you will work on present a carefully structured event, where mounting tensions lead to a climactic moment. While life often meanders along its course, drama condenses and compresses—the dramatic situation lives on the verge of eruption and eventually explodes. The driving energy in the drama is *conflict*.

Conflict

Conflict comes in many forms. Most often characters are pitted against each other because of opposing goals and desires. Sometimes an individual must battle against an external force or situation. Often the conflict is within oneself. In each case, the dramatic situation involves conflict and struggle. It is this confrontation between opposing forces that gives theatre its life.

Objective

Objective is the term usually used to express your goal, purpose, or intention in a dramatic situation. Inherent in the formulation of the objective is the idea that you must overcome an obstacle to achieve your end. Because your objective is always conceived with the idea of winning a conflict, objectives are always expressed in terms of an active verb that can spur you to action and victory. The stronger the verb you choose, the more energized the stage action will be.

Obstacles

The dramatic situation is wrought with **obstacles** to goals and desires. These obstacles intensify the conflict, strengthen our resolve, and increase the energy of the struggle. Dramatic tempo and rhythm change accordingly.

From this driving force of conflict and obstacle the inner life of the actor's work is created. Each choice of action on the stage is a step toward winning the conflict and overcoming the obstacles.

Personalization

A primary goal for you, as an actor, is to make the audience care what happens to your character. You achieve this by internalizing your character's *objectives*—making your character's needs and goals your own. We call this **personalizing a role.**

For a drama to be effective on stage, the conflict must be of great moment to the character. It is your responsibility as an actor to make the conflict compelling. Although not all situations will be of equal importance or magnitude in an objective sense, what is important is the subjective level of significance they hold for your character. For instance, comedy rarely involves a life and death situation, but it is precisely because the characters react and feel as if it were that we find their predicament humorous. More serious drama turns on more significant and meaningful events. A character who is not deeply invested in the outcome of the situation is of little dramatic interest.

Because theatre compresses life, you must play your conflict as if crisis were imminent. You must feel an urgency that directs all your energy toward achieving your goals and winning your struggle. On stage, where a lifetime of meaning is compressed into a two-hour play or a two-minute scene, you must make every moment count. When we see individuals in crisis, they evoke in us a sense of empathy and concern that draws upon our emotions. This is what causes us to identify with characters in a play.

Action

If conflict is the driving force of the dramatic situation, then **action** is the means of resolving the conflict. The choice of action is a consequence of who you are and what you want. Action for an actor should be the most expedient means of achieving an objective within the limitations of character and situation. The actions you take as an actor will lead to the eventual outcome of the dramatic situation. Action then serves your objective, while working toward a victorious resolution of the conflict.

Choice

The ability to make effective and creative *action choices* defines your merit as an actor. These are made in accordance with your character and the circumstances that have shaped him or her, as well as the conditions that are prevalent within the dramatic situation. The range of choice available to you as an actor is determined by:

1. The freedom of your imagination.
2. The ability of your body and voice to give effective expression to your most daring choices.

Given Circumstances

The **given circumstances** are those conditions that determine your choice of action and objective. You can only act in terms of who you are and under what conditions you are operating. The given circumstances of a dramatic situation can be discovered in answer to the questions *who, what, where, when,* and *why.*

Imagination and the "Magic If"

The ability to imagine yourself making choices and taking actions under a set of imaginary conditions is the essential departure point for work in the theatre. If you cannot make the dramatic situation real for you there is no basis from which to act. But if you believe in your circumstances, your actions will have credibility. Stanislavski called this the **"magic if"**— behaving as "if" you were really living within the imaginary conditions of the stage. It is "magic" because the power of such a leap of faith gives truth to the dramatic reality.

When you are on stage with other actors, the *magic if* must be extended to include other characters. You must ask yourself how you would behave if this other person were indeed the king or queen, Juliet or Romeo.

The *magic if* is the fulcrum of your acting technique. It enables you to let your homework on given circumstances propel you into a role. If you believe in the given circumstances, you can live the part as if it were really happening.

These concepts—*conflict, obstacle, action, objective, given circumstances,* and the *magic if*—are the basis of an actor's technique. During our work together you will learn to give physical life to these elements of the dramatic situation.

Acting in the Dramatic Situation

For an actor on stage, the dramatic situation has two components:

1. an objective or goal
2. an action toward the goal

Your job is to analyze the components of the dramatic situation to determine who you are, what you want, what your obstacles are, and what the circumstances are that delimit your behavior. Within the logic of the dramatic situation, you must make coherent action choices that are directed toward achieving your objective. These physical choices must be executed articulately and eloquently by a responsive body and voice.

An actor's work is therefore twofold: an intellectual process and a psychophysical action. Acting students must train their minds as they train their bodies, learning to feel action in the written word and to think with their bodies.

The more integrated our thoughts, feelings, and bodies, the more easily the process of perception—choice—action occurs. This psychokinetic coordination is the focus of actor training. We strive to hone our awareness and sensitivity so the process is energized and quickened.

If your body is inhibited in any way, then no matter how well you have understood the dramatic situation, you will be unable to act to realize the resolution of the conflict that is the essence of the drama. If you cannot correctly analyze dramatic material, then your physical technique will be incorrectly applied. An actor's mind and body must work in creative collaboration.

Understanding Acting Technique

Although the work you are about to begin is geared to prepare you for the successful integration of thought, feeling, and action, it will first be necessary to isolate skills and develop techniques individually before trying to do everything at once. You may feel ready to jump in all at once, so some of this careful technical work may seem frustrating in the beginning. However, if you try to short-circuit the process, your acting will always be technically incomplete. A pianist does not try to play a Beethoven sonata in performance without developing keyboard technique and learning to read music and interpret dynamics. Each skill is learned separately, but the final product is the union of technique, understanding, and inspiration we call art.

Acting technique is less formally structured than other arts, yet it has more component skills than other art forms. Voice, movement, diction, script analysis, and emotional accessibility are all fundamental. Singing, dancing, fencing, gymnastics, and circus may often be expected of today's actor. Remember that technique is an ongoing process, a system toward an end. It is not the end in itself. As you work, you will adapt technical lessons to your strengths and needs.

You are both the artist and the instrument of expression. You must therefore work to expand your creative potential. Acting is a process of self-exploration and discovery, and you are embarking on an exciting adventure into yourself. You will find that you are capable of increasingly dynamic expression. Push your limits. The freer your body, mind, and emotions, the greater the range of artistic choices open to you.

The imagination is fettered to our limitations. An actor cannot choose to do what is feared, so each area of resistance must be addressed. Often breaking down one block releases others. You will be surprised at the changes within you during the course of our work.

Learning Discipline

Progress requires discipline and commitment, so you must be demanding of yourself to make gains. Above all, it is essential to respect the process through which an actor grows. You must value it for yourself and for others. When you work alone, you must do so with diligence and concentration. When you work in a group, the acting classroom must be a safe and protected place, free of judgments. Some have called it a sanctified or holy place; the religious images are used to underscore the basic premise: All efforts are taken seriously and received with respect.

Punctuality, attentiveness, and preparedness are all signs of respect for the work. Coming late to acting class disrupts the creative atmosphere and may cause you to miss the warm-up that readies you for the day's work. Showing interest in other students' efforts encourages progress and fosters mutual trust. Being prepared is essential to maintaining the creative flow. When you work with others, it is upsetting if a scene partner has not studied the material or is consistently late to rehearsal. Antagonism and anxiety engendered by an uncaring actor can stymie the creative process. If you cannot count on your partners to be there, ready and committed, it is impossible to trust them with your feelings. Actors have a special obligation to be responsible to each other and to their work.

To develop acting technique requires *discipline.* You must be demanding of yourself if you are to make gains. All exercise regimens are hard to maintain without the proper attitude. Understanding the challenge is the key to meeting it.

Keeping a Journal

Acting is an immediate and ephemeral experience. A moment passed cannot be re-created. Often technical gains can be equally elusive unless we concretize the lesson in a meaningful way. Keeping a journal of your daily work is an effective means of assessing progress and developing understanding.

Start your acting log in a small notebook that you can easily carry with you regularly. In it should be kept acting class notes, rehearsal notes, scene and character analyses, accounts of personal experiences that affect acting, and a log of your work on exercises in this book. You will be given guidance in making these entries as you work through the text.

The journal will sharpen your thinking and help untangle confusion. You should make an entry after every acting class. Use class time for doing and watching, the journal for evaluating and understanding. Do not attempt to judge your work while you are acting. The critic and the actor cannot coexist simultaneously. That is why the journal is so helpful. It enables you to commit to action in class and then evaluate the experience in a consistent and meaningful way. As questions arise, they should be noted in the log. Some answers will be found as you work. Others will need clarification from your teacher.

An important part of your log should be a section of personal responses to the day's work. Often our performance, or the work of others, provokes strong emotions. Through writing, you can work through these feelings and learn from them. The acting journal should not be confused with a diary, however. Only those emotions and experiences directly related to your acting should be included.

Keeping a journal is an important part of the acting process. Not only does it teach you discipline while clarifying technical lessons, it serves as a chart of your personal growth and gains. Most students feel closely connected to their logs and enjoy referring back to them at later dates to affirm their progress.

Making the Exercises Work

The exercises you will encounter are designed to enhance the perception so necessary for an actor. They work together to develop personal awareness and theatrical sensibility. It is important to understand the lesson implicit in each exercise, *but do not go for results!* It is the working process that counts. You must do each exercise with maximum focus and concentration to derive the optimum benefit.

Read each exercise carefully all the way through, before attempting the work! The directions often have warnings of physical dangers, and moving incorrectly during even relatively stressless work can cause injury, so don't take shortcuts. Make sure you have understood what is being asked of you before you proceed.

Many exercises are best attempted under the guidance of an instructor who can provide objective insight. Because you may often work alone, you will note that exercises are followed by questions designed to aid you in assessing your performance. Answer these questions carefully in your logs. They are keyed to developing your understanding of the evolving technique.

There is no single correct way of performing an exercise! While standards are subjective, there are some objective criteria. If the body is inhibited and the voice blocked, emotions will be forced or contrived, and theatrical energy will be lacking. If you have not understood an exercise or done your homework on a scene, the work will lack clarity. You will know whether you have acted with truth and openness. You will sense whether you could have gone further but held back. It is important to evaluate your own work honestly. The dialogue you have with yourself in your journals will enable you to grow from each exercise.

The exercises you will do are progressive. Each section of the book assumes that lessons have been learned from earlier chapters. As technical demands increase, you will be required to synthesize more skills. Try to work each chapter thoroughly, repeating exercises that gave you difficulty on a first encounter. You will be surprised how earlier exercises become easier when you return to them a week or two later.

Each actor grows and achieves at a different pace. Some students make immediate gains, while others work more slowly and then make a sudden quantum leap forward. It is important to avoid comparing your work to that of other students. Not only does that create unnecessary frustrations or ego-trips, but it ultimately damages the supportive atmosphere necessary for work in the theatre. A competitive ambience in acting class places the focus on results instead of process, destroying the very fabric of an actor's technique.

Accepting Criticism

Acting is a public art. All that we do is seen by others. Public criticism is part of the process. It is important to learn to accept having your work evaluated in front of others, so you can grow from the experience instead of being hurt by it. No one likes to hear critical comments, but without such an evaluation, it is difficult to find a direction in which to work, and a focus for your energy.

An actor's work is personal, so if you criticize others, you must do so constructively and tactfully. Avoid making facile value judgments (I liked X, or Y was no good). Instead make evaluative comments that give the actor a specific point to develop. Criticism must be given thoughtfully if it is to be effective.

Often criticism may feel harsh and unkind. You must learn to take it technically, not personally, or you will be paralyzed by your emotions and close off areas of technical development. The best way to profit from criticism is to take in a spirit of self-interest, constantly asking yourself what comments can be useful. Learning to take advantage of criticism and minimize its sting is part of an actor's training.

Acting Through Improvisation

Working in unscripted improvisations develops your creative skills, for it is *your* acting choices that determine the outcome of the dramatic situation. **Improvisation** teaches the actor to make intelligent, bold, and imaginative choices, while developing the skill and courage to implement ideas. We will use this technique to liberate the creative actor in ourselves.

Michel Saint-Denis, the great director and teacher, underscored that improvisation is "the true essence, the real substance of acting".[1]

Because improvisation does not rely on text, set, or costumes, and is primarily physical, you will learn the need for a responsive body and voice; the importance of letting the imagination flow through the body; and to give in to expressive impulses physically and emotionally. Most importantly, you will come to let thought and feeling inhabit action.

Because you cannot predict your partner's actions, improvisation teaches how to work through the creative process, to listen and "take in"; to establish imaginary relationships, to share the stage, and to develop a sense of "the first time" every time. Improvisation enhances your communciation skills.

Because you can never be sure what will happen next in an improvisation, you will learn to be in a state of centered readiness; to focus and concentrate; to be open, receptive, spontaneous, and ingenious; to develop creative freedom and control; and to trust the impulses of your imagination.

We will use improvisation to draw upon your resources to become actor-creators, with the courage and daring to put your talents to the test. Your work as interpreters of text will be nourished through this process. In the words of Michael Chekhov, "you will eventually be confirmed in the belief that dramatic art is nothing more than constant improvisation, and that there are no moments on stage when an actor can be deprived of his right to improvise."[2]

All the techniques we explore improvisationally will be applied to work with text in Parts III and IV of the book. You will immediately see ways of applying these exercises to enhance and enliven your scenes. Remember, improvisation and scenework are not mutually exclusive, they energize each other.

All that we do as actors is geared to that magic moment when the word is given form and action. To make the play live is the goal of the theatre. Together we will discover how to give life energy to the drama.

[1]Michel Saint-Denis, *Training for the Theatre* (New York: Theatre Arts Books, 1982), pp. 80–86.

[2]Michael Chekhov, *To the Actor* (New York: Harper & Row, 1953), p. 40.

PART I

Preparing the
Body to Act

Figure 1.1 Michael McGuigan demonstrates physical eloquence in the Bond Street Theatre's production of *Pentagon*. (Photo—Joanna Sherman.)

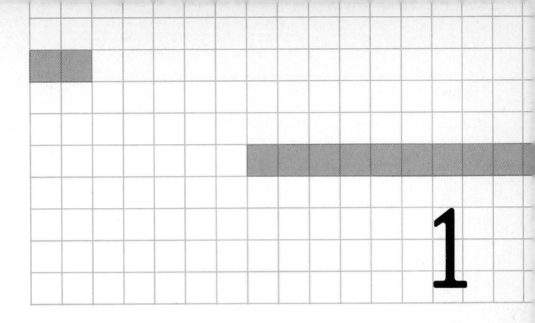

Centering

. . . man's whole body records his emotional thinking.
Mabel Ellsworth Todd, *The Thinking Body*

Physical eloquence is the mark of the trained actor. In the theatre, where the body expresses the language of the heart and mind, the audience knows what we think and feel only through the actor's movement, gesture, and voice. The body must be honed and tuned to attain precision and artistry, for our expressive potential is limited by the range of our physical prowess.

Through our work, you will see that the body is involved in a complex series of relationships with our mental and emotional processes. Alter your physical state, and your emotions shift as well. Our very thoughts affect muscle tension and movement. A change in any facet of our being engenders change in another. These interactions will become the basis of an active and controlled technique.

In this chapter, we will achieve centering and neutrality through work on relaxation, alignment, and respiration, while concurrently developing the qualities that constitute optimum physical function: balance, coordination, flexibility, and strength. Your physical technique takes time and work to develop. Do not feel frustrated if change comes slowly. Enjoy the active dialogue you are beginning with your body as you awaken new sensations.

13

Center

The concept of **center** reflects the belief that the body is capable of achieving an economical and efficient use of its own energy through an integration of physical, emotional, and intellectual activity. Finding a unified source for all expression is the cornerstone of an integrated approach to acting technique, for it permits breath, voice, and movement to accurately reflect an actor's inner life. The work in this chapter leads the body to the centered state.

    Centering is predicated on certain biological facts about animal life:

1. Locomotion and breathing evolved together in a reciprocal relationship.
2. Body rhythms must work in harmony for optimum function.
3. Pulse and respiration increase simultaneously in response to physical, emotional, or intellectual impulses.
4. Changes in movement and respiration create intellectual and emotional changes.
5. A finely tuned internal communication system exists in the body, relaying signals and impulses through the body center.

    These principles form the basis of an integrated acting technique. We will work to coordinate physical and vocal expression of thoughts and feelings through this central switchboard.

    While few of us have ever given serious thought to where the center of our body lies, we all are aware of the sensation of being "off." On an "off" day, things go wrong, repeated accidents or mistakes occur, our thoughts are unclear, and we feel generally incapable of efficient function. These days, when we seem not to control feelings, movements, and thoughts in a productive way, happen to all of us. But an actor cannot be susceptible to such moments. The curtain will go up on our "off" days, and we must know how to harness our energy. The ability to quickly regain optimum use of our resources is called *centering*.

    As a point of reference, let's locate the physical center at our center of gravity, mid-torso, beneath the sternum at its highest point and several inches below the navel at its lowest. This placement of center is crucial to the integrated process, for not only does it mark the physical center, but it is also the point of convergence of the muscular, emotional, and intellectual impulses within our bodies. Most important, it is the point of refueling the body with oxygen that fires all life within us. It is located between an ideally free and flexible upper torso and a strong pelvic region. At center, strength, flexibility, freedom, and balance are coordinated through the respiratory process. Concentration is required to achieve this state of dynamic equilibrium.

    The center is also an emotional locus. All strong emotions alter the state of well-being in the central torso. Think about where your body registers strong feelings, and you will note that the area below the sternum is the first to react to emotional changes. We have come to call these strong emotions "gut feelings" referring to the very point of sensation. "Butterflies in the stomach" and "belly laughs" are ways our language has come to express this sense of emotional center. Eastern cultures have long thought of the center as a source of maximum energy release as well as inner tranquility.

Although intellectual processes find their origin in brain activity, the body takes consciousness of these thoughts as they relate to emotions and movement in the center. Brain function is immediately translated into an impulse. Even purely abstract thought processes will ultimately alter the state of the body center. Think hard about some abstract philosophical problem and note how this is translated into respiratory change in the abdomen.

The exercises in this chapter work together to help you discover the center as the body's central switchboard coordinating integrated use of all your resources.

Exercise 1.1: Mental Impulse and Center

Place a foot-high object on the floor three feet away from where you are standing. Prepare mentally to leap over it. As you take the leap, note all the changes that occur in the torso. Was a breath taken automatically? Did the strong pelvic muscles prepare for the exertion necessary to perform the jump? What was the reaction of the upper torso? Did it freely respond to the body's reorganization?

All these thoughts occurred as a result of the mental thought "to leap." So you now can easily see how mental impulses are sent directly to center to prepare for efficient physical performance. Note your observations in your journal.

Exercise 1.2: Emotion and Center

During the next few days, take note of your body's reaction to emotionally intense situations. Such situations run the gamut from being late to class, to worrying about an exam, to romantic or sexual excitation, to anger at a friend or family member. Observe respiratory changes when you are in these states. What alterations occur? Does the sensation in the lower abdomen change with each new stimulus? You will notice that although these were emotional situations, physiological changes occurred through the body center. Heartbeat, breath, and stomach all respond in some way to our feelings. Enter your observations in your journal, noting carefully the integrated response system of the body.

The dramatic situation is usually emotionally charged. If you are to truly experience the feelings of your character, you must develop the technique to make those responses as organic as your own. The more you grow in awareness of center, the greater the integration of emotional, mental, and physical life on stage.

The Movable Center

Although there is a placement of center that ensures optimum body function, most of us have developed an idiosyncratic sense of center. Observe someone who has placed the body center in the lower pelvis, whose walk and movement lead from that area, or the individual who leads with the head, or the upper chest. While such misplacement is physically ineffi-cient, it reveals much personal data. We receive an immediate impression of a personality from the placement of center. Head centers seem to be cerebral and controlled, whereas pelvic centers sensual and erotic. You may, in fact, change the placement of your own center as a response to mood, emotional state, or situation. Note how your center moves down when you are sexually aroused, or up when you are tense or frightened. If center shifts as a function of personality, emotion, or situation, then as actors, we must work to develop sensitivity to these alterations to heighten our portrayal of character and dramatic context.

Before we can use this concept to establish characterization, it is important to examine ourselves to see where we may have placed our per-sonal center. If we do not know where our center is, how can we alter it for acting purposes?

Exercise 1.3: Finding Your Center

Examine your own behavior. Do you have an instinctive sense of where your center is? Stand with your eyes closed, and sense your breath as it enters the body and flows down. Does it reach all the way down into the pelvic region? If not, then you are probably not properly centered. Now walk around the room in your natural gait. Do you sense yourself leading with any part of the body? Note which part is leading, and try to keep the body on a vertical plane. Note your discoveries in your log. If you cannot find your personal center, do this exercise with a fellow student and see if you can help each other make these determinations. What have you discovered about your center? Is it placed in the optimum position for efficient use of energy?

Over the next few days, observe people around you and see if you can determine where they have placed their centers. Note what impression people give as a result.

You probably had some difficulty locating your center and achieving proper placement. This is to be expected at the beginning. This is a process that takes time and requires learning to think *inside* of your body to coordinate physical and mental life. The exercises we are about to do will improve your sense of center and give you a solid base for more advanced acting technique.

Kinesthetic Awareness

The perception of the relationship of our muscles and bones is **kinesthetic awareness.** This ability enables us to sense our position in space, regulate movement, develop movement memory, and know our thoughts and feelings as they are expressed by the body. These are all crucial skills for actors. Our kinesthetic sense is an information system which enables us to control and adjust our bodies to ensure free and efficient function.

The world we live in has alienated us from our bodies. Machines now do much of the work we did with our hands. In our technological culture, where survival does not depend on physical skills—climbing, leaping, running, throwing—we have grown generally less fit. All the physical fitness regimens and fads of today are a result of the fundamentally sedentary lives we live which have diminished the need for an efficiently operating body. Would a cave man have needed aerobics and exercise classes? His very survival would have depended on his kinesthetic awareness.

Our clothes, dictated by fashion, often impede natural movement and create deformities. High heels and skin-tight jeans do not promote normative posture or movement. How many times have we heard a woman used to wearing heels say that she is uncomfortable walking barefoot, that her legs and back hurt from foreshortened muscles, and that her natural sense of balance is now off? False ideas of ideal masculine or feminine movement distort our perception. Watch young men at the beach and you will see any number of aberrations of natural posture, as macho poses tense the upper chest, back, shoulder, and neck. The amount of energy wasted on a sexy feminine walk, where side-to-side action robs the forward impulse, deprives the body of efficient function. A major price of industrial urban society has been the loss of kinesthetic awareness.

We have become so unaware of our bodies that we no longer recognize how we stand, sit, or walk, nor are we conscious of physical mannerisms. Until some painful reminder of our bodies occurs, we remain oblivious to misplaced tension, faulty alignment, and even the lack of a full and dynamic respiratory process. Because so many processes are occurring in the body simultaneously—we breathe, move, think, feel, talk, and have vital organ function—to achieve optimum function, we need to isolate and explore the way we perform many unconscious acts. As we work, you will sense the enhanced kinesthetic consciousness which is the cornerstone of an integrated acting technique.

Often, our kinesthetic sense is distorted by personal emotions, creating a gap between our body image and reality. Take the case of the fat child who as a slender adult still retains the self-perception of obesity. It is important for the actor to distinguish between psychologically and physiologically based perceptions.

Exercise 1.4: Personal Kinesthesia

Make a detailed journal entry in which you examine your sense of physical self. How do you picture your height, weight, posture, strength, flexibility, grace, and beauty? How do you believe others perceive you? Do you feel that the two perceptions coincide? If there are differences, why do you think that is so? Do you have confidence in your ability to move well and perform physical activities? Why do you feel this way about your physical self? Choose a partner and share perceptions of each other. How closely did they correspond to your self-examination process? Remember that these observations are deeply personal and must be expressed with sensitivity.

To drive home how little we think about our bodies, try the following test for kinesthesia. Lie on the floor on your back. Is your spine straight? Is your head placed exactly between the shoulders? Can you tell where between the shoulders is? Is it turned slightly to the left or right? Is the neck out of alignment pointing the chin toward the ceiling? When you think you are perfectly straight, ask your teacher or a classmate to verify your positioning. You may be surprised at the results.

As we work, you will find a growing and changing self-awareness from which you will be able to release your full expressive potential.

Relaxation

The first step in working toward kinesthetic consciousness is to achieve a state of **relaxation** from which we can more readily sense the workings of the body. Efficient physical function requires a balance between relaxation and tension. Totally relax every muscle in the body, and you fall to the floor like a limp cloth. Completely tense every muscle, and your body assumes a paralytic rigidity. Almost every human activity requires tension and relaxation phases. Think of the beating of the heart. During the relaxed stage following a contraction, the heart rests to harness energy. If a muscle remains tense without a rest stage, strain, fatigue, and even more serious consequences may occur. It is therefore so important to release the areas of habitual tension where rest never occurs and pain may set in. This not only permits renewal of body cells but releases the flow of energy so necessary for our life on stage.

Exercise 1.5: Constructive Rest Position

Lie on the floor on your back. Keeping the feet on the floor at a distance of approximately eighteen inches, bend the knees up toward the ceiling and let the legs fall in against each other so that the knees touch, supporting each other as do two cards in a house of cards. (See Figure 1.2.) This enables the legs to stay up using the forces of gravity and without any tensing muscular intervention. The small of the back should be flat against the floor, and your arms should be folded loosely across the chest or placed by your sides with hands on your abdomen. The face is aimed toward the

Figure 1.2 Constructive Rest Position. Note the arm positions. Some women find it more comfortable to place the arms under rather than across the breast. (Photo—Jim Moore.)

ceiling continuing the horizontal plane of the front of the body. It is a
common error to point the chin at the ceiling instead of the nose, causing
tension at the back of the neck. Sense the weights of the body moving
toward center.

This position enables the body to conserve maximum energy. It is
stressless, requiring minimal muscular holding. The body has all weights
directed toward its center using natural gravitational forces. It is believed
that several minutes in this position with proper respiration can renew the
body almost as well as sleep.

Exercise 1.6: Focused Relaxation—Tension Check

As you lie in constructive rest position, check your body for tension. Slowly
think your way down your body, checking for areas of stress. Start at your
forehead and relax the muscles. Move to the temples, eyelids, cheeks, lips,
jaw, chin, and neck. Think deeply into each point, making sure to let go of
the muscles. Continue working down the body—shoulders, arms, hands,
fingers, chest, abdomen, hips, buttocks, thighs, calves, feet, toes. Take your
time and really observe the changes your mind can cause in the muscle
tissue. Recheck your body to make sure no new tension has crept back in.
Allow a deep relaxed breath into the abdomen, being careful not to
contract the upper chest and shoulders as the breath flows in. Send the
breath into the areas you have just released. Can you feel the effect of the
breath on the muscles? Repeat the process, inverting the direction from
toes to head. How does that change the body kinesthesia?

Exercise 1.7: Relaxation Variation—Tension Release

If you have been unable to send your relaxing thoughts into each part of
your body, try an isolated tension-release process. Working through the
body as before, tense and release the forehead, eyelids, temples, cheeks,
and so on. Hold the tension for approximately three seconds, and release
the breath as you relax the muscles. Often tensing body parts causes an
equal and opposite reaction—contraction followed by decontraction. In
letting go, you can feel the muscles relax. After you have worked through
the body, isolating small muscle groups, experiment with tensing
increasingly larger groups of muscles and then releasing. For example,
tense one side of the face, or one leg from toe to buttocks, then relax.

Exercise 1.8: Relaxation Images

This exercise requires a partner. Let one of you take the constructive rest position. Imagine that your partner has five-pound weights in one-inch cubes. Through fingertip pressure, your partner will place the imaginary weights on the strategic tension areas of the body—forehead, eyelids, temples, cheeks, jaw, neck, shoulders, hands, pelvis, thighs, knees, feet. As the weight is placed, feel it push you deep into the floor and sense the body growing heavier. Relax the muscles under the weight and breathe deeply into the pressure point. Let your partner remove the weights one by one through pressure and release of fingertips. Note the condition of the body. Did you let yourself physically experience the imaginary weight? Make a journal entry recording your ability to surrender to the image. Now change positions and repeat the exercise.

Invent a relaxation image of your own. Note it in your journal. For the next class, try a ten-minute relaxation period using the class's original image ideas.

Alignment

Alignment refers to the balanced arrangement of the skeletal structure which enables it to efficiently counteract the force of gravity. Balance is the key to the dynamic body, so essential to dramatic expression. As we become more and more aware of our physical processes, it becomes clear how all function interrelates. You cannot breathe properly if the spine is misaligned, nor can you relax. Misalignment forces the muscles to compensate for the disequilibrium, creating tension and fatigue, depleting the body's energy and robbing your theatrical performance. The aim of our work on posture is to free the muscles from doing the work of the bones.

NOTE: Some students may have congenital physical problems which inhibit proper alignment. These should be discussed before work begins so as not to cause further stress. If you have a physical impediment, note its effect on your alignment and movement in your journal.

Exercise 1.9: Alignment

To achieve good alignment we must establish a balance of forces along the gravitational axis of the body. Imagine a pole running vertically through the center of the body from the top of the head to the feet. (See Figure 1.3.) As you crystallize this image, arrange your body weight around this axis. If

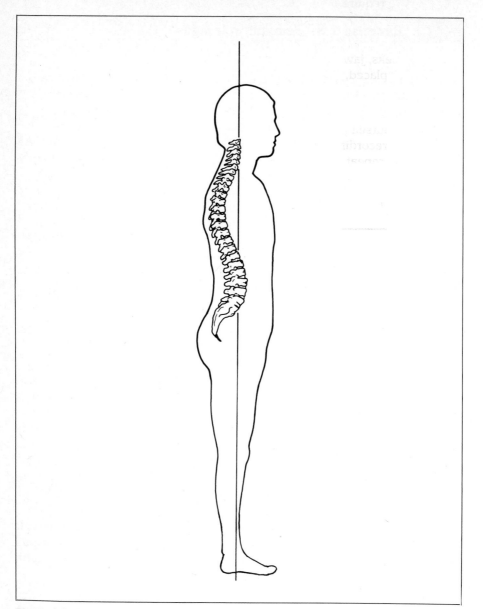

Figure 1.3 Spinal Alignment. Note the natural S curve of the spine.

any weight were suspended from one side of the pole without an equal counterweight, it would topple. The spinal column functions as a central axis in much this way. The body's major weights—head, thorax, and pelvis, must be suspended in a balanced manner off the spine. Note that the spinal column does not run down the back, as we commonly think, but through the center of the body. We often think of the vertebrae as the spine and misplace its position in the body as a result.

As you image your central pole, check to see if the body's weights are equally distributed around the central axis. Nod the head gently to locate the pivotal point that marks the top of the spine. Think up the front of the spine and down the back. Let the ribs hang suspended from the spine. Drop the shoulders. Sense the lower spine and pelvis as a support for the weight of the upper body. As you do this, think through the center of the body where the gravitational axis is located, not along the outside of the body. If the weights are in proper balance, when the spine is seen in profile, it should have a gentle and natural S curve. (See Figure 1.3.) As you "think into" these curves, note that the shallower the curve, the less the body weights are ex-centered, and the less muscular effort required to hold the body. Attempt to straighten slightly the curves of the spine.

Most of you will have some variant of completely normative posture. It may take a long time to correct years of misalignment, and initial adjustments may at first seem uncomfortable or strange and unnatural. Patience is required. After you have had your alignment examined, you should check your posture whenever you think of it during your day's activities. By constantly monitoring your position, you will slowly turn the new pattern into the most natural and comfortable one for your body.

Exercise 1.10: Sensing the Central Axis

Have someone put a mark on the floor where you feel the imaginary axis pole meets the ground. Now close your eyes, fix the pole so that it does not move, and rotate the body 360 degrees around the axis, making small movements of the feet. When you think you have completed the turn, open your eyes. Did you turn completely around? Did you stray from the mark on the floor? Now bending the knees but keeping the upright alignment of the upper torso, move the body up and down the pole as you pliez. Rotate the body around the pole again. Did your kinesthetic sense grow sharper this time?

Exercise 1.11: The Pendulum

Efficient posture enables us to maintain equilibrium with minimal effort. To achieve this, let's use the image of a pendulum. Its stable position lies in the midpoint of its path, where the force of gravity tries to hold it in a vertical position. If you swing a pendulum, it will move in equal time and distance from the midpoint of its path, gradually making smaller and smaller movements around its stable point.

Stand with a firm base, your feet about a foot apart. Imagining the body to be a pendulum, use the ankles as a pivot and swing the body forward and back in a pendulumlike motion. Go as far as you can in each direction without losing balance. Each swing will pass through your most stable point; can you find it? As the movements grow smaller, try to locate the point of dynamic equilibrium. Now swing the body from side to side. Can you sense the stable point in this direction? Is it the same point you experienced when swinging front to back? Use your kinesthetic awareness to discover a common point of balance. Note clearly in your mind the body's position. Now alternate three back-and-forth swings with three side swings. When you come to rest, decide if this was your original point of dynamic equilibrium. Has the increased awareness altered your sense of balance? Note your discoveries in your log.

Exercise 1.12: Building the Spine

The spine can be seen as a series of building blocks which support the weight of the body. To reinforce this concept, let the weight of the head pull off the central axis so that the heavy head hangs in front of the spine with the chin on the chest. Imagine the weight of the head pulling the spine over vertebra by vertebra. Let the arms hang loosely at the side, with no shoulder tension, and with the chin still on the chest. Continue moving

Figure 1.4a–e Building the Spine. Note the progressive straightening of the knees. The jaw remains relaxed and the head comes up last. (Photos—Jim Moore.)

down the spine and, when you reach the last vertebra, be sure to gently release the knees so they are slightly bent (see Figures 1.4a–e). Bounce lightly from the knees, exhaling on each bounce. As you inhale, sense the breath filling the abdomen and pushing against the thigh. Rebuild the spine vertebra by vertebra from the base up. The head, controlled by the upper spine, should be the last part of the body to return to an upright position. Be sure to check for shoulder tension. Try to coordinate the rebuilding with a steady, slow inhalation. Were you able to isolate each vertebra? How accurate were you in differentiating units of the spine? Did you sense a reestablishment of balance as you completed the rebuilding process? How different is this posture from your habitual alignment? Can you locate areas of adjustment?

Respiration

Without proper breath support, an actor is unable to perform the fundamental tasks of the theatre—action and voice. Breath animates movement and is the very material of sound. It is the lifeline of the body, bringing in oxygen to feed the cells and energize human activity. Breath records the changing rhythms of our emotional and mental life, so an open respiratory channel is vital for the actor. Any interference with the flow of air impedes our expressive ability.

Breathing can be facilitated or inhibited by our alignment and tension, which is why we have worked to achieve normative and tension-free posture. Muscle tension from any source will impede the free flow of air, robbing voice and movement of energy, power, and expression. Respiratory rhythm and skeletal movement require coordination for efficient operation.

Understanding this process kinesthetically requires knowledge of our anatomy. Inhalation occurs when the downward movement of the diaphragm lengthens the cavity around the lungs and air rushes in to fill the enlarged space. The most common error is to see the lungs as two small balloons placed in the upper chest. In fact, the lungs fill a large area reaching from a narrow apex near the base of the neck to the diaphragm at the lowest ribs in front, and touching the spinal column posteriorly (see Figure 1.5a–b). The lungs, then, are capable of filling all of the mid-torso with air by expanding the rib cage as we breathe. The diaphragm links respiration with other body processes, for it is attached to the rib cage and the spine, is adjaceant to vital organs—heart, liver, spleen—and is penetrated by the esophagus, aorta, and vena cava. The result is a series of reciprocal relationships:

1. The connection between the diaphragm and the spine and ribs causes misalignment to affect respiration and vice versa.
2. The proximity of the viscera and the breathing apparatus affects body sensation, well-being, and emotional and digestive processes.

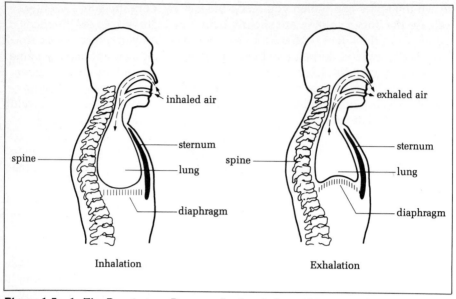

Figure 1.5a–b The Respiratory Process. As the air flows down into the lungs, the diaphragm lowers.

3. When we alter respiration through strong emotional changes or mental impulses, the diaphragm movement affects the stomach and heart.
4. All movement must be linked to breath because the diaphragm is attached to the twelfth thoracic vertebra, to which are also attached the large trapezius muscle, which connects head, shoulder, arm, and rib movements, and the psoas muscle, which controls the movement of the legs, pelvis, and lumbar spine. Through sharing this common vertebral linkage, almost all major body movement can be directly linked to a respiratory impulse.

Thus our very biology underscores the necessity of an integrated process for optimum function. It is important to work to develop kinesthetic awareness of these vital connections.

Exercise 1.13: Sensing the Respiratory Process

Lie on the floor in constructive rest position. As you breathe, trace the flow of air as it enters your nostrils, passes along the back of the palate, enters the windpipe, down the bronchial tubes, into the lungs. Feel it fill the lungs. Then trace the path in reverse as you exhale. Repeat this consciousness exercise for two minutes. How has this affected your breathing?

Now, as you breathe, become aware of the downward movement of the diaphragm displacing vital organs as you inhale. Sense all the skeletal movements in the torso. Feel the ribs expand and the sternum lift. Feel in how many directions the expansion occurs. Be aware of any tension in the muscles of the neck and shoulder and work to release holding. As you exhale, sense the rising of the diaphragm, the contraction of the ribcage, the lowering of the sternum.

Try to breathe through an integrated awareness of the skeletal and muscular changes engendered by respiration. Be cautious to release tension and keep the upper chest and shoulders relaxed. The process should be slow and natural. Do you notice any accompanying change in emotional state as you work?

Exercise 1.14: Integrating Breath and Skeletal Action

In constructive rest position, let the arms lie at the sides with hands placed gently on the lower abdomen, just below the navel. Breathe deeply, imaging the movement of the diaphragm inside of you. Exhale completely on an "fff" sound. Force out the last bits of air within you. As you do this, note what happens to the spine. Are you able to completely empty the body without an adjustment of the spinal position? Repeat this exercise on a hissing sound, watching the spine's movement, then exhale through the mouth, then through the nose. Did you notice how the spine responded to each alteration? Your observations should tell you a great deal about the relationship between spinal movement and respiration.

Balance, Coordination, Flexibility, and Strength

Navigation through crowded sets, group scenes, and stressful dramatic situation, while manipulating props or moving in limiting costumes are all part of the demands placed on the actor. Often these problems are complicated by physical character traits: think how many characters suffer from physical disabilities, from Richard III to Laura in *The Glass Menagerie*. Unless you are the master of your body, a wide range of physical character and action is removed from your repertory. There is nothing more distracting than a clumsy actor on stage. The audience becomes painfully aware of the actor as a person playing a part, and the theatrical illusion is shattered. Because the actor's body is the very material of artistic expression, it is important to develop the skills that permit aesthetic movement—balance, coordination, flexibility, and strength. The goal of movement training is to provide a disciplined body free to respond to your creative impulses.

Flexibility—Limbering the Joints

We will begin our physical workout with loosening exercises designed to limber the body. Loosening can be achieved through rotations, flexions, stretches, swings, and shakes. You will note how much easier it is to rotate and flex than it is to shake. This is because shaking requires a complete letting go and releasing of tension in the muscles. Many of you will be able to shake out the wrists and ankles, yet will have difficulty in shimmying the shoulders and hips. There is an initial resistance to letting go of the muscles of the torso, as we are psychologically more protective of this area. As we proceed through these exercises, note where your movement is inhibited and explore these psychophysical connections in your journals.

Exercise 1.15: Head Rolls

Let your head grow heavy. Drop the weight of your head forward, chin on chest, but do not allow any movement in the upper torso or lower spine in response to the weight of the head. Isolating the head and neck, slowly bring the head around over the right shoulder, facing front, and elongating and stretching the left side of the neck. Circle the head to the back, letting it hang straight back, while checking to make sure that there is no lower spine movement. (See Figures 1.6a–c.) If you dropped the head back with a clenched jaw and closed mouth, you should feel a pull down the front of the neck. Relax the jaw and open the mouth, feeling a release of tension as you let go of these areas. Slowly circle the head around the back over the left shoulder. With the head facing front, stretch the right side of the neck. Come around full circle to the front, dropping the heavy head so the chin rests on the chest. Maintain proper torso alignment as you circle. Repeat this circle slowly, making sure you feel the complete stretch at each point. Complete three circles to the right, then circle three times to the left. Let the head float up into proper alignment when you have finished. Sense the

Figure 1.6a–c Head Rolls. Remember to keep the jaw relaxed as you drop the head back. (Photos—Jim Moore.)

warmth of the blood flowing into the relaxed muscles of the neck and the new lightness of the head.

Exercise 1.16: Rotations

Now that you have released tension in the neck, let's move down to the shoulders. Bring the shoulders up to the ears as far as they will go. Circle them around to the back, attempting to have the shoulder blades meet. Lower the shoulders as far as possible and circle around as far as possible to the front. Repeat three times, then circle in the opposite direction. As you do this, you may hear the sounds of the joints loosening. Have you been breathing as you work?

Rotate the arms at the elbow, first left then right, supporting each elbow with the opposite hand. Rotate the wrists, even the fingers.

Keeping the upper torso still, rotate the pelvis in a circle around your imagined center. Rotate three times to the right, then change directions. How does this broad torso movement make you feel?

Rotate the legs one at a time from the hip joint, making large circles with the feet. Rotate the lower leg from the knees; rotate the feet from the ankles. Rotate four times in each direction.

Exercise 1.17: Torso Stretches

Standing with good alignment, feet about a foot apart, extend the left arm out to the side, then gently arc it over the head, leaning the body to the right (see Figure 1.7). The spine will curve to the right while the muscles of the left side stretch. Be careful not to let the extended arm go forward of the frontal plane of the body. Breathe into the stretch and feel the muscles release. Return to neutral and repeat with the right arm to the left side. The stretch should be felt along the arm, down the entire side of the torso past the hip joint.

Repeat Exercise 1.12, "Building the Spine." When you have rolled down the spine, take care to get a good stretch and lengthening of the spine through *small* bounces in the knees while releasing the breath. Come up slowly, rebuilding the vetebrae one by one.

To invert the spinal stretch, lie on your back on the floor. Bend the knees, bringing the feet up to the torso (see Figure 1.8a). As you inhale, raise the spine off the floor, vertebra by vertebra into an arch. As you exhale, lower the spine, rolling down the vertebrae. Repeat several times, increasing the arch on each lift. Grab your ankles and repeat. Note how

Figure 1.7 Torso Stretch. (Photo—Jim Moore.)

Figure 1.8a–c Inverted Spinal Stretch. Note the increase in the arch of the spine in each position. (Photos—Jim Moore.)

much higher the arch becomes (see Figure 1.8b). Slowly lower the back, rolling down the spine. This exercise can be extended into a full back-lift (see Figure 1.8c).

	Exercise 1.18:	Swings										

Arm Swings: Stand with the legs comfortably spaced about a foot apart with a slight give in the knees. Swing the arms from the shoulder joints back and forth. Let the momentum carry you up on your tiptoes as you

Figure 1.9a–d Torso Swings. (Photos—Jim Moore.)

swing the arms forward. Inhale as you come up on your toes; exhale as you come down, and swing the arms back. Repeat eight times. Now make large circles with the arms from the shoulders, clapping the hands as they meet in front of the body. Repeat eight times. Now swing the arms in alternation so the right arm is circling forward as the left arm is circling back. Did you have trouble coordinating the alternating swings? Now swing the arms laterally across the front of the body eight times. Did you hit into anything on these arm swings? If you did, it should indicate that you need to develop a sense of yourself in space.

Torso Swings: Stand with the legs spaced about eighteen inches apart, knees slightly bent. Drop down the spine so your fingertips are brushing the floor, head hanging down with a relaxed neck. (See Figures 1.9a–d.) Swing gently from side to side, keeping the head relaxed so it sways with each swing. Gradually increase your momentum until your arms pull you upright to the left. Let the force of gravity take you down again as you swing upright to the right. Repeat the full torso swing six times, making sure to exhale on each downward movement. Come up slowly, rebuilding the spine.

Leg swings: Stand neutrally. Find your balance center in the right pelvis. Swing the left leg from the hip, coming up as high as possible in front of the body, and as far as possible in the rear. Repeat eight times, increasing the arc on each swing. Were you able to maintain your balance?

Exercise 1.19: Shakes

Work up the arms, flutter the fingers, shake the wrists, shake from the elbows. *As you shake and flex, remember to release the breath.* Feel the exhalation carrying away body tension. Try shaking out the wrists without breathing, then shake again while exhaling. Which releases more tension? What did you discover about the relationships between breath and movement?

Lift the right leg and shake out the ankle. Really feel it loosen. Flex from the knee. Shake out the whole leg. Repeat the process with the left leg. Did you remember to exhale as you shook? Now shimmy up and down the torso, shaking out the breath as you go. What happens to the breath?

Face shake: Standing neutrally, let the head fall, chin on chest. Quickly shake the head from side to side, as if you were rapidly signaling "no," releasing sound as you shake. Did you feel all the skin on the face fall away from the bones? Did you get full vibration of the lips, of the voice?

Full-body shake: Image yourself to be a marionette whose strings are all tugged from above and then relaxed. Jump around, letting go of all the muscles. Try to release breath and sound as you jump. Did the head bob freely?

Balance and Coordination

Developing balance and coordination permits control of movement, facilitating difficult action and work with complicated props and costumes. It adds grace and beauty to gesture.

Exercise 1.20: Slow Motion

Walk around the room at normal speed, sensing the movements of your body. Now walk in slow motion. As you slow down the walk, note all the components of walking you have been performing unconsciously. Slow down the movement even more. You will discover that walking is actually a result of placing the body in disequilibrium and then recovering. When we walk at normal speed, we are unaware of the constant peril of falling in which we are placed. Etienne Decroux, the great French mime, called walking the first drama of man for this very reason. Sense the shifting weights, balance, and coordination necessary to perform this act we take for granted. Take care not to tense as you work.

Sit down in a chair. Now stand up and sit down again in slow motion. Be aware of all that the body does as you slow this action down. As you move the lower torso behind you, note the counterweight compensation of the upper torso. Feel how the swing off center must have a just balance. What does your body do to maintain equilibrium?

Exercise 1.21: Balance Through Sensing Center

Stand neutrally, breathing deeply into center. On an inhalation, turn out and lift the left leg, bending the knee out to the side. Take hold of the left foot with the right hand and bring the foot up to rest on the thigh of the leg on which you are now standing (see Figures 1.10a–c). Let go of the foot and maintain your balance. Feel how your center has moved, how your body weight has been redistributed to maintain balance. Now slowly extend the arms in front of you and raise them straight up over the head, linking thumbs. Again, feel your center's displacement. As you exhale, concentrate on your center, and keeping thumbs linked, slowly bend to touch your toes. Inhale, and return to the upright position, arms extended overhead, exhale as you bring the arms down to the sides. Lower the left leg. Repeat, raising the right leg. Were you equally balanced on each side? Try to perform this exercise without thinking of the body center or using respiratory

Figure 1.10a–c Balance Through Sensing Center. Some men find it difficult to lift the leg onto the front of the thigh. Use the modified position shown instead. (Photos— Jim Moore.)

coordination. You will find that you lose your balance without a strong mental sense of center.

Strength

Although an actor does not need the strength of a weight lifter, certain muscles of the actor's body are called upon to aid centering through the coordination of movement with breath, voice, and feeling. The muscles of the pelvic girdle support respiration while giving control for movement at our center of gravity.

Exercise 1.22: Strengthening Center

Lie on your back on the floor. Bring the knees to the chest, dangling the legs loosely. Flatten the spine against the floor, bringing the weight of the

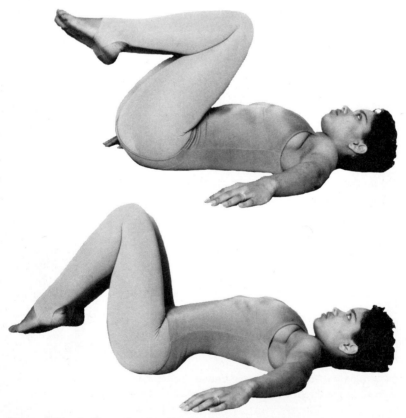

Figure 1.11a–b Strengthening Center. (Photos—Jim Moore.)

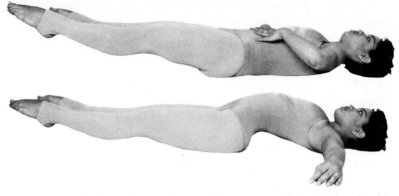

Figure 1.12a–b Strengthening Center. Be sure your abdominal and pelvic muscles are strong enough to support this exercise or you will put strain on the lower back. (Photos—Jim Moore.)

legs in toward the torso. Slowly arch the back, excentering the weight of the legs. As the arch grows deeper, you should feel the tug of the weight of the legs. Find the point at which your muscles can no longer support the weight of the legs without stress, then slowly flatten the spine, bringing the weight back to center. (See Figures 1.11a–b.) Repeat this eight times.

Still lying on the floor, extend the legs. You will find the spine naturally arches as the legs are extended. Flatten the spine against the floor, drawing the legs up toward the body. Slowly arch the back, allowing the weight of the legs to pull away from center. You should feel the muscles of the pelvis and abdomen working to perform this exercise. Repeat eight times.

When you have grown sufficiently strong, you should be able to perform this variation on the above exercises. **Do not proceed if you feel lower back stress.** Lying on the back with the legs extended, lift the legs four inches off the floor. Keeping the legs elevated and extended, slowly flatten the spine to the floor, drawing the extended legs toward the torso. Slowly arch, allowing the weight of the legs to excenter. Repeat eight times, never lowering the legs to the floor between these arch-and-flatten sequences. As you do this, be sure to check the upper torso for tension. (See Figures 1.12a–b.) This exercise should be done without any shoulder and chest involvement, with the strength coming from the pelvic region without neck or shoulder strain. Check for strain by attempting to sing from the diaphragm as you perform the exercise.

Rediscovering Center

After working through this chapter, you should begin to feel a new sense of body center. Stand in proper alignment and feel your breath drop down to center. As you breathe, feel the tension flowing from your body on the exhalation, and the energy filling your center on the inhalation. Relax the jaw and shoulders and let the ribs expand to receive this infusion of creative power. Enjoy your new sense of integration and wholeness as you sigh out a feeling of physical pleasure on your next exhalation. Feel your body glowing with new-found energy. Repeat Exercise 1.3. As you walk across the room, what changes do you feel? Are they physical or emotional? Can you tell them apart? Note your new sense of self in your log.

The Actor's Neutral

When your body enters a state of integrated readiness for action and response, you have achieved the actor's **neutral.** Neutral does not mean empty, it means ready and open. Think of a car. engine revving, ready to be put into gear. Neutralizing the body frees it from our personal limitations, both psychological and physical, by breaking down emotional blocks and expanding physical awareness and prowess. When we are physically neutral, we appear free of those aspects of our personalities that mark our physical presence and prevent us from fully assuming a role. Neutrality is thus the first step toward characterization. All of the work in this chapter has prepared us to enter the neutral state, free of the inhibitions that limit our range of expression. The energy conserved when the body is working efficiently through centering can be released in the creative process. When you have achieved internal harmony, and the ability to coordinate feeling and function, you are ready to explore more advanced acting technique.

Summary

In this chapter, we have explored the concept of centering as a basis for acting technique. Through the development of kinesthetic awareness, we have worked to achieve integration of feeling and physical life in the body center. Using relaxation, alignment, and respiration to achieve neutrality, we freed ourselves of personal limitations to harness and channel our energy toward theatrical expression. The exercises keyed to balance, coordination, flexibility, and strength, have introduced us to the skills necessary for optimum movement. We have just begun a process that requires continued effort. As your acting progresses, you will need to pursue more advanced work in stage movement to achieve the control, range, and freedom necessary for the complete actor.

Voice

Proper stage speech is largely a consequence of right thinking,
of understanding the operative words in sentences, and partly of
feeling language and literature and being aware of sound and
rhythm in relation to meaning.

Harold Clurman, *On Directing*

Over the centuries, quality of voice has been considered the actor's most
important attribute. Until the modern era, most actor training was dedi-
cated to the art of oratory. In ancient Greece, where it was traditional for
the playwright to take the lead role in the performance, Sophocles made
history when he withdrew, claiming his weak voice prevented his doing
justice to the play. Some claim this act signaled the birth of professionalism
in acting, where now highly skilled and vocally trained actors would compete for the lead role formerly taken by the playwright. Cicero tells us that
orators often trained actors, and that orators went to see actors perform to
hone their respective skills. We know that in more recent eras, the art of
declamation was the dominant principle in acting, that actors scored
"points" with bravura renditions of their speeches, provoking audience
applause much the way opera audiences applaud after brilliantly sung
arias. Although in recent times, the emphasis has shifted to a more
rounded concept of acting technique, and voice training has changed from
work on vocal pyrotechnics to releasing expressive power, a voice capable

of communicating thoughts and feelings and of stirring the audience remains a necessary asset for all actors.

Feeling the Voice

The goal of this chapter is to open the channel for emotional expression through voice. We will begin by examining the actual physical process of producing sound, then hone the muscles of articulation, and explore the relationship between sound, feeling, speech, and text. The by-product of our work will be an improvement in the basic qualities of voice: beauty, power, clarity, and interest. You will learn the principle that sustains all voice work: *There is no substitute for the energy of free breath.*

As we work on our voices, we must keep in mind the central idea of integration, for much of the vocal training process can appear purely mechanical if we do not see the connections between technical exercises and how we think and feel. Each exercise has a physical, emotional, and intellectual component, so it is important to work with an active mind and responsive emotions. While you work, observe how you feel, what responses are evoked, what was blocked and what was freed. Use these exercises to enhance your self-perception. The freedom these exercises will give you may make you feel giddy and silly—enjoy it! Although this work is serious and demands discipline, exploring new sensations is exhilarating and fun. Our goal is to extend the development of kinesthetic awareness we began in Chapter 1 to include a sensitivity to our vocal apparatus.

You will quickly learn that you cannot depend upon your ears to tell you how you sound. You have grown attached to the sounds of your own voice and cannot make objective judgments on its quality. Further, we do not hear ourselves as others hear us, increasing the possibility of a faulty aural evaluation of how we sound. You must learn to sense how the vocal apparatus is performing through the body and not through your ears, and come to think of voice as a kinesthetic process created by certain muscular movements. This enables you to assess how you are producing sound and to make necessary adjustments. If you become aware of throat tension, you know that the voice cannot be achieving full resonance. If you feel constriction in the shoulders or chest, then the breath cannot have reached center. Do not use your ears to obtain this data, but instead work to develop advanced kinesthetic awareness that gives a read-out on your physical state from which you can determine not only that there is a problem, but where it is located and how you can restore healthy operation. As you work through the exercises in this chapter, consistently monitor the body for inhibiting tension.

Each voice is personal and individual. There is no objective standard of how the voice should sound. The only operative rule is that your voice must freely reflect all that you think and feel to become an effective tool for you, the actor. In the words of voice teacher Cicely Berry, "Your voice must be accurate to yourself." Most of us have lost contact with the experience of our free and natural voices. At birth, we came into this world free to emit whatever sound expressed the emotion of the moment. We slowly learned to channel our direct emotional cries into words, and then learned socially acceptable patterns of expression which cut us off from the direct flow of sound. As time went on, under the influence of family and peer groups, we learned to shape our voice to fit an external image of our behavior—artificially high voices to reflect femininity, forced low voices as a sign of masculinity. Life's tensions created patterns of muscular holding that physically blocked the free flow of sound. Although some of this is a necessary consequence of living in a civilized world, an actor must strip away the barriers to free emotional expression to release full vocal power.

The Process of Vocal Production

How do we produce sound? The brain receives a need to communicate. This in turn is translated into an impulse to breathe. The outgoing breath passes through the vocal chords, causing vibration in the breath stream. These vibrations create sound. The quality and tone of the sound is determined by the resonators—the bony and muscular area where the sound waves vibrate. Speech occurs when the articulating muscles of the lips and tongue shape the sound into recognizable words. Voice is the result of the translation of thoughts and feelings into physical impulses and movement—it is by its very nature an integrated process.

Breath and Voice

Breath is the animating force of the voice. If the breath does not flow, there is neither sound nor feeling expressed. Worse, we compensate for the absence of respiratory energy with muscular force, causing tension and obstruction to the free flow of emotion on breath. Any attempt to replace respiratory energy with muscularity is always counterproductive. With this in mind, we worked in Chapter 1 to ready the body to produce sound through relaxation, centering, alignment, and respiration exercises. Our goal was to produce an open respiratory pathway unimpeded by tension or faulty posture, so that an energetic breath is available to us for the creation of sound. Through relaxation we readied the body to receive impulses, while providing free passage for the breath to touch our emotional center and infuse our voices with feeling.

For optimum sound, the breath must enter a free and open respiratory passage and flow down to center, where it finds emotional content. The exhalation must flow unobstructed to the vocal chords, where, in a tension-free throat, maximum vibration may be obtained. Faulty alignment and muscle tension inhibit respiration and the free flow of sound and feeling.

Exercise 2.1: Breathing Naturally

Stand comfortably in neutral position, feet eighteen inches apart. Study Figure 2.1. Let a breath come in and mentally trace its passage down to center and its release on exhalation. Allow the breath to flow in and out without attempting to alter your normal respiratory pattern. Now inhale and hold your breath. As you do, sense the body's need to resume natural

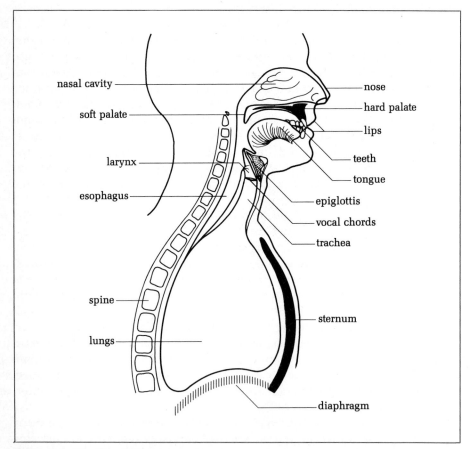

Figure 2.1 The Vocal Process.

breathing. Exhale, and wait for a strong message from the body to take in air before inhaling again. Note how unnatural such manipulations feel. Your body will breathe in response to organic needs if you do not interfere with the process. Your breath will naturally alter in response to emotion or tension.

Exercise 2.2: Breath and Sound

Take the constructive rest position (see Exercise 1.5). Slowly breathe in and out, tracing the path of the air as it enters the body and travels down to the center. Imagine that the breath is coming in to warm your belly. Let the breath enter, filling the body with a warm glow. As you exhale release the breath on a warm aspirated "huh" sound. Repeat until you feel the breath reaching as far into the body as possible.

Slowly rise, keeping the steady warm flow of breath. Bathe the air in front of you with a warm "huh" sound. As you breathe, observe the relationship between breath and sound. Note how the body moves to let in the air that will create sound. Play with your respiration. Place your hand gently on the stomach under the rib cage. Begin to lightly pant through an open mouth with a relaxed jaw. Feel with your hand the movements of the stomach in response to the rapid respiration. Close your eyes and sense the connection of breath to the body center. See if you can add a gentle release of sound on each exhalation of the panting process. Release the sound through an open and relaxed mouth. Return to normal breathing and reestablish a relaxed respiratory pattern.

Now, instead of exhaling on a steady stream, stop and start in a staccato fashion. Once again, sense the relationship between breath and body center. Now release a "huh" sound on the exhalations. Note the interplay between breath and sound. Alternate between staccato and legato exhalation while releasing the "huh" sound. Sense how organic the connections are.

Nasal or Mouth Breathing

The question always arises as to the advisability of nose or mouth breathing. In fact the method of respiration depends upon the body's emotional and physical needs at any given moment. When you are relaxed, sleeping, or engaged in nonstressful activity, the body benefits from nasal respiration which permits an adequate oxygen supply while filtering and warming the air. However, it is easier to take in more air rapidly when breathing through the mouth, and in addition, mouth breathing maintains a more direct pathway to the deeper emotional center. Under the emotionally charged conditions of the stage, breathing through the mouth allows better vocal support while more easily tapping the actor's emotional well.

| | **Exercise 2.3: Sensing Nasal and Mouth Breathing** | |

Stand in neutral position. Breathe in through the nose, letting the air flow in to the body center. Do not force the air flow. Repeat three times. Now breathe in through the mouth, once again permitting the air to reach the body center. As you repeat this exercise with mouth breathing, do you sense any difference in the physical sensation of breath when breathing through the nose or mouth? In which process did you feel you took in more air? Describe this difference in your journals.

   Now take a partner. Stand about three feet apart. Look deep into your partner's eyes and trade breaths, one of you inhaling as the other exhales, both breathing through the nose. When you have shared several exhanges of breath, repeat the exercise, breathing through the mouth. This time, inhale and exhale through the mouth. Did you notice any difference in the flow of energy between nasal or mouth respiration? In which did you feel a more direct connection to your partner? Record the results in your journals. Most of you will feel a stronger contact when breathing through the mouth. For some of you the difference may be quite pronounced. You should keep this in mind while working on your scenes, when it is important to keep the channels of feeling as open as possible.

Sound and Speech

Let's begin the process of voice production by differentiating between sounding and speaking. The human body is capable of producing many sounds that are not part of sophisticated language structure. Yet these sounds often clearly and directly express emotional states. At birth, we all freely scream, cry, and coo as a function of our needs and feelings. Slowly language develops and offers a more precise method of communicating our thoughts and feelings. However, precision and subtlety are often achieved at the expense of more direct emotional and visceral expression. It is easy to hide your feelings behind words, but almost impossible to disguise the emotional content of a cry, scream, or laugh. When strong feelings overwhelm us, we often cannot control our exclamations. Sounds of fear, joy, pain, or excitation will flow directly in response to certain stimuli. The need to emit a sound precedes the need to speak a word in highly charged emotional situations. The content of such sounds is immediately perceived by an audience, so as actors, we must develop the capacity to express pure emotion directly on voice.

| | **Exercise 2.4:** Releasing Sound | | | | | | | |

Stand in neutral position and check your alignment. Once again follow the passage of breath down to center and its release on an exhalation. As you do this, check for any areas of tension you may have blocking the free flow of air. Know that as the breath touches center it can tap your emotional well and express what you feel. Allow your current emotional state to infuse your breath and let your next exhalation be a sigh that expresses your state of mind. Repeat this, letting the sigh flow out of you. How fully can you express what you feel? Are you holding back? Is the sigh on an open vowel sound? Be careful not to collapse the upper chest as you release sound. Let the body move with the sigh. We should be able to sense your mood from the sound and movement of your body.

If you find you are too inhibited to fully release the breath, make note of this in your journal. As the work moves ahead, you will be surprised how easy this exercise will become, so it's good to have a barometer of your progress through a notation made at different points in the work.

Taking Pleasure from Sound

We must work to free ourselves of any negative feelings we may have about our voices and learn to take pleasure from the sensation of our feelings expressed on sound. We all have socially learned inhibitions against such direct expression of emotion, but you will find that overcoming reservations about the sounds of feelings relieves psychologically induced vocal tension. Let's think of the vibrations that create sound as something tangible and enjoy the vibrations of sound as they reverberate through the vocal channel.

| | **Exercise 2.5:** Taking Pleasure from Sound | | | □ | |

Give yourself a sound massage. Start with a head roll as in exercise. This time, as you release the head, release a sound. Send the sound around the neck and think of it as releasing tension everywhere it goes. Send the sound down your spine, into the shoulder blades. Let the body move with the sound. Does it feel good?

Imagine the most scrumptious dessert before you. See it in every detail. Take a taste and savor the flavor in your mouth, on your tongue. Swirl it around inside your mouth. Lick your lips. When you have fully experienced how delicious it is, release your enjoyment on the sound

"Yummummummumm." Repeat this sound, and as you do, make sure it expresses how you feel about this dessert. Now savor the vibrations in your mouth, on your tongue, between your lips. Feel your pleasure expressed in the vibrations on your lips and enjoy the sensation. "Yummummummumm."

Opening the Vocal Passage

Through your kinesthetic sense of the vocal process, you should now feel aware of the connection between relaxation and respiration, respiration and sound, sound and feeling. Now let us focus on the specific physiological areas that must be released to produce a free sound. Think of the pathway that sound takes: center → chest → neck → throat → mouth. If any interference occurs in the open respiratory channel, the result is a cutting off of the breath energy and diminished vocal return.

If you have properly followed the alignment work in Chapter 1, chest blockage should not occur. Be careful not to collapse the upper chest on exhalation or sound release. The major area of obstruction of breath and sound usually occurs in the throat, where we often register tension and muscular holding. The throat is the passage at the neck that contains both the larynx and vocal chords. The consequences of inhibiting the passage at the throat are of monumental concern to the actor. Throat tension will cut off vibrations and reduce both volume and resonance, especially the warm resonance of the chest. To compensate for the loss of power and tone, the tendency is to push the sound out, creating new tensions, moving the voice up in pitch and away from your inner emotional connection to sound. The result is a hollow sound that communicates little of your emotional life.

The jaw controls the opening of the mouth and permits the outward flow of sound. A clenched jaw results when you hold back against feeling. Imagine trying to scream with the jaw tightly clenched. What would be the result of such an effort? Even our language has images that relate to withholding through the clenching of teeth—bite your tongue, grin and bear it—are expressions of repressive behavior that use the image of the tightened jaw. In the famous Edvard Munch painting *The Cry*, the screaming woman whose cries reverberate is depicted with a wide oval mouth through which the full impact of her emotional state can be expressed by sound.

The soft palate is the fleshy area at the back of the roof of the mouth from which hangs the appendage called the uvula. If you look in the mirror you can see it and notice how you can manipulate its movements. As you lift the soft palate, you become aware of the potential for blocking of air flow that exists if the soft palate has become lazy. It can bar the path of air and vibrations and cut off complete resonance and sound.

The tongue's primary function in voice is to aid in articulation. But the tongue is a responsive organ and will register tension. You may have experienced the sensation of a thickening of the tongue in a particularly stressful situation. When the tongue tenses, it has a reflexive effect upon the larynx to which it is attached. Tongue tension may lead to laryngial and throat tension, so it is important to keep the tongue relaxed when it is not needed for specific tasks.

The following series of exercises is designed to develop awareness of the areas of the vocal pathway we have just discussed.

Exercise 2.6: Jaw Release

Place your fingers on your cheeks just forward of the ears. Open and close your mouth, feeling to find the hinge of the lower jaw. Open the mouth as wide as you can. Do you feel inhibiting tension under your fingers? Stretch the mouth out to the side. Check again for tension. Clench the teeth and relax repeatedly, noting the feeling of tension and release. Feed in an impulse to yawn. As you do, open the mouth as wide as possible. Let the body stretch with the yawn. Did you let out a sound without even trying? Yawn and stretch again, making sure to get maximum aperture of the mouth in all directions. If the impulse to yawn occurs again, give in and enjoy the sensation of stretching and releasing the jaw.

Exercise 2.7: Soft Palate Lift

Breathe in through an open mouth, and sense the cool air coming into the mouth. Feel the cold sensation as it hits the soft palate. Continue tracing the breath through the throat and down to center. Repeat this several times until you can feel a lift of the soft palate as the air comes in. The sound "k" is actually made when the tongue and soft palate meet. If you breathe in and out on the sound "kaaah" you can feel the movement of these two areas as well as the cool breath as it crosses the soft palate.

Exercise 2.8: Tongue Stretching

Stick your tongue out as far as possible. Get past all the inhibitions you may have about this antisocial act by taking pleasure in it. If you are in class, combine sticking your tongue out with making a face and a noise directed toward another member of the class. Find the childlike quality of this activity and communicate with others with your tongue stuck out. Now return the tongue to the inside of the mouth. Placing the tip of your tongue behind your bottom front teeth, stretch the tongue forward on a roll so you can feel the stretch at the back and middle of the tongue. Roll back and forth, keeping the tip of the tongue firmly in place behind the front teeth.

Exercise 2.9: Lip Loosening

Wet the lips with the tongue. Blow through the lips, making what is commonly referred to as a "raspberry." Blow through the lips again, this time adding sound. As you do, imagine that you are making the sound of a motor boat. Your lips should tingle from these vibrations.

Exercise 2.10: Throat Opening

The upper throat is the point where air and vibrations must round a bend. It is therefore susceptible to congestion. In order to unblock this area, let's take out the turn by dropping the head back. As you do this, be careful to involve only those vertebrae at the top of the neck. Do not arch your back or you will inhibit respiration. With the head dropped back, sense that you have straightened out the respiratory pathway. With this sensation in mind, inhale through an open and relaxed mouth, tracing the path of air as it enters and flows down to center. As you exhale, release a "haa" sound. Do not let the jaw intervene in the release of sound or you will feel constriction and tension in the throat. Keep the mouth wide open and see how free your "haa" sound can be. Slowly return the head to an upright position, making certain to keep everything relaxed. Keep the image of the open throat and repeat the "haa" sound. Is it as free as it was with the head dropped back? If not, drop the head back again and see if you can find a free sound, then once again, slowly bring the head back up. Repeat several times until you feel secure that you can keep the throat open.

What have you learned through this series of exercises? Do you feel any physical changes in the body? Record your sensations in your journal.

Resonance

The tonal quality of the voice is achieved through full use of the **resonators**. Vocal amplification occurs as sound waves hit the bony structures of the resonators and start them vibrating much like a tuning fork. If sound is properly formed, the vibrations will travel up the hard palate to the nasal bone and forehead for full head resonance, then proceed through the skull, down the spine and into the ribs to create chest resonance. The unimpeded flow of vibrations gives our voice volume without strain, while adding the aesthetic qualities of warmth and depth. It permits the full realization of vowel sounds in our speech. If the vibrations are inhibited in any way, the lack of resonance gives the voice a thin quality, limiting our ability to communicate emotions. The following exercises are designed to enhance kinesthetic awareness of your resonators.

Exercise 2.11: Head, Nose, and Mouth Resonance

Make an elongated "Y-y-y-y-yuh" sound. As you do so, feel the vibrations on the hard palate. Add to the "Y" sound a prolonged "eee." Sound on "Y-y-y-eeee" with the mouth closed and feel the vibrations in your teeth. Now open the mouth and feel the vibrations move into the nasal bone. If you cannot feel the vibrations from within, place your fingers on the sides of the nose where it meets the cheeks and repeat the "Y-y-yeee" sound. Can you feel the vibrations? This time make the "eee" part of the sound occur on a falsetto and feel the vibrations up into the forehead and skull. Repeat this series of sounds in rapid succession until you can clearly feel the path of vibrations. Keeping your fingers in place, send out the following sounds with nasal resonance: "Mee, may, mee, may, meemeemeemay-maymay."

Exercise 2.12: Chest Resonance

Place your hands on the chest at the sternum and release a deep "huh" sound. As you do, feel the vibrations in your chest. Without pushing or forcing the sound, see if you can increase the vibrations in the chest as you repeat "huh." Now lie on your stomach with your head turned to the side. Release a "huh" sound, and feel your chest vibrate against the floor. Hum in this position, then sing, then recite a few lines of text. Can you feel the chest resonance?

Articulation

Articulation refers to the way vibrations are shaped into sounds. These sounds are strung together to make words. Our discussion is concerned with one all-important goal—clarity. The aim of good articulation is to ensure that you will be understood. Of course there are other factors that influence communication—whether or not you have had a clear understanding of the material or a strong connection to the character's needs and situation. But assuming you have done your acting homework, sloppy enunciation can still muddle your message. What we will work toward in this section is proper mechanical action of the organs of speech. There will be no normative standard of proper speech set forth, for there is no one way to speak English. Ours is a diverse language. Accents vary from country to country, city to city, neighborhood to neighborhood. These differences have fed the expressive power of our language. We do not want to eradicate individual speech patterns, but instead work for an understanding of how your personal speech habits may impede clarity or the full realization of the meaning of a text. You will need articulatory control to create the accents and dialects necessary for complete characterization.

The basic organs of speech are the vocal chords, lips, tongue, and soft palate, so let's prepare for this work by loosening the muscles we need to work. Repeat Exercises 2.6–2.10 in preparation for articulatory work. Open the mouth as wide as you can and feel the jaw relax as you slowly return to a normal aperture. You should feel a change in your state of muscular preparedness.

Think of how many different sounds we are capable of making, and then realize that they are all given their form in the small area between the back of the tongue and the lips (with the exception of the distinction between voiced and unvoiced sounds created by the vocal chords). The smallest movements of any muscles in this area will change the way we produce sound. It is so easy to see why it is important to develop precision for optimum articulation.

Our speech is made up of combinations of vowels and consonants. Vowels are unimpeded sounds that flow freely through the mouth and are always vocalized. Some are pure vowels, which means that the shape through which the sounds pass is constant. Others are dipthongal, that is, they are made up of movement from one vowel sound to another through intermediating sounds. All are shaped by the tongue, others are coarticulated using the lips.

lip and tongue coarticulated vowels

oo	(booth)
oo	(book)
OH	(boat)
AW	(ball)
o	(bottle)
OW	(bounce)
OI	(boy)

tongue-shaped vowels

AH	(barge)
u	(bud)

a	(bad)
e	(bet)
i	(bid)
ER	(burn)
EE	(beef)
AY	(bay)
I	(buy)
EAR	(beer)
AIR	(bare)

Exercise 2.13: Vowel Articulation

Repeat these vowel sounds in order. As you speak them, feel the changes in the shape of the mouth and position of the tongue. Try to pronounce the lip-tongue coarticulated vowels without any movement of the lips. Is it possible to do this? What were your results? Now try to say the tongue-shaped vowels without any movement of the lips. How did you fare? Was it possible to isolate these vowels on the tongue without any lip movement? You should have discovered the impossibility of uttering coarticulated vowels without lip movement. Now repeat this exercise withholding tongue movement. What did you discover? Notice how small the changes are for each sound and how precise each tiny movement must be to achieve a clear distinctive vowel sound. Use this exercise to develop awareness of your idiosyncratic speech patterns. Do you habitually articulate clear vowels? Are there some that you notice you do not always form clearly? Where are your areas of lazy articulation? Take your time with this. Savor the full enunciation of each vowel.

Exercise 2.14: Linking Vowels and Resonance

Go through the long vowel tones, "a, e, i, o, u," and as you project them, feel where each sound is resonating. Did you notice how each vowel falls naturally onto a different pitch? Then try the following series of words: keep, meek, week; hate, mate, wait; my, high, why; mode, load, poke; moot, booth, tube. As you repeat these words, stay aware of the resonating areas. Feel how they change with the varying vowel sounds. Make sure you are achieving full resonance on each word. Stand neutrally and look at the wall farthest from you. If you have a partner available to work with, you may direct your sounds to a partner some distance away. Throw vowel sounds across the room. Pretend they are in a ball of sound in your hand. As you release the sound, throw the ball with the force of your body behind it. How does this affect the quality of the sound? Once again, "a, e, i, o, u."

Consonants shape the intelligibility of our speech through their capacity to provide interruptions in the flow of air in the vocal passage. They define the skeletal structure of words, permit contrast, and are rhythm and tempo controls. To understand the importance of good consonant articulation, we need only take a simple sentence: "Take the dog to the park." If we remove the vowels, we are left with "Tk th dg t th prk." It is possible to surmise from this the content of the original sentence. However, if we removed the consonants and left only the vowels, we would have "a e e o o e a," from which we would have no inkling of content. You may try this with other sentences to see the significance of consonants in intelligible speech. Because consonants frame the meaning of words, there is very little room for error in articulation. The smallest mispositioning of the tongue and lips in consonant enunciation can obscure clarity. The following chart demonstrates the minute position changes required for each consonant:

lips	lips and teeth	tongue tip and teeth	tongue tip and fr. palate	tongue blade and palate	tongue back and soft palate
b/p, m,w	v/f	z/s,ds/ts, θ/th,1	d/t,n	zh/sh,dg/ch ny,y,r	g/k,ng,h

The top line of the chart refers to the point in the breath passage where the flow of air is interrupted, constricted, or stopped to produce the consonant sound listed below. The degree of interruption in the flow of air varies for different consonants. Note that some of the consonants are separated from the next symbol by a slash. These indicate cognates—sounds that are produced in an identical manner—only one is voiced and the other is unvoiced. Try to whisper both sounds and you will understand the difference between a voiced and unvoiced consonant. The consonants b, p, d, t, g, k are called stops, or plosives, because the air passage is cut off completely, followed by an explosive release of sound. Other consonants are called continuants because it is possible to sustain their sounds.

Exercise 2.15: Consonant Articulation

Using the above chart, slowly make each of the sounds listed, making certain to carefully observe how you are producing each consonant. Are you using the articulators according to the chart? Have you discovered sounds you have difficulty differentiating in your speech? Are there areas of sloppiness in your usual enunciation? Sense the difference between the plosives and continuants, between voiced and unvoiced consonants. Try "tetetetetetetah, dedededededah, tedahtedahtedahtedah, buhbuhbuhbuhbuhbuhbah, puhpuhpuhpuhpuhpuhpah, buhpahbuhpahbuhpahbuhpah; kuhkuhkuhkuhkuhkuhkah, guhguhguhguhguhgah, guhkahguhkahguhkahguhkah." Try a series of tongue twisters: "Peter Piper picked a peck of pickled peppers," "She sells sea shells by the sea shore;" "Billy Button bought a bunch of beautiful bananas." Invent others. You will see that the firmer your articulation, the less apt you are to get tongue twisted.

Sound and Emotion

As we observe human expression, it is apparent that certain sounds are best suited to specific emotions and, reciprocally, particular sounds evoke certain feelings. It is hard to imagine giving full vent to anguish, pain, or passion on a consonant, because such strong emotions require an open and uninterrupted flow of sound. If you try to give vent to such feelings on consonants, the resulting sound gives the impression that we cannot let the feelings out, that we are inhibited by character or situation. It is interesting to note that classical Greek tragedy was written in a language replete with open vowel sounds and exclamations suitable to the portrayal of powerful emotions. Take the famous cry of Cassandra as she goes to meet her death, "Oh to to toi po poi da Ōpollon Ōpollon" As we think about sound and feeling it is important to remember that we expressed all our needs and emotions through sounds when we first came into this world, and language came later in our development and permitted specificity, not immediacy. Sound was all we needed as babies for direct emotional expression.

Exercise 2.16: Discovering the Feelings of Sound

Standing in neutral position, with relaxed respiration, release the long vowel sounds in slow succession, each on a new breath. As you do so, elongate the sounds as much as possible—"ay, eee, aye, ohhh, ooooo." Fill the room with each sound. Let the feeling of the sounds flow through your body. Repeat them if the feelings do not immediately come. Did you feel any emotional changes? Try this with the shorter vowel sounds. How different are the feelings of the short and long vowels? Can you describe the difference in sensation evoked by each?

Consonants have an important role in emotional expression. Let's look at the plosives b, p, d, t, g, k. Repeating each plosive five times, see how the repetition of the sound makes you feel. Does each one also suggest a movement? If you feel like moving, give in to that feeling. Now repeat each sound five times on a crescendo. Did this intensify the feeling of the sound? Note your findings.

Let's look at the continuant *m*. Let the sound roll on your lips, "mmmmmmmmmmmmmmmmmm," for a few seconds. How does it feel? What does it make you want to do? Add the "ah" sound. Repeat the sound "mahmah" five times. Do any feelings come over you? Try this with "sh, nya, w." Then add connecting vowel sounds. What are your results? Take some time to play with all the sounds on the vowel and consonant charts. Try making unusual combinations and note what happens to your emotional state. When you have played with these sounds enough to sense their emotional connections, try variations in pitch and resonance. Try "heehee" down low, then try "heehee" up high. Do the same with "lala, mymy, soso, foofoo." What happened when you changed pitch? Did you notice that as the feelings changed, there was an accompanying psychological change. This should give you some insight into the connection between sound, vocal placement, and characterization.

Sound and Movement Integration

Sound and movement find their source in the same impulse center in the body, making possible organic unity in our kinetic and vocal responses. Voice actually begins within the respiratory system as a movement impulse that reverberates in our muscles. You may have noticed that many of the vocal exercises contained a movement component. It is often difficult to isolate the need to produce a sound from the need to move. You may have found yourself moving during an exercise because it felt right, although no such reaction was suggested.

Sounds themselves can inspire movement. Think how easily we respond to sounds external to us. Music often provokes an irresistible urge to move. Think about your response to loud or abrasive noises. It is important to develop sensitivity to the movement impulses that come from sounds we produce internally. You must sense the breath as the source of both movement and voice. Feel movement as a need to have a kinetic follow-through of the breath impulse.

Finding this integrated responsiveness in the body will allow you to fully physicalize a verbal image as we begin our work with text. If the body does not support the intellectual and emotional content of a word there is a sense of disjointedness in our acting. Sometimes it leads to disconnection of dialogue from action in your scene work. I have all too often seen an actor enter the stage with a strong action choice, spend the emotional impulse on action, and then deliver a disembodied line after the action was completed. The words were no longer connected to the original impulse. When the reverse occurs—the line is delivered out of the initial impulse, and the action occurs as an afterthought. This separation of sound from action destroys your credibility as a character and disperses energy while at the same time diminishing your ability to fully communicate all the elements of your dramatic situation.

Exercise 2.17: The Ripple of a Yawn

Let's start with a yawn. As you yawn, feel the desire to stretch. Trace the impulse to move as it ripples up the spine and out to the limbs. Sense the integration of sound and movement as you let out the yawn. Repeat this, luxuriating in the feeling of organic unity.

Exercise 2.18: Vowel and Consonant Sound and Movement

Release some long vowel sounds. As you do, shake out your hands and notice the effect of movement on voice. Is it possible to separate the two completely as you shake? What have you observed? Now release vowel sounds and simultaneously let the feeling of each vowel flow from the breath to the spine and out through the body. See how each sound evokes a different movement. Make sure the movement originates with the breath impulse in the body center, rooting the kinetic response in the torso, letting the limbs move only as a follow-through. Switch to consonant sounds. Let the impulse simultaneously feed movement in the same way you proceeded for the vowels. Experiment with various consonant sounds and movement. Did the quality of the movement change as a function of the sound? Did you observe a relationship between the feeling of the sound and the kinetic responses in the body?

Exercise 2.19: Animal Sound and Movement

Let's use this technique to create an animal. Choose a specific animal and lie on the floor in fetal position, imagining you are this animal's embryonic form. Feel yourself slowly develop into the fully formed animal. As you do, think about how this animal breathes, and let the breath feed the movement. Take your time. To do this exercise correctly, you must let your mind slowly feed your kinesthetic sense. When you find yourself fully formed with an organic respiratory pattern, simultaneously find the animal's method of locomotion as you release the animal's sound. Move around the room as the animal, holding onto an organic sense of sound and movement. Keeping this process totally integrated requires time, patience, and a heightened awareness of voice and body. It should not be attempted without a proper warm-up and relaxation period. When you have successfully completed this exercise solo, it can be expanded into a group exercise, creating animal habitats as a class. A specific environment (jungle, swamp, northern forest) must be chosen so that members of the class can create the animal life of a region.

Words and Feelings

From the exercises we have just done, it is clear that sounds and feelings are intimately connected. If we look at language as a systematic collection of sounds, it should follow that by selectively emphasizing those sounds which release the emotion we are feeling as actors, we can clearly express the needs of a character through words. Our work with text is the point of integration for all the techniques we have worked on so far. The body must be free, centered and properly aligned so we can achieve proper breath support for sound released through an open vocal pathway into clearly articulated and fully resonated words; words must be felt as physical images in the body; and the phonemes or sound components of words must be explored and indulged for their full emotional and intellectual expression.

Good writing often strings together the sounds that best express the content of the text. The ability of words to reflect their meaning phonically is called *onomatopoeia*. Words like *whack* or *crash* give the feeling of the thought they are conveying by their very sound. Some words can intone an emotion through their sounds. It is important to develop a sensitivity to this quality of language if you are to infuse words with life on stage.

To illustrate this point, let's look at the following lines from *Twelfth Night*: "If music be the food of love, play on." Note the repetition of long vowel sounds and continuant consonants that serve to illustrate the feeling of the music. To say this line and accent the plosive final "c" in music would be to go against the very meaning of the line. If we allow ourselves to indulge those sounds which support the meaning of the words, we find an emotional connection to the text through the physical feeling of the language. Try saying this line, emphasizing the sounds which support the central idea. Indulge the sensual feeling they evoke. What have you experienced? Try the same with this Shakespearean line: "Blow, blow, thou winter wind!" What sounds support the central image? Did you notice the repeated "w" and the plosive "b"?

It is important to have a strong physical image to support the language. Close your eyes and feel the "winter wind." Let it pass through your body. Hear it blowing. Take your time to be sure the image has been thoroughly experienced by all your senses. Try saying the line, "Blow, blow, thou winter wind!" again. How did the physical image work feed into your ability to indulge the sounds? To fully experience text, it is important to work through the senses to infuse voice and body with the full content of your words. This enables the audience to see your images.

| | **Exercise 2.20:** Finding the Image in the Sound | | | |

Choose a short poem that has strong physical images and a sensual use of language and sound. Close your eyes and slowly let each image fill your sensations. Work word by word. When you have experienced a word clearly, say the word with a movement that expresses the feeling evoked by the image. This is a slow process, but it is important not to shortchange any word. Even *but* and *and* can have emotional significance. When you have fully experienced every word, open your eyes and string them all together. You will notice that each new word now takes on a different quality both inside of you and vocally. The text has come alive!

Although poetry is richest in sound-image-feeling connection, most plays benefit from this kind of exploration of text. Take a look at any scene or monologue on which you are currently working. What are the significant words? Which words most strongly express your character's needs, emotions, and objectives? Ask yourself if there are sounds in these words that can feed the feelings, then let the body respond to the sounds and images. Explore the relationship between sound, movement, and feeling as you rehearse this material.

Summary

We have just explored the basic principles of voice production. Our emphasis has been to develop kinesthetic awareness of the vocal process, while working to integrate voice with other components of acting technique. Our work has been predicated on the idea of the free breath as the sustaining physical and emotional energy source for the voice. We have laid the groundwork for more advanced vocal training, which can be developed in specialized classes and through continued readings. The bibliography provides sources for further study.

The skills and awareness you have gained will serve as the building blocks for more advanced technique. Remember, you must condition your instrument through constant work. The exercises in this chapter must be part of a regimen of voice and movement work.

3

Filling the Theatrical Space

To know that the soul has corporeal expression permits the actor to unite with his soul.
Antonin Artaud, *The Theater and Its Double*

The houselights dim, the stagelights go up, to reveal a solitary actor in an empty space. Our eyes are glued to this physical presence. In seconds we have received a strong impression of the essence of this character and yet not one word has been spoken. Even the audience seated in the last rows of the balcony has learned much in these few silent moments. Exposition has occurred through the ability of the actor to radiate thoughts and feelings across the theatrical space.

Energized Performance

A vital stage presence results when internal energy is freely released through breath, voice, and movement. If an actor relies on text to do the work of the body, the performance will be lifeless and empty. Thoughts and feelings must be translated into a physical dynamic to successfully project across space.

Energy, the intensity or vigor of expression, is an essential component of the actor's technique. Although we have no precise method of measurement, a languid performance is easily recognized. It inverts the usual energy flow as the audience must strain to reach the actor. Energized performance is not automatic. Invariably, in beginning acting classes, even those held in spacious studios, actors will set up their scenes in the closest possible proximity to the audience, eliminating the need to project across space. It is important to resist this temptation and work to stretch our expressive range. We all have the potential to become exciting performers once the blocks to energy release have been removed. Then we can experience the pleasure of mastery and control of the theatrical environment, the thrill of touching the audience through the power of our performance. The ability to do this is won when we have developed a free and open channel for energy flow.

Breath, the Conduit of Internal Energy

The connecting link between our internal energy source and the external environment is the breath. Breath must come all the way in and touch the body center and then be completely and freely released in order to animate stage behavior. To understand this vital connection, you need only watch actors perform without attention to the respiratory process. The action appears lifeless and empty. Often tension makes actors breathe shallowly or forget to let in air altogether. Such performances never connect to the energy center in the body and therefore cannot fill the theatrical space.

Breath is part of a series of reciprocal relationships in the body. The relationship between breath and physical activity level is evident. It is not possible to run a mile without proper respiratory support, and, reciprocally, running a mile will alter the depth and tempo of respiration. A similar correlation occurs with emotional level. Antonin Artaud, the great theatrical theorist and actor, went so far as to describe the components of respiration—inhalation, exhalation, and retention—as the primary color palette of emotion. Artaud believed you could alter emotional state through the manipulation of the respiratory process. Experimentation with his theory proves him correct, a fact which yogis have known for centuries. If changes in respiration alter internal emotional energy, it is also true that internal emotional change induces respiratory alteration.

The actor must develop awareness of these physical, emotional, and respiratory interrelationships. This is why we gave so much attention in Chapters 1 and 2 to the proper mechanics of the respiratory process—to facilitate a free exchange of these reciprocal relationships and permit a greater release of energy on breath.

The exercises in this chapter are geared toward the integration of respiration with movement and feeling, as they should all ideally emanate from the same source—the actor's center. For this reason, many improvisations begin with breath before a voiced sound is added. You must be aware of your breathing and correct it if it is uncentered before beginning to work. Attentiveness to the respiratory process must become a natural part of an actor's technique.

Life Energy and Theatrical Energy

In life, energy is a result of personality, mood, and physical well-being interacting with environment and situation. Although energy level may occasionally be consciously altered to meet the demands of stressful situations (for example, job interviews, important dates, sports events, auditions), our general energy level in life is most often the unconscious result of existing conditions. Stage energy too is the result of the meeting of character with environment and situation; however, in contrast to life, the actor's stage energy must be characterized by the following five qualities:

1. Control
2. Focus
3. Purpose
4. Dynamics
5. Enlargement

Control. The actor must work to obtain mastery of voice and movement as well as the open respiratory process through which energy is released. The exercises presented in Chapters 1 and 2 developed the strength, flexibility, and centering that begin the road toward increased control.

Focus. Acting demands a heightened awareness and level of concentration. The body is on the alert in the theatrical environment, and attention cannot wander from the dramatic situation.

Purpose. All action on stage, including the smallest movement, is purposeful and motivated by the objectives of the character in the given situation. Aimless action detracts from the central idea of a scene and diffuses energy.

Dynamics. Although all stage movement must be energized and forceful, it is important to achieve texture and variety to broaden the range of expression and hold the attention of the audience.

Enlargement. In most life situations, we are unconcerned with filling big spaces and communicating with large groups of people. Acting requires the expression of common emotions in an uncommon way. Feelings expressed through breath, voice, and movement must penetrate large spaces without losing truth or sincerity.

The exercises in this chapter work together to achieve these five fundamental qualities of stage energy.

Enlarging Expression

The theatrical event is a compression of life, emotionally and intellectually charged. Although as actors we talk of "living the part," what we do on stage is not a duplication of our everyday life experience.

Although most forms of theatre require that you perform as if the audience does not exist, there will always be a peripheral awareness of the audience's presence: you hear coughs and rustling of programs, and you learn to hold lines for laughs or applause. Although you focus attention on your objective within the dramatic situation on stage, you are also involved in a reciprocal energy flow with the audience. You can feel from the audience's responses whether you are reaching the public, and you adjust your energy level accordingly. The mere presence of the audience demands that you enlarge your portrayal and radiate emotions beyond the playing space. To do this, you cannot behave as you would in life, where your behavior is not a spectator event. You must learn to express your character's feelings with sincerity, in a form that is larger than life, through a radiation of energy.

Exercise 3.1: Enlarging Energy

Stand in the middle of the room. Do you feel small or large in relation to the space? Send your inner thoughts out to the walls of the room. Check for points of energy blockage in the body. Use your eyes, your breath, your spine, your chest, and pelvis. Did you remember the back wall? Now extend your arms out from the side to transmit your emotions. Let your feelings energize your fingertips. Sense the breath flowing out through the fingers, the toes, the chest. Imagine your fingertips have laser beams from which they can send messages to the furthest reaches of space. Send a message through the walls to an area outside the room. Return to neutral.

Have these images altered your physical condition? How? Check for changes in respiration and body center. Do you feel larger or smaller now in relation to the space?

The Actor in Space

Learning to feel comfortable in your work space is essential. You need to develop a sense of yourself in relationship to the size, limits, acoustics, and audience-performer configuration of the theatrical environment. Exploring the space will permit physical freedom and the ability to assess the degree of projection and enlargement required to fill the space.

Exercise 3.2: Meeting the Space

Let's explore the room you are in. How big does it feel? What do you see, smell, and hear in this space? Walk around and touch the surfaces. How do you feel about this space? Is it clean and cared for? If it is not, as a group ready the space for your work. Is it flexible? Can you rearrange it? Discuss as a group how you feel about the physical setup of the space.

Adjusting to New Environments

Over a course of time, you often unknowingly develop a strong attachment to the work space. Although this familiarity helps create the feeling of a safe environment for creative work, it is important not to grow dependent on the comfort of the space to the point you cannot adjust to new conditions. Often plays are rehearsed in studios and moved into the theatre late in the rehearsal process, and actors are expected to make immediate adjustments to the new and usually larger space. Similar demands are placed on actors on tour, or at an audition, when you may walk into the theatre or studio only moments before being called upon to perform.

Exercise 3.3: Adjusting to New Environments

To prepare for these situations, sometime during the semester move the class to a new space. Note the general reaction. Are you tense? Do the actors hesitate in setting up their scenes? If it is not possible to move the class, turn your current room around, inverting the audience and performance space. How did this affect your performance. Note in your journal how you felt and what adjustments were made.

Centering and Energy

The Torso as Energy Source

The source of physical and emotional energy is in the torso. As the center of breath and gravity, it is a vital area for the actor. Because the most vulnerable parts of our being—heart, guts, respiration, and sexuality are situated in the trunk of the body, most of us tend to protect and inhibit that region. Some of our earlier exercises may have made you aware of just how protected you are. It is crucial to remove our inhibitions related to torso movement in order to expand our potential for expressive energy release.

For this reason, we have worked on increasing flexibility, strength and freedom in this area. We must strive to avoid using facial mugging and indicative gesture from the limbs as a substitute for more centered expression.

We often describe with our hands what we should feel with our torso. Etienne Decroux, the father of the modern mime form, put it succinctly when he said, "It is the trunk that suffers while the arms complain." To underscore this point, think of the great sculptures of antiquity such as the *Winged Victory of Samothrace*. Many have lost limbs and heads through the centuries, yet from the torso alone we are able to determine the emotional content of the work.

The torso dervies its expressive power from changes in alignment of the spine, paired with breath. Note how spinal position in people around you is a reflection of character, age, mood, and emotion.

Exercise 3.4: Freeing the Torso

Shake the top of your torso in a shimmying movement. As you do, shake out the breath. Shimmy the bottom of your torso. Let the movements release sound. Shimmy up and down the torso, releasing sounds. Notice how pitch lowers on the bottom shimmy.

With hands on hips, rotate the pelvis, making circular movements with the lower half of the torso. Now thrust the pelvis behind the spine and then thrust forward in a "bump and grind" motion. Inhale on each movement back, and release a sound on each forward pelvic thrust.

How did you feel as you made these torso movements? Were you aware of inhibitions during pelvic thrusts? Because of the sexual connotations of such movements, we are all somewhat reticent to perform them in public, but as actors, we must strive to free our bodies from these constraints. Remember, theatre often deals with private emotions in public. As we liberate our bodies, we liberate our minds and feelings.

Viewing the Body in Three Dimensions

Because we so rarely see a rear view of ourselves, there is a tendency to think of ourselves two-dimensionally. We view ourselves frontally, forgetting the expressive potential of our backs and profiles. Today, actors are so often required to work in the round or on thrust stages, where their bodies are required to provide meaningful images from all sides, that it has become crucial to think of energy emission as a three-dimensional process emanating from the torso. Observe carefully the next time you attend a performance in thrust or arena staging. Were the actors using their bodies effectively?

Exercise 3.5: Viewing the Body in Three Dimensions

Stand with your back to the audience. Keeping in mind the position of the spine as a reflection of emotions and a source of energy, communicate the following information to the audience, using breath and movement without words:

1. You have just won a ten-million-dollar lottery.
2. You were turned down for the part of your dreams.
3. You have fallen in love.
4. You have just escaped from an armed robber.

Directing Energy

Energy Never Stops

Energy flow in the theatrical space must be a directed continuum. One actor gives out, the other receives, reacts, and changes the energy, which is returned to the other actor, who in turn takes the energy in, reacts, transforms it, and then emits again. Usually such emissions and reactions are correlated with the flow of breath, transmitting on exhalation, receiving on inhalation. If at any point the energy flow stops, the scene will be rendered lifeless. Actors must think of their emotions as a constant energy flow on stage.

Various theatrical thinkers have categorized this flow with different terminologies. The great Russian director Vsevolod Meyerhold, when developing his principles of biomechanics for the actor, saw acting as continual sequences of stimulus and response. He believed the actor needed to develop the capacity for "reflex excitability," which would facilitate a circular process:

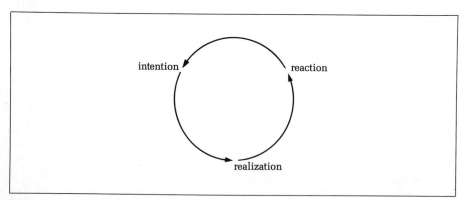

Figure 3.1 Energy Never Stops.

Each reaction engenders a new intention, creating an energy continuum. According to Meyerhold, each part of the process must be realized physically. The intention, realization, and reaction all induce physical changes in the body, which in turn produce emotional change and then evoke an emotional reflex in the audience.

Constantin Stanislavski,[1] whose theories and techniques serve as the basis for most approaches to acting in the twentieth century, emphasized the concept of "an unbroken line" of communication through the transmission of "invisible currents" of energy. He called this the process of "irradiation."

Terminology may differ, but the concept remains fundamental: Actors are involved in an uninterrupted flow of feeling and action on stage which is realized as a transmission of energy through breath, voice, and movement.

Exercise 3.6: Keeping the Energy Flow

Stand facing a partner. Decide who will be actor one. Trade breaths as you did in Exercise 2.4 so that when one of you inhales, the other exhales. Let actor one focus on a strong message you wish to communicate to your partner. Communicate your feelings on a prolonged exhalation on "f." Actor two must inhale as actor one exhales, trying to absorb something vital from your partner. Actor two must communicate his response to the message received on his next exhalation on "f," and actor one must respond in turn in a continual process. Keep the energy flowing. Do not let time elapse between exchanges.

Were you able to keep the energy flow? Did the inhaling and exhaling connect you emotionally to your partner? Note in your journal any feelings of increased openness and vulnerability. Repeat the exercise on a voiced "huh" sound. Check for vocal tension.

What did your bodies do during the exhange? Often there is an unconscious leaning forward as you transmit and a rocking back as you receive. Did this happen?

Exercise 3.7: Group Energy Flow—Passing Sound and Movement

This exercise should be approached with childlike fun! Let the class stand in a circle. One person begins, sending a sound and movement to the

[1]The theories of Stanislavski will be discussed in detail in Parts II and III of the text.

person to his or her right. That person must receive the sound and movement, take it in on an inhalation, respond, and send it out to the next actor to the right until the response system has sent the sound and movement around the circle several times. It is important to involve the torso in every movement. The taking in and reaction time must be rapid to keep the energy alive. There should be a split second of elapsed time between members of the class. Anyone who stops to think before reacting will lower the energy level of the group. Note when this happens. What is the effect of such a delay? Notice that people often stop the flow because they feel inhibited. See how inhibition creates tension and blocks energy flow, communication, and stage life. The movement and sounds should be free and open. If the class completes this exercise successfully, be aware of the change of energy in the room.

Mental Image and Energy Control

The actor's thought process can direct energy flow and even induce a physiological change. It is important to think in terms of powerful images formulated with vivid language to produce an effect on the body. The following exercise should enable the actor to alter body weight through mental energy direction. It is crucial to paint strong images in the mind's eye.

Exercise 3.8: Image and Energy—Changing Weight

Choose a partner close to you in size. Try to lift each other with arms around the waist. Is your partner heavy or light? Let one of you be the imager, the other, the lifter. The imager must close his eyes and think of his body as a giant oak tree, with roots going deep into the ground, covered over with cement. Feel yourself attached to the earth. When you have found the image in the body, let your partner try to lift you. Has the directing of energy downward changed your weight?

Now think of yourself as a feather floating in the air. Air currents lift you upward like a bird. When you have found the image and sent your energy upward let your partner try to lift you. Has your body weight changed? What can be learned about the power of mental direction of energy from this exercise?

Exercise 3.9: Feelings and Energy Through Color

Choose two colors of the same hue in different intensities. Pale blue and royal blue, for example. Make a sound that expresses the lighter color. Find a movement that matches the sound and radiates the energy level of the sound and color. Become the color. Let this movement take you around the room. With your voice and body paint the room the color. Let the body and sound flow. Repeat the exercise with the higher-intensity color. What changes occurred in voice and movement to reflect the variation in color intensity? Turn the exercise into a guessing game. Can the class guess the color you are thinking of? What is it about the energy of your portrayal that will enable them to identify your color? Note the results in your journal.

NOTE: Often college students find this exercise embarrassing. They find it difficult to express an abstract feeling devoid of literal content. It must be underscored that unless this inhibition can be overcome, there develops an overdependency on text and literal meanings. An entire range of the actor's expressive potential is precluded. Interestingly, children adore this exercise. Emil Jaques Dalcroze, the creator of eurhythmics, used a scarf exercise to awaken a sense of the power of color energy in the very young. Children would choose scarves of various colors, then move, dance, and make sounds in response to the emotions the colors evoked. In the twentieth century, we understand through abstract art the powerful communication potential of pure color and form.

Purpose, Concentration, and Energy

The first time you find yourself alone on stage can be exciting, intimidating, inspirational, or terrifying. Eyes are upon you, watching your every move. If you focus on your feelings about being watched, you will grow increasingly self-conscious, and your energy will be directed internally toward your negative emotions. But once you find a purpose for your presence on stage, you can justify your actions and direct positive energy toward achieving your goal or objective. This becomes clear if you imagine being told to stand on stage without receiving any further information on your reason for being there. What would you do to fill the space? How would you determine your actions? Let a member of the class stand in the middle of your playing space without any direction. Observe carefully. What does this person do to cope with this assignment? Is it enough just to stand there and be yourself? Is "being" dramatically interesting? Does it produce an energized performance?

If we were to watch the average evening at home of an American salesman's family, most likely the scene would be far removed from an Arthur Miller play. Unless we were there to gather sociological data, the events would shortly fail to hold our interest, as life is filled with insignificant activities. The actors would seem listless and lacking in focus and energy, even though they would be experiencing genuine emotions and feelings, truly "living the part." Life does not always meet the requirements of an artistically crafted dramatic situation, often lacking form, purpose, action, control, and significant content. Life experiences hold spectator interest only when they reflect dramatic elements such as conflict, crisis, and obstacles. For this reason, crowds will gather to watch a street brawl or a rescue operation, activities that are dramatic in content. During these situations, the participants are forced to harness and direct their energy and to focus on their immediate purpose. The redoubling of energy output for purposeful action acts like a magnet for the spectator.

Exercise 3.10: Moving Walls

Imagine that the walls of the room are closing in on you, that unless you push with all your might they will crush you. Stop the movement of the walls!

How did this crisis affect the purpose of your movement and influence energy direction?

Focusing on a Point of Attention

Interesting characters are constantly animated by their active goals. On stage, you must always feel you have a task to accomplish, and getting that job done is of foremost importance. This objective is your **point of attention.** Everything else within your range of perception is of secondary interest. Not only does this focus your energy, but it directs the audience's attention as well.

When you are on stage, there are forces pulling you away from your focus within the dramatic situation. The omnipresent audience and your own fears and self-consciousness, even problems from daily life can dominate your thoughts. It is important to learn to concentrate on your objectives. You may be aware of the audience, the set, the lights, backstage personnel, but they must recede into the background of your attention. Think of focusing the lens of a camera. You have an object of primary attention. There are other objects in the picture, you know they are there, but you adjust your focus according to the object of interest. Concentration is a process of selecting focus.

Exercise 3.11: Concentration and Obstacle

Your objective is to recite the alphabet backwards. Your partner's objective is to break your concentration in any way possible. Can you hold concentration on your objective?

You may have discovered that general noise was easy to ignore. The more specifically your partner tried to engage you in conversation the more difficult it was to concentrate. The more involved you were in maintaining your focus, the less you worried about your performance.

Repeat the same exercise, using a Shakespearean sonnet or poem of similar length. Your objective is to deliver it with clarity and meaning, and your partner's to upset your concentration. Note your level of success in your log.

The audience's focus always follows the actor's. If your concentration is scattered, the audience will not be able to follow the action of the drama. Through your ability to direct focus and energy you can make the reality of the stage palpable to your audience.

Exercise 3.12: Directing Attention

You are a member of the nighttime cleaning staff of a large corporation. While cleaning the corporate president's outer office at 10 P.M., you hear voices and discover that the president is still in his office with someone. Eavesdrop on what is happening. By watching you listen and respond, we should know what you are overhearing. During the course of this exercise, your point of attention should change from cleaning the outer office to discovering what is happening inside the inner office. Could your audience guess what you overheard?

Purpose and Energy

All action on the stage must be meaningful, purposeful, and controlled, and must serve the needs of the character. Economy of energy is crucial to sustained theatrical effort. The actor who is unaware of what he is doing inserts distracting gestures into the flow of meaningful data. You must be careful not to scatter energy through poor concentration. Often after performing a scene, actors reveal that they are unaware of having made crosses or gestures, or may admit that they chose particular actions because they did not know what else to do and felt a need to move or do something to avoid standing still too long. You cannot permit either unconscious or contentless action on stage, as it dissipates energy and confuses the audience. All action must be carefully selected as a means of fulfilling an actor's purpose on stage or as a revelation of character. As you work on scenes, it is important to think about energized actions that will help achieve your purpose for being on stage.

Exercise 3.13: Evaluating Purposeful Action

Consider your last work on stage. Were all you actions meaningfully chosen? Did you pace or meander without purpose? Were you aware of what your fingers were doing, your face, your feet? Do you personally have nervous habits? Do you indulge them on stage? The next time you perform, note whether you have a greater awareness of gesture and movement.

Purpose and Enlargement

A strong purpose can facilitate enlargement. The more powerful the intention, the more forceful the energy output. Often when your energy is low in acting class, the students will inform you that you could not be heard, or that your actions appeared languid. To correct this, the temptation is to simply raise volume and exaggerate movement. This often results in an externally transfused performance, which loses emotional truth and sincerity. In order to successfully enlarge voice and movement without loss of truth, it is important to intensify your sense of purpose. Increasing the strength of a character's needs and objectives increases the energy of the portrayal.

Exercise 3.14: Enlarging Through Purpose

Return to Exercise 3.6, "Keeping the Energy Flow." Begin the energy flow on the "huh" sound, trying once again to absorb something vital from your partner. When you feel that you and your partner are successfully sharing the energy, increase the distance between you by five feet. Continually increase the distance between you until you are separated by the entire span of the room. Were you able to transmit energy over the increased space without forcing volume? Did pitch rise? Remember that increase in pitch is often a result of tension. Did the distance cause you to strain to communicate?

Begin the exercise again. This time actor one must focus on a strong purpose; try to get your partner to leave. Actor two must oppose this objective and try to alter actor one's purpose. As you increase distance, intensify the desire to make your partner go. Attempt to keep the sound on the same pitch. What effect did a strong purpose have on the ability to project across the room? Were you able to control pitch?

Environment as Physical Energy

Each scene takes place in an imaginary environment. The body is responsive to the physical conditions which surround it. Setting, climate, weather, location—indoors or outdoors, the particular room and decor all affect energy level. Some conditions rob the body of vigor; others infuse it. Some create stress, some inhibit, some stimulate. Often an actor is faced with an empty stage upon which to build the illusion of an imagined environment. To communicate the setting to the audience, actors will often turn to pantomimed indication, wiping the sweat off the brow to suggest that it is hot out, shivering in the cold, or touching imaginary objects to suggest place. Although this serves to communicate an intellectual message to the audience, in order to have the audience feel what the actor feels, energy must be altered through an internal change to project the stage environment. To achieve this, let the image affect your respiration and muscle tension as you imagine where you are.

Exercise 3.15: Creating an Environment

Lie on the floor in constructive rest position. Imagine yourself in some beautiful location with which you are familiar. See, smell, touch, hear, and taste all that is around you. Use all five senses to create a complete image of the environment. Take your time. When the image is clear, release a sound that expresses how this place makes you feel. Do not force or hold back this sound. Open your eyes. Can you hold onto the image? Rise to a standing position. Let your body, breath, and movement all express how it feels to be in this favorite spot. How do you move or walk? How has your original energy state been altered by the power of the image? Let out a sound that expresses how good it feels to be in this place. Enjoy it!

Exercise 3.16: Weather and Energy

Divide the classroom into various weather zones. Examine the energy changes induced by each climatic variable as you move from zone to zone. Initiate each change with an adjustment of respiration in order to center your feelings. Does the atmosphere affect your emotional state? Be careful not to indicate the changes externally. As you perform this exercise, be aware of the reciprocal relationship between emotion and environment. Think about the climate and weather of the scene you are working on. Have you let this affect your energy, voice, and movement in the scene?

If you have trouble centering this exercise in the body and tend to indicate, imagine your hands are tied and that you may only use your torso to express these variables. How did eliminating hand movement affect your ability to produce an internal change?

Exercise 3.17: Setting and Energy

Divide the playing space up into two imaginary spaces. Let one be a comfortable family room, the other a formal living room overfurnished and filled with priceless, fragile antiques. Move from space to space. What changes occur in the body in each space. Can your classmates easily guess which half of the room is which space even without your indicating the presence of particular objects in the room? Could they tell from the way you breathe, move, and walk where you have placed your center? These are all alterations in your energy field. Create new spatial dualities of your own choosing. Can the class guess where you are? Be cautious at each turn to avoid indicating the nature of the place. Let your body energy create the ambience.

Try the above exercise with partners. Can you share the energy?

Character and Energy

Finding a Neutral Energy Base

Your body must be prepared to create a character. We have already worked to attain a relaxed body free of blocks to energy flow as well as a neutral posture and center that can be altered as a reflection of character. Your creative work must not be trapped by the physical traits of your own identity. Your personal energy must become a tool, not a limitation of character work. Let's try to neutralize our energy base and create a free and dynamic body, ready to transmit and receive energy flow.

Exercise 3.18: Evaluating Personal Energy

Examine yourself. Are you a high- or low-energy person? Are you lethargic or quick? Focused or scattered? Do you have trouble motivating yourself? Be careful not to confuse nervous energy, which is often scattered and wasteful, with high-intensity focus! When you are on stage, do you alter your personal energy or impose it on the character or situation? Has your creative work been imprisoned by your personal energy level? Write the results of this self-examination in your journal. How does the energy of the character on which you are working vary from your own?

Passive and Active Characters

Jean-Louis Barrault, the great French actor, director, and pantomimist, has written extensively about what he calls a "magnetic halo," a radiation field that surrounds every human being and varies in its vibrations depending on the nature of the individual psyche or personality and the person's interaction with the outside world. We each possess this halo, and it is this we examined in our discussion of personal energy level. Each character that we encounter in a play also owns a magnetic halo. It is important to examine and determine the nature of this radiation for each role we play. More assertive characters move with greater ease, often consuming the external environment within their own magnetic field. More passive characters tend to have weaker radiation. This means that the weight of the outer world comes in closer to them. Their movement therefore requires a greater push from within as they are in a struggle to assert themselves against the external environment, which in dramatic situations is often a hostile one. Viewed this way, actors who play weaker characters cannot be passive in their energy field, for they must muster up greater internal force in order to function in the impinging environment. Therefore passive becomes active from the point of view of the actor's inner life. This technical approach avoids the perennial problems involved in making passive characters physically interesting and dynamic on stage.

Exercise 3.19: Character Energy Flow

You are lying in bed asleep in the morning. Deal with the difficulties of waking up to face the day for a passive personality. Remember that the passive personality feels the air around him as if it had great weight. It is a force that must be reckoned with. Find strength from within and push out. What adjustments did you need to make for this person to rise and face the day? How did this affect respiration? Attempt the same exercise as an aggressive character who imposes himself on his environment. What was the effect upon your movement? Analyze the difference between these two personalities performing the same task.

Substitute other simple actions and repeat the problem with opposite characters. Keep the energy force flowing for the passive personality at all times.

Repeat the exercise with specific characters from scenes you are working on in mind.

Color as Character Energy

We have already seen how colors have an energy field around them that is determined by hue and intensity. Colors have emotional qualities that we can associate with certain personalities. Most of us choose to wear colors that reflect how we feel about ourselves. What color best reveals your sense of self? Costumers make similar judgments when they select colors for particular characters. Is there a character in a play you have read who could never wear scarlet? Pink? Black? What is it about this character that makes these choices impossible? Understanding the relationship between color and character provides a technique for determining a character's energy.

Exercise 3.20: Color as Character Energy

Using a character you are working on in scene study, decide what color best suits this person. Using this color, repeat Exercise 3.9, "Feelings and Energy." After you have gotten a strong sense of how that color moves and sounds, return to your scene. Say your lines and perform your actions, infusing them with the energy of the color you have chosen for this character. Were you able to connect these two processes? How did it affect the quality of your movement and voice? Was pitch or volume altered?

Summary

We have examined the source of energized performance and worked to develop focused, controlled, and dynamic expression using breath as a conduit for energy emanating from our body center. We have seen how purposeful direction of energy functions as the key to dynamic stage presence and the development of characterization. These concepts will be integrated with our work on text. You should now feel increased confidence, freedom, and command of your resources as you fill the theatrical space.

Developing Trust Through Physical Sharing

Intimacy requires courage because risk is inescapable.
Rollo May, *The Courage to Create*

Trust is the cornerstone of relationships. In the theatre, where every creative act is tied to a complex network of relationships among actors, directors, designers, playwrights, technicians, and spectators, trust, and the connected feelings of respect, responsibility, sharing, and caring, are crucial to the artistic process. If the chain of trust breaks down anywhere within this sytem, theatre cannot take place. Ultimately, it is respect for the art itself that bonds its participants into a creative ensemble.

Rollo May, in his book *The Courage to Create*, describes social courage as "the courage to relate to other human beings, the capacity to risk one's self over a period of time in a relationship that will demand increasing openness." This is the courage of the actor, whose very work demands the plunge into new relationships as a matter of routine. Actors gain this courage through trust. Trust is an actor's faith.

Your emotions and your physical self are your stock-in-trade. To offer such personal wares you must feel that your efforts will be received in an atmosphere of support and concern. You will learn to be open and vulnerable so that your feelings are available to you and can be expressed easily in public. Simultaneously, you will open affective channels of communication.

As you experiment in your scenes and improvisations, you will need to take emotional risks. You cannot tell what works in the theatre until you do it. This means that you must be willing to take chances and fail, and try again. You may be asked to do things that seem emotionally scary, but you must find the courage to try. Remember that you are always in control. You can open to new feelings or maintain blocks. This requires courage and *trust*—trust in yourself, and trust in the acceptance of your classmates and teacher. Later on, when you work on productions, trust will be an implicit part of your relationships with directors and other members of the cast.

Acting class is a place to test your creative limits, and the ambience must be conducive to emotional freedom, risk taking, and growth. This does not mean there will not be criticism, only that all criticism will be aimed constructively and creatively to foster learning. To make acting class a safe place, we need to develop bonds among the members of the class. We will build upon individual relationships to achieve a positive group dynamic.

The exercises you will be performing in this chapter work to establish trust through physical encounters with others. Although the result is emotional bonding and psychological support, the method is physical. Once you have exchanged a heartfelt touch with someone, you are never complete strangers again. This is one of the great pleasures of acting—the sense of relationship that develops from each experience with another actor. The more we engage in this kind of sharing, the easier it is to touch and to be touched, to exchange feelings, to create an affective relationship. It is what permits us to play intimate scenes with someone we barely know.

The material in this chapter will help you find connections to other people and open new channels for interpersonal expression. You may discover that there is a carry-over from acting class into your personal life; that is an extra dividend, and such new awareness should be noted in your acting log. However, the primary focus of these exercises is not therapeutic, but creative, and you must work to use your new openness to enhance your acting. Because the work in this chapter is geared to deepen your relationships with others, all the exercises require at least two people. As you work, try to find different partners for each experience so that bonding will occur with as many people as possible.

Breaking Down Barriers

The first step in the process is to tear down the barriers that society teaches us to place between us. It is much easier to be judgmental of someone you are not connected to in a deep way. What you will discover is that there is a basis for more meaningful communication with every member of your class. Once you have tapped that common well of human emotions in other people, they will never seem quite the same to you again. A new closeness will join you.

It is extraordinary how little profound contact we allow ourselves with others. We often harbor the illusion that we are open, accessible, and free to express ourselves emotionally. Yet the simple act of looking a stranger in the eye provokes fear, embarrassment, and uneasiness.

Exercise 4.1: The Penetrating Gaze

During the course of this exercise no words must be exchanged; communication must be nonverbal. There will be temptations to break silence, but they must be resisted. Pair yourself off with a member of your class. Gaze deeply into one another's eyes. What happens? Is there a

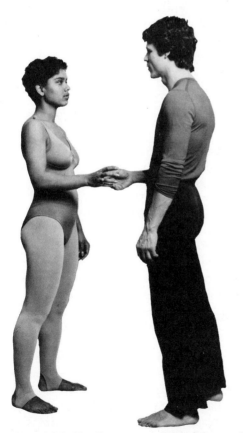

Figure 4.1 The Penetrating Gaze. (Photo—Jim Moore.)

tendency to giggle to cover the discomfiture of feeling someone probe inside of you? Think about how often your eyes squarely meet others. Hold your gaze on your partner. Try to discover some aspect of this person you never noticed. Ask yourself why this side of your partner has gone unobserved. Now find something in your partner that attracts you, that creates warm feelings. When you have found it, communicate your sensations through your breath, through your body, through your expression. When you feel that a real exchange of feelings has taken place between you and your partner, release a sound that expresses your feelings. As you sound, exchange a touch that reflects the feelings. If no sound flows, simply exchange a touch. (See Figure 4.1.)

What did you discover as you went through this exercise? Were you uncomfortable? Did the feelings intensify or dissipate? What changes occurred as you released breath, sound, and touch? Was touching your partner easy or difficult? Note your reactions in your log.

Many of you may be familiar with mirror exercises. This exercise forces us to focus intensely on our partners as we try to enter their thought processes and anticipate their behavior. Several variations on the mirror can lead to opening new channels of communication and freeing expression.

Exercise 4.2: The Mirror

Let's begin with a simple mirror. The class should divide into pairs. Decide which one of you initiates and who will follow. In this exercise, the actor playing the mirror tries to replicate all that the initiator does as closely as a mirror reflection. Begin the mirror. (See Figure 4.2.) The person playing the mirror must focus deeply on the initiator and try to stay as close as possible to the movements. After a minute or so, your teacher will indicate a switch of initiators. Then switch again, alternating roles. The key is to make the transition smoothly when a new initiator takes over. You should be so connected to your partner that you can anticipate where he or she would have gone with the next movement and easily continue the trajectory of the initial choice. If partners are really connected, it is often difficult for an observer to tell who is the initiator and who is the mirror.

If you observed the pattern of movement during the preceding exercise, you would probably notice that most gestures occurred in the arms and hands and that almost no movement occurred in the torso. This is because we are still protective of our body center. We therefore have to work hard to involve the torso in expressive activity. This is a point to which we will return repeatedly throughout our work.

Figure 4.2 The Mirror. Note the involvement of the entire body. (Photo—Jim Moore.)

Exercise 4.3: Variation—Torso Mirror

Repeat the original mirror exercise, this time rooting all your movements in the torso. Be sure to use the pelvis as well as the upper torso. The limbs may move, but only as a natural follow-through of movements initiated in the body center. How do you feel after mirroring torso movements? Was the connection between you and your partner any deeper? Did you feel yourself more exposed to your partner? More inhibited? More connected to the exercise?

Exercise 4.4: Variation—Torso and Breath Mirror

Repeat the torso-rooted mirror, adding audible respiration to the movement patterns. Be sure to mirror breath with gesture.

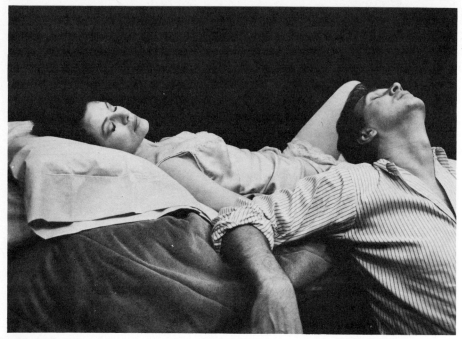

Figure 4.3 Diane Weist and Frank Langella in *After the Fall* by Arthur Miller, directed by John Tillinger. The actors have established the intimate nature of their relationship. (Photo—Peter Cunningham.)

Exercise 4.5: Variation—Torso and Sound Mirror

Repeat the torso-rooted mirror, adding sounds that flow from the movement. See if you can connect the sound and movement to the same source as you did in Chapter 2.

Exercise 4.6: Variation—Emotional Mirror

Prepare for the mirror as in the original mirror exercise. Look deeply at your partner. When you have a sense of having communicated an emotional state of mind, begin the mirror. Change feelings and intensity as you work. At first the emotions will feel external, but as you and your partner become more and more connected the feelings will become real. Continue this switching of initiators. What did you discover about the power of a shared experience?

Eliminating the Fear of Touching

As you discovered during "The Penetrating Gaze" exercise, exchanging touch is difficult, given all our social conditioning to avoid physical contact with people we do not know well. The physical barriers between us often cause or reflect emotional ones. The ability to touch correlates with our ability to relate, to empathize, to communicate. Desmond Morris, in his book *Intimate Behaviour*, underscores this point when he reminds us that "We cannot be close physically without becoming 'close' emotionally." It is important for actors to erase fear of touching and permit the intimacy with other actors that is crucial to ensemble work and the portrayal of intimate relationships on stage. At the same time, we must be sensitive to our partners' private space and not violate them in any way, or trust is broken.

Exercise 4.7: The Group Massage

Arrange yourselves in a small circle, keeping people of similar sizes grouped together. Turn sideways to the right (see Figures 4.4a–b) and massage the upper back and neck of the person standing next to you. The teacher or a group leader can direct the massage so that the class is experiencing the same sensations simultaneously.

Start at the upper neck and make circular movements with the thumb on either side of the spinal column, working down along the spine. Use a firm touch. Massage along the shoulders, then along the shoulder blades. As you work, feel for areas of tension and work them through. Breathe deeply

Figure 4.4a–b Group Massage. (Photos—Jim Moore.)

to gain maximum benefit and release from the massage. Using a more gentle pressure, place the hands mid-spine, and run one hand up the spine and the other down. Repeat this stroking of the spine several times. As you are massaged, try releasing sound to relieve tension and express sensation. The massage should last about fifteen minutes. How does the class mood feel after the massage when compared with how you all felt when class began? Are you all freer with one another and more comfortable within yourselves?

Exercise 4.8: Group Breath

Stand in a circle. Place the palms of your hands over the lower abdomen (at the body center) of the persons on either side of you. Feel the warmth of the hands on your belly. As you breathe, sense your breath finding its energy from the touch of the person next to you. See if the group can find a common respiratory rhythm. Share the sense of a common energy source. Can you feel the intensification of the group dynamic?

WARNING: Some of the exercises in this section can cause injury if proper precautions are not taken. Read all warnings carefully! It is important to ensure the safety of every student. Care must be taken to inspect the environment to make sure it is free of danger points. Careful directions must be given that impress upon the participants the extent of their responsibility toward each other. Do not hesitate to interrupt an exercise if it appears that safety is in jeopardy. An injury can reverse all the gains of a group.

Exercise 4.9: Touch Identification

This exercise must be performed in total silence in a room cleared of all physical obstacles. Choose a partner and study each other carefully. Note various physical attributes: size, weight, hair length, and texture. Observe clothing and style. Now separate from your partner.

Everyone in the class must be blindfolded except a group leader, who observes to alert actors of any danger. Turn the lights off in the room. In the dark, walk around, sensing where other people are through sound and energy. Can you avoid colliding with others through an instinctive sense of where people are? How quickly can you move without running into anyone? After you have wandered in the dark for a few minutes, it is time to find your original partner. Using only your sense of touch, comb the space in search of your partner. There must be no verbal communication to confirm your impressions of whom you have identified. Only the sense of touch may be used. If you believe you have found your partner, take his or her hand. If one of you believes the other has made a mistake, you may refuse to give your hand and move on in search of your partner. After about five minutes, the class should be told to freeze, the blindfolds removed, and the lights turned on. How many of you found your partners? Was it difficult to allow yourself adequate touching to make an identification? Did you feel violated by the touching or did you enjoy it? Did your sense of intimacy with other members of the class change after touching? What did you learn about the power of your tactile sense?

Surrendering Physical Control

Trust implies a confident reliance on other people—a sense that they will act responsibly toward us. Faith in the caring and considerate responses of others is an implicit part of any creative relationship in the theatre. Too often we are taught to mistrust, to keep up our guard, to take the defensive posture. These behavior patterns serve to block an open emotional channel. The following exercises test the limits of our ability to trust others.

Exercise 4.10: Surrendering the Head

Partner one should lie in constructive rest position while partner two kneels behind the head, placing thumbs at the jaw hinge and the other fingers under the head around the upper vertebrae of the neck (see Figure 4.5). The object is to completely surrender control of the head to your partner. Gently lift the head *just two inches* off the ground. If it does not feel very heavy, then the other person is assisting you and has not surrendered control. Sometimes you can feel a contraction of the muscles at the back of the neck, which indicates that complete relaxation has not been achieved. Release the head and lift again. Move the head gently to the left, to the right, up, down, in small circles.

Do you feel that the other person has let go, or do you feel a holding, that the head has not been completely released? Communicate to your partner what you feel and coax him or her into complete confidence in your hold. Tell them, "I've got you. Trust me." When you feel complete surrender has been achieved, exchange positions. Most people are surprised at how difficult this simple exercise can be. We associate the head with control of our body functions and feelings, so giving it up to someone else is not easy. This is a first step in learning to trust your fellow actors.

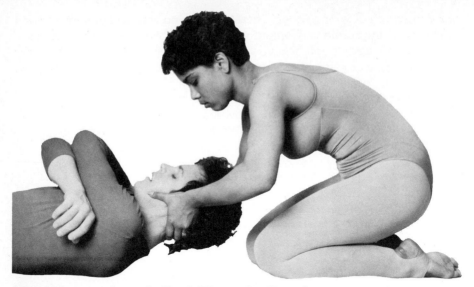

Figure 4.5 Surrendering the Head. (Photo—Jim Moore.)

Exercise 4.11: Falling Backward*

Form couples with people of similar size. One of you stands behind the other with feet spread comfortably, one foot two feet behind the other. Make sure you establish firm footing. **Do not do this exercise in stocking feet or you will have no grip on the floor.** Place your palms on the back of your partner. Slowly withdraw your hands so that they are four inches from the back of your partner. Your partner must fall backward until meeting your hands, which will gently return your partner to a standing position upon contact. Repeat this, moving the hands several inches further away. Move the hands *only* one foot from the back and repeat. At this point your partner will have gone past the point on the axis of the body at which retaining balance is possible. (See Figure 4.6.)

In order to fully let go, a strong sense of trust in your ability and responsibility for catching your partner must be felt, or apprehension will prevent a complete release. If your partner brakes, take the exercise back to the beginning, bringing the palms only a few inches from the back to try and build trust again. Reassure your partner of his or her safety. Work slowly toward the one-foot mark again. It is impossible to fall backward without some degree of anxiety. The moment we pass the point at which our ability to recover balance is lost, there is an automatic moment of anxiety. The question is, can our trust in our partner become stronger than our fear of falling? Switch positions and repeat the exercise.

Figure 4.6 Falling Backward. (Photo—Jim Moore.)

*WARNING: This exercise is potentially dangerous and should not be done unless a teacher is present. You must pair carefully to be sure that each partner is capable of catching the other. If there is an unusually heavy student, care should be taken to either place two people in the catching position or to omit this exercise. There is no need to push this exercise beyond the one-foot fall limit. Once the ability to recover balance is passed, an actor's trust is tested.

Exercise 4.12: Flying**

This exercise requires at least eleven people. Ten of you should pair off with someone close in size to you, but try to match the weaker people with someone stronger. Remove all watches, bracelets, pins, belts, and pendants. **Do not do this exercise in stocking feet!** Stand at one end of the

Figure 4.7 Flying. (Photo—Jim Moore.)

room, facing each other, with arms joined in a wrist lock (see Figure 4.7). Place strong couples in first, third, and fifth positions. The eleventh person, the flier, should be one of the smaller, lighter people in the class. The flier should stand as far across the room from the group as possible. Thinking of yourself as an airplane gaining speed down a runway at take-off, run across the room and leap onto the linked arms of your classmates. Rotate the role of flier, starting with the smaller members of the class so the group can develop a catching rhythm and build confidence in its ability to catch increasingly more weight. How did you feel as you prepared for take-off? Was there apprehension about leaving the ground? How did you feel after you did it? Did you feel free? When you were catching, did you feel confident in your ability to receive the flier?

WARNING: If there is an unusually heavy person in the class do not risk injury by attempting to catch this flier, unless you have a good number of strong people to form the landing pad.

Exercise 4.13: Leading the Blind

Divide into pairs and place a blindfold on one person. The seeing person must function as a seeing-eye dog. Using just touch, *no words,* lead your blindfolded partner around. Start slowly at first, but as you gain confidence in your ability to lead and follow, begin to move more quickly. If the situation permits, leave the classroom and travel more difficult courses. Return to the starting point and switch roles. Did you trust your partner's ability to lead you? Did you follow well? Did the guide feel comfortable touching the blindfolded actor to give directions? Were you sensitive to the messages you received from the guide? Did the blindfold help to increase your level of concentration?

Exercise 4.14: The Obstacle Course

Using chairs to delineate the perimeters, mark off an area about five feet wide by fifteen to twenty feet long which will function as the obstacle course. Choose one student to be the guide and another to run the course. Blindfold the course runner. Arrange a series of obstacles in the delineated area—using bookbags, chairs, clothes, and the bodies of other students. Anything handy and not inherently dangerous may be used. Create variety in the course so that some things must be circled, others stepped over or under, but leave room to actually make it through. The course runner must remain silent throughout the entire exercise and any comments or responses from members of the class must be held in check. The only person who may speak is the guide. Let one student lead the runner to the starting position (see Figure 4.8).

The guide must give careful directions in leading the runner through the course. The runner may ask no questions and may only follow instructions. The guide must make every effort to avoid a collision with the obstacles. This exercise tests the ability of the guide to articulate the relationship of the body to the space as well as the specificity of his desired response. The runner must learn to listen with extraordinary care and interpret verbal commands physically, while giving complete trust to the guide. This exercise can be repeated with different partners, but each time,

Figure 4.8 The Obstacle Course. (Photo—Jim Moore.)

a new obstacle course must be created so the runner has no preconceived ideas about the space.

Exercise 4.15: Obstacle Course Variation

Before attempting this variation, make sure you have carefully read and worked through the sections "Sound and Emotion" and "Sound and Movement Integration" in Chapter 2.

Prepare for the obstacle course as before. Everything remains the same except for one key change. The guide is now forbidden to use words to direct the runner and may only use sounds. This requires a real integration of sound, movement, and feeling within the guide. The sound released must accurately express what you want the runner to do. The runner must listen with a degree of concentration even greater than that demanded before. It may take a minute for the guide and the runner to get attuned to each other's communication system. Be patient; trust yourself and your partner. How did the guide relate directions through sound? How did the runner know when to move? Please note your reactions to this exercise in your logs.

Shaping and Sharing an Improvisation

Shaping an improvisation is a skill that we will develop progressively. At this point it is important to learn how to share an imaginary reality and establish a relationship with a partner. This requires honing communication skills. We will build upon this work in Chapter 6.

	Exercise 4.16: Tug-of-War							

Two actors must play tug-of-war with an imaginary rope. "See" the rope on the floor between you. Look your opponent in the eye. Get ready to compete for possession of the rope. Each of you picks up an end. On your mark, get set, go! (See Figure 4.9.) If you each believe in the imaginary reality and object, you should be expending as much energy as if the rope were real. The body should be centered. There should be tension in the arms, strain on respiration, real feelings of competition between you. Were you able to achieve all the above sensations? Did you feel that you and your partner successfully shared the imaginary reality? Did the length and shape of the rope remain constant? Who won?

Once you feel you can establish the rope and the imaginary circumstances, you must examine how well you shared with your partner. Did you both want to win so much that neither one of you could win or the rope grew because you both insisted on winning and pulled at the same time? Did you establish a give-and-take? Although you both may want to win, in a shared improvisation you must be willing to surrender some ground to your partner while trying to defeat them within the exercise.

Try the exercise again, this time focusing on the inner thoughts of your partner. Sense when one or the other of you has the advantage, let that redouble the other's efforts. How well did you communicate silently with your partner during the exercise? Did you feel you began to read each other's thoughts on the give-and-take? You may have noticed that when

Figure 4.9 Tug-of-War. (Photo—Jim Moore.)

you played this exercise with more internal focus a deeper concentration was required and another level of sharing was reached.

This exercise can be extended into a team tug-of-war. This requires that every member of the group sense what all the others are doing at every moment. If one person decides a particular team has won and no one else perceives this, the sharing within the exercise has failed. Extreme concentration is required for group communication.

Sharing emotions is fundamental to acting. As we work to open up the channels of communication, we develop a sensitivity to the feelings of others. Often actors are obliged to make an entrance during an intense scene on stage and are expected to immediately adjust to the emotional level of the performance. This requires sensitivity and accessibility of feelings as well as tremendous technical control. The more blocks we strip away in our work with other actors, the better able we are to respond to the feelings they give us. The following scale exercise is predicated on the ability to give and take emotional states and intensify them while maintaining control.

Exercise 4.17: Scale of Laughter

Five students sit in five chairs placed one beside the other, facing the class. Start staring straight ahead, completely neutral and unemotional. When everyone has reached neutrality, the first actor must make a slight change of expression, moving toward a smile. The change should be almost imperceptible, perhaps just a slight upturn of the corners of the lips. Turn to the actor next to you, who will face you, mirror your change, turn forward, raise it slightly further toward a smile, and turn to the next actor, who will face you, mirror you, turn forward, raise the level, and turn to the actor next to him or her, who repeats the process. The actors on the end must take from the person next to them, turn forward, raise the level, then hand it right back, intensified, to the person they just took from. These actors have the most difficult job, for they must take, raise the level, and give back in rapid succession. It may take several times back and forth across the group to arrive at a full smile. As you work, it is important to increase tempo, reducing the time between exchanges. As the smile works toward giggles and laughter, it is harder to sustain emotional level if too much time elapses between actors raising the level. By the time laughter is reached, there should be barely one second between exchanges. Let the laughter grow until actors are laughing so hard they can't go on. Were you able to reach hysterical laughter? Did anyone in the group short-circuit the feelings and cut off the intensifying emotions? If someone takes too long, or stops to judge what he or she is receiving instead of immediately responding, this exercise can fizzle out. This is an exercise that can only work with completely open channels of communication among everyone present. If there were difficulties, try a new configuration of five, and put your most accessible and open actors on the ends and in the middle seat. What was the reaction of the class during this exercise? Were the feelings so contagious that they affected everyone in the room? Did shared physical impulses generate real feelings? Analyze your own reactions to this exercise and make a note of how open you felt in your log.

Summary

The creative environment in your class should reflect the gains made through these exercises. You have established a sense of caring and mutual responsibility, have broken down emotional blocks within yourself and between you and your classmates, and have allowed a level of physical and emotional intimacy to enter the work. Now that open channels of communication have been established, you are ready to create a scene.

The Warm-Up

Your body must be ready to act, to yield up emotions, to give them energized physical expression. Before every acting situation—class, rehearsal, and performance—you must prepare your body to deliver the actor's work articulately and efficiently. The warm-up ideally integrates all that you have learned to put your body in gear.

An actor who goes on stage without proper physical preparation will struggle to find an energized state during performance. Concentration will suffer; intensity of expression will fall. It is hard to recapture what you lose from the moment of an entrance, so it is essential to come on stage ready to act, or you will play catch-up throughout an entire performance.

Warm-ups must be developed according to the body's logic. The work we have done in earlier chapters provides the basis for constructing intelligent and effective preparatory exercises. The goals of the warm-up are:

1. to relieve tension that blocks emotional flow, full respiration, and voice
2. to loosen and limber
3. to connect voice, movement, and feeling at the body center.

The warm-up should be structured to achieve a centered state; therefore, all acting warm-ups must include a respiratory and vocal component. Many of the exercises we worked on in earlier chapters can be organized into a warm-up designed to achieve these goals.

There is no set way to conduct a warm-up. The choice of exercises and duration should be determined by the work to follow, the physical conditions of the work space, the number of people working, and the nature of the interpersonal dynamic. It is important to develop sensitivity to all of these factors, for they affect you physically and must be taken into account as you work if you are to reach optimum expressive potential. Often, I have completely altered a planned warm-up based on new conditions I found when I entered a classroom. On a cold winter day in a poorly heated room, I may cut short quiet floor time and choose more active exercises to get the blood flowing. Sometimes, I can feel a group is emotionally down, so I infuse the warm-up with psychologically active, fun exercises to lift the mood and get actors focused on the work. Clearly, a mime class needs more rigorous physical work, and Shakespeare requires more emphasis on voice. Warm-ups before a performance should never end with actors lying prone on the floor, but should help harness and direct the energy needed for that first entrance. Thought and sensitivity are necessary if the warm-up is to achieve its desired goal—a centered, energized, integrated actor.

Initially, you may need supervision as you warm-up—someone to check tension and alignment, to remind you to breathe, to feed helpful images into the exercises. If you are warming up with a scene partner in rehearsal, you should help each other to think through these items. As your kinesthetic awareness grows, you will be increasingly able to work alone, able to adjust to your sense of tension, posture, and respiration.

Getting Focused

Because actors are people, you bring to each work situation the emotional baggage of your lives. You may have had a particularly stressful day, are in personal emotional difficulty, or perhaps you just don't feel up to par. The warm-up is a place to rid yourself of these weights so you can enter a creative state. *This means learning to focus on what you are doing, not what you are feeling.* This is a rule of thumb applicable to your life on stage.

Let's get your attention focused where it needs to be. Most warm-ups in acting class are done standing. As you stand in a circle check your alignment. Were you physically sloppy? Was your energy dispersed? Correct your posture, using your kinesthetic awareness. Make a mental note of any old bad habits that have slipped back in and try to correct them during the day.

If your warm-up begins on the floor, take a look at how you were lying. Were you just spread-eagle, permitting energy to dissipate from the center? Take the constructive rest position and think through the body, letting weight return to rest on the center, harnessing your energy. Check to see that the spine is straight and that shoulders are dropped.

Standing or lying down, take a relaxed deep breath. Is the respiratory channel open? Note where the areas of tension are and pay special attention to releasing them as you warm-up.

This process should take no more than a minute and serves to place your attention in the body so you can get the most out of the warm-up that follows.

Creating the Warm-Up

I have arranged a series of exercises divided into six categories according to their primary emphasis:

1. Relaxation
2. Limbering
3. Respiration
4. Balance
5. Voice
6. Integration

These categories are somewhat arbitrary in that there are always overlaps among them. Limbering helps to relax; relaxation helps the breath; breath and voice are organically linked; balance requires limbering, relaxation, and respiration. So linked are the functions of our bodies, that it is almost impossible to totally isolate any component of the warm-up from the others. In fact, if you do not breathe as you limber, you lose the benefits of the loosening. The fact that breath must be linked to every movement and every sound is evidence of the inevitable cross-over among the exercise categories.

If you choose several exercises from each group, you will have created an adequate warm-up. You may vary the selection from day to day to give variety and interest to your warm-ups; however, in situations where there is a lack of time, it may be convenient to have a more ritualized warm-up that a group can go through without stopping to learn new exercises. If a routine warm-up is used, it is important to avoid the trap of running through the exercises by rote without focus and kinesthetic awareness. To make gains, you must constantly remind yourself to "think inside" your body.

After you have understood the purpose of each exercise group, you will be able to create some of your own exercises, which will lead to feeling centered. If you are warming up alone, choose exercises that concentrate on your areas of need. *A warm-up is effective if you feel centered, energized, and physically, vocally, and emotionally ready to act.*

Exercises described in earlier chapters are included in each group and can be located by the numerical notation. Following this listing are descriptions of the exercises introduced in this chapter. Remember to check your respiration and alignment as you work.

Relaxation

1.6 Focused Relaxation—Tension check
1.7 Relaxation Variation—Tense-release
5.1 Throw the Breath Away
5.2 Facial Stretch
5.3 Body Stretch-Contract

Exercise 5.1: Throw the Breath Away

Stand neutrally. Think about your areas of tension, problems you have carried with you from your life outside, and any negative feelings you may be indulging. Now imagine you could rid yourself of all these limitations by sending them out of the body on a strong exhalation. Place your hands at the mouth, and as you exhale, when the breath hits the hands, use a strong throwing motion to throw away your negative feelings on the exhalation. Watch the path of your breath. As you inhale, take in positive sensations. Repeat this five times, increasing the force of the exhalation and the thrust of the hands.

Exercise 5.2: Facial Stretch

Imagine that your face is made of clay and that you could stretch it toward the outside in all directions. Stretch, opening the eyes as wide as you can, dropping the jaw, and stretching laterally toward the ears and temple. Sensing a lift in the soft palate, feel the cool air in the back of the throat as you inhale. Now as you relax the face, pass neutral and imagine it shriveling into as small and compact a glob as possible—a facial prune. Add the image of having bitten into a sour lemon. Tighten, tighten, until you feel you can hardly take a breath. Now stretch your face back out as far as you can, breathe, and contract again. Repeat four times. Now move the entire face to the upper left-hand corner, now to the lower right, now upper right, then lower left. Return to neutral. How does your face feel? Have you felt muscles you never knew you had? Is it warm from the flow of blood into these areas? Just think about all the expressive movements of the face you never use!

Exercise 5.3: Body Stretch-Contract

This exercise extends the facial stretch to the body. Imagine that your body is elastic. Stretch it to its outer limits, opening the arms, legs, fingers and toes wide, stretching the buttocks, feeling open at the chest. Simultaneously stretch the face. Now quickly move from the stretch into a fully contracted, shriveled body. You should find yourself in a small crouch, all neatly tucked, fists, toes, buttocks, arms, and legs tightened, with your facial prune. Now jump back into the full stretch, like a stretched rubber band. Focus on your respiration. Is it free? Try and release sound. What did you discover? Shrivel again into a complete contraction. Try and release sound again. What did you discover? Stretch and contract three more times.

Limbering

1.12 Building the Spine
1.15 Head Rolls
1.16 Rotations
1.17 Torso Stretches
1.18 Swings
1.19 Shakes
2.6 Jaw Release
2.7 Soft Palate Lift
2.8 Tongue Stretching
2.9 Lip Loosening
2.10 Throat Opening
2.17 The Ripple of a Yawn
3.4 Freeing the Torso
5.4 Spinal Whip

Exercise 5.4: Spinal Whip

Stand neutrally, legs about a foot and a half apart. Slowly drop down the spine so that the head and arms are hanging between the feet, knees are slightly bent. In this position, begin a strong undulating movement of the pelvis, letting the undulation ripple through the spine up to the neck, throwing the head up and out at the end of the follow-through. Think of the spine as a whip you are cracking and imagine the rippling S curve. Be sure to release the breath on each undulation. Pause between each new breath to avoid getting dizzy. Be sure to come up the spine slowly, rebuilding vertebra by vertebra.

Respiration

1.13 Sensing the Respiratory Process
2.1   Breathing Naturally
2.3   Respiration and Center
5.5   Panting

Exercise 5.5: Panting

Standing neutrally, begin a gentle pant. The goal is to take in as much air as
you release so you can continue the panting breath at will. If you find
yourself gasping for air, then you have not found a balanced respiratory
pattern. Once you have settled into the pant, try to quicken the breath and
maintain control. You should feel little quivering movements at the body
center.

Balance

1.11 The Pendulum
1.18 Swings
1.20 Slow Motion
1.21 Balance through Sensing Center
5.6   Pliés

Exercise 5.6: Pliés

Stand neutrally, feet about ten inches apart. Check your alignment. Bring
your palms to rest crossed against the chest. On a count of eight you will
perform a full plié (deep bend of the knees), maintaining torso alignment.
On the four count you will feel your heels lift off the ground. Be sure you
keep proper posture during the entire descent. Rise on a count of eight.
Repeat four times. Did you have trouble holding proper torso alignment and
balance?

Voice

2.2   Breath and Sound
2.5   Taking Pleasure from Sound—The Sound Massage
2.11 Head, Nose, and Mouth Resonance
2.12 Chest Resonance
2.13 Vowel Articulation

Exercise 5.7: Running Through Your Resonators

Stand neutrally. Begin with your deepest chest resonance, run through your range, moving from chest to mouth to head resonance as you move up in pitch. You will feel that there is a natural change in the sound from "huh" to "ah" to "ee" as you change from chest to mouth to head resonance. Note the point at which the resonators change. Were you able to relax the vocal passage so completely that no break in the voice occurs as you switch resonators? If you felt the voice crack it means that tension occurred in the vocal channel. Go back to releasing a free breath and then try this exercise again.

Integration Exercises

Exercise 5.8: Up and Down the Spine with Resonator Scales

When you have mastered the run through the resonators, try adding movement up and down the spine. Drop down the spine and as you run up the resonators, rebuild the spine vertebra by vertebra. When you reach the top, raise the arms overhead. Descend down your resonators as you release the hands, wrists, elbows, and head, dropping down the spine as you flow down the resonators. Did the inclusion of movement free the voice? Invert the process and go down the resonators as you go up the spine and go up the resonators as you rebuild the spine. How did this feel? Did it help to release the "eee" sound to have the head hung over?

Group Warm-Ups

Most of the exercises you have just performed can be done individually or in a group. There are times when group warm-ups are necessary or desirable. Often the warm-up can be a time to build a supportive group dynamic, to break down barriers, or to unite a group for a communal creative effort. Group work helps to foster a shared energy level, rhythm, and focus. A successful warm-up can encourage a positive ambience. Although many professional actors prefer to warm up on their own, having honed a personal warm-up over years of work, student actors benefit from group exercises and the ensuing esprit de corps. This is especially necessary before a performance or class, when a united team effort is essential to success. To achieve group solidarity, return to the following exercises:

3.7   Group Energy Flow—Passing Sound and Movement
4.7   Group Massage
4.8   Group Breath
5.9   Rhythmic Group Sounding
5.10 Group Mirror

The next exercises are particularly useful before a performance, rehearsal, or group improvisation.

Exercise 5.9: Rhythmic Group Sounding

This exercise should only be done after a thorough vocal and physical warm-up. Select one person as the leader. Return to the group breath with hands on neighbors' bellies providing the breath impulse. When group respiration is coordinated, the leader should release a rhythmically repeated "huh" sound. The entire group must join the leader's rhythm. Slowly increase the tempo of the sounding with energy increasing with pace. When the group has reached a point of maximum energy release on sound, remove the hands from stomachs and raise the arms shoulder height, bent up at the elbows. With outward elbow flexions at the moment of vocal release, turn the group sounding into a group cheer. Now run around the room in a circle with sound, movement, and voice all on the same rhythmic pattern. This exercise was inspired by watching a high school football team workout before a game, shouting in unison, "kill, kill, kill, kill." Often, before a performance, I have ended a cast warm-up with this exercise, substituting the word *go* for the "huh" sound, and sent a group of revved-up actors running rhythmically like a football team into the dressing-rooms.

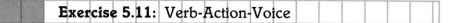

Exercise 5.10: Group Mirror

Choose a leader who is particularly physically and vocally expressive. After a complete warm-up, have the leader stand before the class or cast. The group must attempt to mirror the leader's every sound and movement, following the guidelines for mirror exercises provided in Chapter 3. The leader must take care that all movement and sound are connected at the center, involve the torso, and offer complete vocal release. The more expansive the sounds and movements the better. The leader must be energized or the group energy will fall.

Relating the Warm-Up to the Work

After you have worked through the warm-up sequence, you should feel physically and vocally ready. To achieve the total centered state, you must work to connect your thoughts and feelings to your body. The following exercises will provide these vital links.

5.11 Verb-Action-Voice
5.12 Character Walks and Words
5.13 Opening Line Warm-up

Exercise 5.11: Verb-Action-Voice

This exercise works best with a partner or in a group, but can be done alone with an imaginary partner. Choose a strong action verb. Good examples are: stop, go, hit me, give me, take it, do it, say it, run, kick, jump, kill, help, and so forth. Say each verb with a particular objective in mind. As you speak, perform a simultaneous movement. All movements must be centered and originate in the torso. A disconnected hand gesture will not help you integrate feeling with voice and movement. If you are working alone, make sure you direct your verb to an imaginary partner. Try saying each verb with four different intentions, noting each time how the movement and voice changed with alterations in thought and feeling. If you are working in a group, let several different people try different intentions with the same verb, each jumping in in rapid succession. As you move from verb to verb, see how expansive and free you can be in your voice and action choices.

This exercise can be tied directly to scene work if you choose a verb that represents your character's objective. Try experimenting with different actions to achieve the objective as you say your verb. Use your character's voice.

The following character warm-up exercises are best incorporated after you have completed the exercises in Chapters 12 and 13.

Exercise 5.12: Character Walks and Words

Each individual has a walk peculiar to personality structure. The manner in which this walk coordinates with breath can help to define who you are on stage. Chapters 12 and 13 will teach you to analyze a character you are working on in terms of how the walk and respiratory connection reflects identity. As you think through your character, start circling the room, letting your feelings pervade your movement. Continue walking until you feel you have found a walk that expresses who your character is. When you feel right about the movement, choose a short phrase, expression, maybe just one word that your character would use as an expression of something central to his or her personality. Examples might be "gee whiz," "go away," "damn it," "cool," "neat," "go to hell." Try to coordinate the walk with the verbal expression, linking the two through respiration. When you have found the connections, we should have a strong impression of who your character is. This work will give more vital stage life to your scene work.

Exercise 5.13: Opening Line Warm-Up

This exercise follows logically from the two preceding ones. After you have found your character's walk and word, think about your scene and choose a strong action verb to express your character's objective on the opening line. With this verb in mind subtextually, say your opening line accompanied by a strong centered action. Repeat the line, experimenting with readings and actions until you feel centered in the life of the character. Try saying the line as you do your character walk. Note in your journals how this exercise affected the next performance of the scene.

Summary

A good warm-up works to unite body, voice, feeling, and thought at the actor's center. The warm-up connects you to your expressive self, expands creative potential, and facilitates energized performance. It synthesizes all the lessons of earlier work to prepare your body to act. Be sure to warm up before every performance situation.

PART II

Internalizing the Dramatic Situation

Communicating on Stage

For the actor the whole thing is to give of himself. In order to give of himself, he must first possess himself.
Jacques Copeau, *Notes sur le métier de comédien*

When we are on stage, we are involved in the process of communication—with other actors, with the audience, with ourselves. We have talked of this process as an unbroken energy flow, as a chain of stimuli and response, as continuous action. Implicit in each is the image of unending cycles. Unlike everyday life, the theatre demands an ongoing uninterrupted communication process.

In this chapter, we will explore the way we transmit and receive communication on stage, learning those skills which enhance our ability to make the play come alive within us and for others. We will learn to focus and concentrate, to be open and responsive, and to create the inner images for a role.

Listening and Taking In

Two concepts that dominate our work with acting partners are **listening** and **taking in.** We listen with our ears, our minds, our hearts, our feelings, our bodies. Taking in means that what we hear and feel we let inside of us to affect us physically, emotionally, and mentally. When actors talk of the "illusion of the first time," they are referring to listening with new ears each time they perform, so that their responses are fresh. If we have really taken in our partner's thoughts and feelings, they will provoke a change inside of us. This change requires an adjustment of our next message to our partner, who in turn adjusts to what is received from us. We have created yet another circular flow: listen—take in—adjust—transmit. We will work on our ability to receive and respond to our partners so our adjustments will be sensitive and efficacious.

Communication is a source of action! Because conflict of wills is a fundamental part of the dramatic situation, you must relate well to further your objectives. On stage, the communication process requires an effective reading of thoughts, feelings, and actions in order to advance your character's goals.

Figure 6.1 Jamila Perry and Delroy Lindo in *Joe Turner's Come and Gone* by August Wilson, directed by Lloyd Richards. Observe the deep communication between the two actors. (Photo—Peter Cunningham.)

Exercise 6.1: Communicating Sensations

This exercise is done in pairs. Decide which one of you will be the initiator. Sit facing your partner in silence. Take your partner's hand and close your eyes. Choose an objective you wish to communicate to your partner. Using only the touch of your hands, communicate your objective. Since your eyes are closed you must sense the response by touch, listening for respiratory changes, sensing body tension and vibrations in the air between you. Pursue your objective for three minutes in this way, adjusting all the time to the response you are receiving from your partner.

How much could you feel from your touch and intuition? Did you feel a deep communication process between you? Discuss with your partner what you thought the objective was. How effectively was it communicated with these limitations?

VARIATION I: Repeat this exercise with your eyes open but maintain silence. How did the return of vision affect your communication process? Did you use your face more to communicate, or your eyes to receive? Did your torso express your objective? Was the major source of information still coming from touch?

VARIATION II: Repeat this exercise, adding sound and language so that you now have all of your expressive channels available. Be careful not to rely on words to do the job of touch, sight, and body language. You must continue to make optimum use of the means of communication you developed before, while listening carefully to the meaning of what your partner says and taking in the response. Make certain sound and action are integrated. Using all of your senses to communicate makes this a vital process to watch.

Did you feel that you and your partner had an uninterrupted communication flow? Was that easier to maintain when your eyes were closed? Did you feel outside external stimuli upset concentration and invaded your communication process as we added the other senses?

Concentration and communication are inextricably intertwined. You may have sensed how much you needed to concentrate on reading and transmitting messages in order to perform the last exercise. The more intense your focus on your objective, the more belief you will evoke from your fellow actors and the audience. The techniques we study are effective only if you perform them with focused energy.

Too often, we confuse concentration with tension and think we must stare with paralytic rigidity at our object of attention. In fact, to communicate with your partner you must be relaxed and open, free of any interfering tension. The exchanges you share should be based on the energy that flows between you.

Exercise 6.2: Shared Story Telling

Sit facing your partner. One of you begins to tell a completely fantasized story—the wilder the better. Make it rich in imagery. Tell the story using your voice and body to communicate all the sensory details. At a signal, the person listening will pick up the story without so much as missing a beat, as if he or she were inside the head of the other and can finish a partner's sentences without hesitation. Continue the story, switching the roles of raconteur and listener several times until you have perfected your listening abilities to such a degree that the switches are effortless.

    VARIATION I: A more difficult version of this exercise is the story-telling mirror. This requires that the listener simultaneously mimic action and repeat the story as it is told by the initiator and be ready to jump in at the signal to switch roles. You need to feel how your partner translates the story content into physical impulses. Use all your senses to enter your partner's thoughts and body. Did you notice how much you had to concentrate on listening to make sure you could jump in at any time? Did you feel the flow of energy between you?

You have discovered that actors need all their expressive organs for maximum communication. We often let language compensate for weaknesses in our other expressive channels. Words are really the icing on the cake. It is possible to hide our feelings behind our words, but much more difficult to hide what we feel as our eyes and breath express it. Learn to communicate your thoughts and feelings through all the means available to you.

Learning to Be Vulnerable

The essence of acting is communication so it is important to recognize our personal inhibitions and work to let down blocks. Because of the difficult world in which we live, we learn to build elaborate systems of emotional defense. While this protects us from getting hurt, it impedes the communication process. Acting requires freedom; our feelings must be accessible to us so we can respond to the messages we receive from other actors. *Taking in means allowing ourselves to be **vulnerable**.*

    We can abandon ourselves without fear when we recognize that we are only imagining the stage reality, that we are pretending while simultaneously acting with belief and conviction. This seemingly paradoxical statement is at the core of acting technique. We must live fully within the imaginary world of the drama with total emotional commitment, while remaining aware of its artifice and maintaining artistic control.

Figure 6.2 Rhoda Feuer and Marvin Scott in the Hunter College production of *The Sea Gull* by Anton Chekhov, directed by Mira Felner. Note the vulnerability of the actress as she reveals her unrequited love.

Exercise 6.3: Communicating Through Free Association

We constantly censor our visceral responses and choose what we consider to be socially acceptable behavior. This exercise makes you aware of how much you inhibit your deepest communication flow for self-protection.

Sit facing a partner. You will free-associate off each other's words. One of you says the first word that comes into your head, the other says the first word he or she associates with that word, the initiator free-associates with the second word, and so on, both going back and forth with your immediate word associations. The key is to say the first thing that comes to mind without any time lapse between words. Say only one word at a time. This should be done as a rapid-fire exercise. If anyone hesitates, you will discover that it was to censor the immediate response because it revealed too much about you. See how long you can keep this up and how free you can be in your associations.

This exercise can be done in round-robin fashion, with the group sitting in a circle. To do this exercise well, everyone must concentrate, listen, take in, and respond freely.

Personalizing

Personalization is the process through which you make the dramatic situation personally meaningful so you can believe in what is happening and respond with truth and sincerity. It enables you to find an inner connection to your character's objectives. Personalization makes the communication process work on stage. It requires allowing the imaginary circumstances of the play to elicit concrete inner images for your words, while letting the words of the other characters touch you. To personalize, you must concentrate on the dramatic reality and let each element call forth a response from your inner being. The techniques that help us personalize are sense memory, substitution, emotional recall, and imaging. These work together to make the play come alive inside us.

Sense Memory

Sense memory, the ability to recall and recreate experiences through our senses, helps form the images so vital for the actor's personalization process. We all have a storehouse of memories that can serve to stimulate our imagination and aid in the creation of character and dramatic circumstances.

The ability to evoke a responsive chord in others depends on how freely and accurately we can express the sensation of an event. To see, feel, hear, taste, and smell things that are not really there is crucial if you are to communicate their existence to the audience. Objects on stage often may not be exactly what they are supposed to represent. Tea may substitute for whiskey, a cheap plaster copy for a great sculpture, a window supposedly looking out on a garden may face a brick wall or a painted flat. The ability to make the audience believe that these objects are real depends upon the skill with which you can reconstruct the sensory experience that each is meant to simulate. You need to sharpen your powers of observation in life so you can more easily recall like experiences. Sense memory allows the free play of associations to take place within you, stimulating your imagination and facilitating communication.

You may be surprised to discover how generalized your sense of awareness is. We go through life with relatively little focus on things around us. We take in general impressions without specific detail. Learning to zero in on objects and people gives you a great deal of useful data to incorporate in performance. To emphasize how little we pay attention to these things, try to describe a pencil. Can you remember every detail?

Exercise 6.4: Honing Sensory Observation

Pick up any small familiar object; a pencil or a fork or a piece of candy will do. Really examine it for details—color, weight, size, shape, texture. Notice how many qualities are present in this object that you never really noticed before. Increasing your level of concentration on the object enables you to discover things in the commonplace and familiar of which you were never aware. Take in all the visual elements, then move on to the tactile. Examine the relationship between sight and touch. Does your object have an odor or distinct taste. Does it make any noise? How does it sound when you touch it, hit it, knock it? When you believe you have truly studied all the sensory details of your object, put it away out of sight.

Can you recreate the feel of the object in your hand? Can you see it in all its detail? Can you experience in your imagination its smell and taste? The noise it makes? Do you believe you were able to totally recreate the object in your mind's eye? Go back to the real object and check your sense memory. Were there any details you forgot?

Put your object away again. Without divulging what your object is, describe it in great sensory detail to your class, or to a partner. Make them feel what you felt, see what you saw, hear what you heard, and so on. In order to truly communicate the nature of your object, you will discover that you have to relive the experience of your object in your imagination. You need a specific inner image if your audience is to truly share all that you felt. Were you able to communicate the true nature of your object to someone else?

You may find it helpful to repeat Exercise 3.13, using a familiar place from your past. Focus on sensory data and see how much more you can recall this time.

While it is good practice to try to relive the sensory details of real experiences, on stage, you will be relating to experiences that take place only in your imagination. It is important to learn to construct imaginary experiences with the same detail and specificity as those from real life.

Substitution

Substitution is the use of people and events from your own life in place of characters and events in a play. When we substitute people, we pretend the actor in the scene is someone else. If I'm playing the balcony scene from *Romeo and Juliet,* I may decide to substitute for Romeo my real life boyfriend with whom I am madly in love. Often this helps identify with the feelings of a character and determine an appropriate emotional response.

While substitution is useful as we personalize a scene, there are pitfalls in the technique when used in performance. First, in the example above, I have to work to conjure up my boyfriend, which takes me out of the stage reality and into my own mind. Second, my energy is directed inward toward my personal emotions, depleting the vitality of my performance. Third, if I am playing the scene to my boyfriend, who is not there, how much am I relating to the Romeo who is on stage with me? Substitution puts a screen between you and your fellow actor, breaking down the communication process. How can you react to Romeo if you are thinking about someone else?

The recurring question from beginning actors is, "What do I do if my stage partner doesn't give me what I need to play off? What if I find Romeo unattractive or cold, shouldn't I put someone in his place who turns me on?" Learning to find what you need in your acting partners is part of an actor's job. Use the power of your imagination to create what you need! Look at your Romeo and find something appealing about this person, however subtle, and build upon it, allowing all that you know about passionate love to flow. You must learn to discover and use the aspects of other actors that feed your stage relationshp, or else all that happens between you will be empty. Communication can only take place if you are sharing the reality of the stage with your partner.

Exercise 6.5: Discovering Your Partner

No words may be exchanged during this exercise, and total concentration and communication is required. You must never reveal to your partner what attribute you chose for each emotion. Knowing that your thought processes are to remain private lets you think and feel without inhibition.

Stand facing your partner. Looking deeply at each other, find the thing you like best about your partner. When you have found it, let your imagination enhance it as the feelings flow between you. Keep focusing on the thing you like best. When you feel you have really established contact, exchange a sound and a touch that express how you feel.

Return to neutral. Still with the same partner, this time find the thing that angers you most about this person. Really think about what it is as you

Figure 6.3a–c Discovering Your Partner. (Photos—Jim Moore.)

feed it to your imagination. When the feelings come let them flow and express them to your partner on a sound and touch.

Return to neutral. Look at your partner anew. This time find the thing about this person you could most easily love. Let the feelings of love grow between you. When you have really connected to this attribute of your partner, exchange the feelings on a sound and touch. (See Figures 6.3a–c.)

In doing this exercise, you may at first have felt a bit self-conscious and protective. Once you got past those feelings you should have discovered how easy it is to find everything you need in your acting partner when the proper focus and imagination are at work. As a result, do you feel closer and more accessible to each other? Did this enhance your ability to communicate?

If you can successfully perform the above exercise, you will be able to find the qualities you need in other actors. You can still use substitution in your homework on a scene as you try to gain understanding of your character's feelings and situation. Used this way, substitution can inform your action choices and intensify your responses.

Emotional Memory

Emotional or ***affective memory*** is a form of substitution. It requires recalling an event from your life that is analagous to the event or emotions required in a play in order to substitute your real emotions for the character's. Affective memory works much like sense memory to render tangible and meaningful in personal terms the imaginary circumstances of a play. It can provide the images necessary for personalization.

It is rare that actors have had experiences that resemble those of a character in every way. Emotional memory work seeks those experiences that approximate the situation of the character. In Act I of *The Seagull*, when the audience mocks Treplev's play, causing him anger and pain, you the actor may never have written a failed play, but perhaps you have acted in a play that was poorly received, or have written a poem or a term paper that was scoffed at. These personal analogous experiences can help you empathize with Treplev's pain and rejection.

In an emotional memory exercise, you would select a powerful experience from the past and recall the physical details that surrounded the event, much as you recalled the physical details of a special place in Exercise 3.15. As more and more specific data are recalled, you are transported back to the initial experience which grows increasingly vivid through sensory recollection until it is so real that you actually feel an emotional response strongly akin to the original.

Sometimes, events in our life come back as a natural response to the given circumstances of the play. The character's situation triggers a responsive chord precisely because we have had a parallel experience. When this happens, our acting is enriched, but only if we shape those tapped feelings to fit the specific needs of the role and the given circumstances. The play must dominate the form we give to a part, not our personal emotional life, or we risk shaping a character around ourselves instead of realizing the playwright's vision. This can diminish the dramatic power of the play. Reliving our own experiences in the guise of a character is not in and of itself good acting.

Emotional memory cannot replace the work of the imagination. It is a good place to begin your search for a personal reference point for a role as part of your acting homework. It does not belong in a performance when you must be directing your energy outward for effective communication and focusing on your actions and objectives.

The pitfalls of this technique in performance are clear from the following story. I once watched an actor play Eben in *Desire Under the Elms*. In the scene where he learns that Abbie has killed their son, his grief at the loss of the child seemed inadequate to the magnitude of the event. I asked the actor if he had really worked through the given circumstances of this scene and grasped the complex emotions of his character, who had wished the child dead and triggered the murder. The actor told me he had been trained to use affective memory for such a scene. Since no significant person in his life had ever died, he remembered the death of his cat whom he had really loved, and substituted the cat for the child. The substitution of the cat for the baby reduced the drama to the banal, while the actor played a general sense of grief and loss that in no way took into account the guilt and anger also present for Eben, the character, within the context of the play.

This actor did not use his imagination to build upon his personal experience, so the use of emotional memory engendered an inadequate, generalized emotion not specific to the given circumstances. The actor, focusing inward to conjure up this experience from his life, lost sight of his objectives and left the actress playing Abbie alone on the stage while he was busy working inside of himself. He forgot about his rage, love, and hatred of her. The entire communication process between them broke down while he was having a private emotional experience.

Affective memory should be used to spur your imagination, not to replace creative work with text. When emotional recall is properly used, it can enhance your connection to a character's plight and help in the process of personalizing a role, providing useful information upon which to base our choice of action. Emotional memory is probably best used as an exercise to make your emotions more accessible—a kind of emotional warm-up.

Creating Images

You will notice that when you communicate in everyday life, your mind provides a mental image for the words you say. It is as if you visualize people, places, and events and your relationship to them as you speak. This same process continues when you are on stage. Envision the images your character would have to fill your words with life. If you are talking about your lover in a scene, you must have someone specific in mind. See your lover in detail as you describe him or her so that your words can portray the internal image. In *The Glass Menagerie*, an actress playing Amanda would need to paint an inner picture of her life in Blue Mountain in order to make her reminiscences meaningful. These images create an emotional connection to a role. To achieve this connection, the images cannot be general. The more detail you create, the more your emotions are evoked. This deepens your expressive power and permits communication of what you think and feel so the text of a play can arouse feelings, thoughts, and sensations in the audience. Our work on sense memory facilitates the imaging process.

Exercise 6.6: Creating Inner Images

Repeat each of the words below with three different internal images. Notice how your thoughts change the way you expressed the word. Were you able to communicate your image?

1. water
2. cloud
3. sex
4. star
5. rose
6. fire
7. sunrise
8. devil
9. money

Personalization and Subtext

The internal images that determine the significance of your words and reveal your inner objective, what you really want at a given moment, are your **subtext**. Sometimes the words in a play express a character's thoughts directly, but often there is a contradiction between the words we say and what we actually feel. Subtextual meanings are subtly expressed by a gesture, an action, an intonation, a breath, a pause. What you are experiencing and doing as you say a line colors the significance of the words. If we are listening only to the objective content of dialogue, we may mistake the message.

Whereas substitution and sensory memory work call upon the life experiences an actor can bring to the play, subtext requires that the inner images be created on the basis of the given circumstances of the drama. In *A Streetcar Named Desire*, when Stanley returns home from the hospital in scene 10 and tells Blanche they sent him home for the night, Blanche's line "Does that mean we are to be alone here?" can be made to express an entire gamut of thoughts from a warning, to disgust, to seduction. The choice of Blanche's inner thoughts must be rooted in an understanding of the play. Your subtext becomes the basis for action. Effective communication requires learning to express and read subtextual meaning.

Exercise 6.7: Subtext—What's in a Word?

Take the statement "I need you." Say this line to a partner with each of the following objectives:

1. To make your partner realize how much you depend on him or her.
2. To convince your partner you are completely independent.
3. To communicate to your partner that you despise him or her.
4. To persuade your partner that he or she is the most wonderful person in the world.

Notice how you had to change your inner thoughts to communicate each change in objective. Did your subtext inspire action? Did your partner listen with the ears and eyes to read your subtext?

Often singing puts us more directly in touch with our feelings than speech. It has been speculated that the elongated vowel sounds of song allow for greater emotional flow than the more clipped sounds of speech where consonants have greater play. Often we burst into spontaneous song when we are happy as a direct expression of intense feeling. For this reason, coupled with concern for aesthetics, many of us hesitate to sing in public, although we enjoy the emotional release of song in the shower. Singing beautifully is in fact a subjective judgment. Many wonderful singers have voices that are objectively unpleasing, but because of the great emotional connection they make to the subtextual content of each song, they move us deeply. Louis Armstrong comes to mind at once. If you create inner images for the words of a song and work to communicate their meaning as you sing, you can be touching and affecting no matter what the objective quality of your voice.

Exercise 6.8: Personalization—Communicate in
Song

Choose a song with lyrics that express something meaningful to you. Go over the words to make sure that each line is clear. Fill each word with a full image, taking care to define your subtext. Stand or sit facing your partner and recite the words of your song, trying to communicate meaning. Maintaining eye contact, begin again, this time singing the song to your partner while keeping your focus on communicating the meaning of the lyrics.

Were you able to personalize the words? Describe the difference in the experience of reciting the lyrics versus singing the lyrics. Did you feel the song enabled you to make a deeper connection with your partner than did speaking these same words? Try singing your song to a group.

Summary

The ability to communicate is essential to the theatrical experience. Effective communication means listening and taking in the messages you receive from other actors, while remaining personally open and vulnerable. The process requires concentration and focus. The dramatic situation must touch us, the words we speak must be meaningful, we must have strong inner images if we are to successfully communicate the feelings of our character. Various techniques can sensitize us, but ultimately, we need the power of our imagination to make the dramatic reality live.

Given Circumstances

In everyday life "if" is an evasion, in the theatre "if" is the truth.

Peter Brook, *The Empty Space*

The *magic if*, the ability to act as "if" the circumstances of the play were real, is the measure of your theatrical imagination. The logic of the given circumstances, the *who, what, where,* and *when* of the dramatic situation must shape your behavior and inspire creative acting choices. The given circumstances are an imperative to action.

Physicalizing the Given Circumstances

The given circumstances are expressed through your physical life on stage. Your voice and body provide the vital information an audience needs to understand the play. The exercises in this chapter will teach you to make the imaginary world of your character tangible and real to you and to the audience. You will learn to behave appropriately within the the reality of the stage and to interact with characters and objects by treating them as you wish the audience to believe they are. This is done through *physicalizing* the given circumstances.

116

The exercises in this chapter are deceptive. Be·careful not to fall in the trap of externally indicating shifts in given circumstances. Respond to them from a centered state, allowing the breath to lead the body and voice. If you remain physically unchanged during these exercises, then you have not internalized the given circumstances and are indicating your reactions externally. Your thoughts should feed your feelings, affecting respiration and alignment, altering your energy. Your actions must come naturally out of these changes.

As you work through this chapter, you will find the sense memory and personalization work from Chapter 6 helpful in avoiding playing the cliché. Take the following example. If you tell an untrained actor to go on stage and wait for a job interview in a hot humid office, the immediate reaction may be to start fanning and wiping perspiration off the brow. If you recreate such an experience for yourself, you will see that you actually behave quite differently. You do not simply react to the heat, but are aware of your desire to get the job and make a good impression. Your objective dominates even the way you respond to physical circumstances. You may try to keep cool and relaxed, take deep breaths, stay very still, or check to make sure there's no embarrassing perspiration stain. These actions, all geared to achieve your objective, are not the obvious choices; however, if you go through a sense memory exercise, recalling when you were actually in a similar circumstances, these possibilities will come back to you.

The key is to be as specific as possible in your imaginary painting of the given circumstances. Just as details evoked feelings in our sense memory exercises in the preceding chapter, such focus on the specifics of the given circumstances inspires action, awakens emotions, and enlivens your performance. Because it is so easy to succumb to impulses toward generality, we will address the *who, what, where,* and *when,* separately, learning to enrich our stage life through focusing on physicalizing each independently.

Justification

As circumstances justify action, often actions need to be made plausible through **justification.** You, the actor, are therefore involved in a dual relationship between circumstances and action.

1. Some circumstances demand and justify taking certain actions.
2. Some actions require that you provide the imaginary circumstances to justify them.

In your work in the theatre, you will be asked to perform actions because they are in the script, or because a director tells you to do something, or some pragmatic necessity obliges you to cross the stage or take a specific position. None of these actions may be performed without reason.

It is your job as an actor to imagine a circumstance that would justify your behaving in the specific way required.

Justification enables you to use known and imagined circumstances to create a sense of truth and belief in your actions. This, in the words of Stanislavski, will "awaken your sense of faith" in what you are doing on stage. Every detail you add to the given circumstances reinforces the truth of what you are doing.

We free ourselves from personal limitations on stage by letting the circumstances justify behavior that is not natural to us. If the situation is compelling, it will command action; so you can achieve a level of characterization, simply by imagining circumstances powerful enough to motivate behavior not usually within your personal pattern of action. The *magic if* is also the departure point for characterization.

The exercises in this chapter are meant to develop your ability to physicalize the circumstances of a scene by feeding your imagination and teaching you to justify stage behavior. In some cases, circumstances will be provided as justifications for action, in others, actions will be given and you will provide the justification. As you work, you must examine your acting to be certain that your actions were accompanied by an organic physical response and a sense of truth.

Improvising the Given Circumstances

Who

Who begins the search for your character's identity and an understanding of your relationship to the other characters on stage. Who you are is a result of the confluence of circumstances that have shaped your character's life. Whether they are experiences from the distant past or events immediately antecedent to the dramatic situation on stage, these physical and emotional conditions shape your character and are made tangible to the audience through your behavior on stage.

Since character is established on stage through our physical impression of an actor, you must define as much as you can of a person's past by the physical choices you make. Energy, center, voice, alignment, and action reveal aspects of personality.

To determine who you are, you must pose a series of pertinent questions: How old am I? What do I look like physically—height, weight, attractiveness? How am I dressed? What is my occupation? What are my sexual proclivities? What is my social, familial, and political status? What was my childhood like? Did I suffer any trauma? Am I loved? Am I fulfilled? How do I feel about myself? Am I aggressive? Passive? Extroverted? What are my ambitions? My secret desires and fears? Certain roles will suggest additional questions, and you must give thought to the information you need for each character you will play. If I am in a scene or "improv" with another actor, I need to know who that person is. What is the nature of our relationship? How do I feel about him or her? How does that character feel about me?

More than any other of the given circumstances, the *who* is given to portrayal through cliché and stereotype. Ask an inexperienced actor to portray an old person, and immediately the back is hunched and a tremor and cane are added. Yet if you look at many of the elderly people you know, you will see that neither stoop, nor cane, nor tremor can be seen. So what makes a person appear young or old? Why do some old people appear young? Observe people of various ages around you to see if you can determine what it is that defines age. Focus on energy, tempo, and center. Enter your observations in your log. Make similar observations of people in various professions. Use all that you learned about kinesthetic awareness. Can you tell what they do from their physical comportment? Look at people whose occupations you know and see if there is anything about them that helps fix their identity. After you have carefully observed those you know, try a guessing game next time you are on a bus or train, or in a restaurant. What qualities were you looking at?

Exercise 7.1: How Old Am I?

Make a wish and blow out the candles on your birthday cake at age 4, 8, 14, 16, 21, 30, 40, 55, 70, 80, 90, 100. Make the wish specific and know how much you want it to come true. What adjustments did you make for each age? Were you playing externals, or did you really think about how life circumstances would alter thoughts and behavior and affect the wish you would make at each age? Did something inside change as you thought about each wish? Did your respiratory rhythm change? Did your energy change? Did you allow the changes to run through your entire body?

Exercise 7.2: What Is My Occupation?

Choose a specific age and occupation for your character. Be as specific as possible. Substitute "corporate attorney" or "construction worker" for general terms like "professional" or "blue collar." Enter a bank and stand on line to make a withdrawal or deposit. As you stand on line, observe other actors as they enter the bank. Who do you think they are? When actors have clearly established their identities, try to create an interaction that involves the group. One actor might try to sneak ahead in line and see what happens. Share the improvisation allowing the best idea to become the focus of the scene. Did everyone react in character?

Exercise 7.3: Am I Attractive?

You must decide exactly how your character looks by answering the following questions in terms of the character you will play. Are you facially attractive? What kind of body do you have? Are you short or tall, fat or thin, athletic, or gone to seed? What is your best physical feature? Your worst? Is there anything about you that you think others are turned off by or drawn to? How do you feel about yourself? When you have answered all of these questions, let your body respond to the choices you have made, altering center, respiration, and alignment accordingly. Enter the playing space that has become a singles' disco. How did your entrance reflect what you know about your level of attractiveness? Wait for someone to ask you to dance, or do the asking yourself, depending on how you feel about yourself. This exercise can be done as a solo or group improv. When done as a group exercise, all the actors must be aware of listening to the same music, being influenced by the same shared environment. When the exercise is over, ask the observers if they can describe who you were physically? How accurately were your intentions portrayed?

Where

Where describes the physical and social conditions in which your character lives. Where sets the scene and actively interacts with the who and what of the given circumstances. Where determines actions and is simultaneously defined by action.

How we behave is a function of where we are. Think how different your behavior is when you are alone in your room or out on a dinner date. The same person can radically alter actions because of where he or she happens to be. Since normative behavior is a function of environment, it is important to define the environment in which your character acts as specifically as possible. Ask those questions that enable you to determine the factors that will influence conduct. Are you indoors or out? If you are inside, in what room are you? How is it furnished? If you are outside, what is the specific locale? Are you in upper- or lower-class surroundings? What is considered acceptable behavior where you are? What is the weather? Where have you just come from and how does that influence how you act? How do you physically interact with the place you are in? Examine how environment is portrayed through action.

Exercise 7.4: *Where* Through Action

Perform each action listed below in the different WHERES:

1. Browse through books and magazines in:
   a. the library
   b. a bookstore
   c. a porno shop
2. Thoroughly dust and clean:
   a. your living room
   b. an antique shop
   c. a doctor's office
   d. a sculpture gallery in the Louvre
3. You are starved. Eat a meal:
   a. at McDonalds
   b. in a four-star French restaurant
   c. at home
   d. at a picnic

Did the WHERES change your actions? Your objectives? Your energy? Did you feel different in each location?

Exercise 7.5: *Where*—Group Activity

Begin this exercise in silence. One actor chooses a specific place, enters, and commences a purposeful action. As other actors believe they know where the scene is, they should enter the stage and perform an action appropriate to the place, joining the first actor. When five or six actors have entered, we should have a strong sense of the *where*. If the second actor misjudges the *where* and chooses an inappropriate action, the first actor should try to adjust the action to fit the mistake. Often this cannot be done and the exercise is effectively ended by the misunderstanding. It is therefore important for the first actor to be as specific as possible with every action, and other members of the group must learn to be equally good observers to avoid confusion.

When everyone has established a good sense of the *where,* you may break the silence and initiate appropriate dialogue. What was the effect of words on the scene?

This exercise can be done with a great deal of imagination. I will never forget a particularly creative class I taught who turned this exercise into flights of fantasy. One day, the initial action was to bowl for a strike. As soon as the class understood the *where,* they quickly jumped in, becoming bowling pins, somersaulting balls, as well as the human elements of the game. It was a wondrous bowling alley.

Exercise 7.6: *Where* with Group Rhythm

Set up the playing space with chairs to resemble a car, bus, plane, boat, roller coaster, or other moving vehicles. Actors should fill the available seats. Working in silence, imagine you are all on a trip together. Try and find a common rhythm to express speed, the smoothness of the ride, rough spots, curves, and other elements that effect body rhythms and movement. Were you able to establish a common *where?*

Exercise 7.7: *Where* Through the Senses

This exercise enables you to establish a strong feeling of place. Our sense memory work will be helpful here. How well you choose the *where* for each sense will affect the success of each exercise. Learning to make interesting and intelligent choices for every improv puts you on the road to wise action choices for your scenes.

Choose a specific place with lots of visual stimuli—a toy store or a museum would provide such an atmosphere. Enter the place and look at everything in it. Really let your eyes take in everything you imagine would be there. Allow yourself to respond fully to what you see. Take your time, giving full play to all your reactions. Were you able to establish the *where* through what you saw?

This time, try to establish place through smell. Choose a *where* with strong olfactory stimuli and repeat the above exercise. Let the smell flow through your body. Did observers know where you were?

Repeat the above exercise, using your sense of hearing to establish the *where.* Was this easier or harder than sight and smell?

Now establish the *where* by touching all the imaginary objects present in your *where.* Do not indicate; really touch and feel what is there. Let yourself respond internally to the tactile stimuli.

Try to establish the *where,* using any combination of two senses. Notice how adding a second sense makes the problem easier. Now add a third sense and repeat the exercise. Your portrayal of the *where* should be even sharper.

Figure 7.1 Kyra Sedgwick and Raphael Sbarge in *Ah, Wilderness!* by Eugene O'Neill, directed by Arvin Brown. Observe how the actors create the moonlit night. (Photo—Peter Cunningham.)

Remember that when you are performing scenes you must use all your senses to establish *where* you are. If you can do it well with one or two, imagine what you can achieve with all five!

Exercise 7.8: Environment and Behavior

To underscore how environment affects behavior, in each of these two character improvisations, one actor will feel comfortable in the environment, the other will be ill at ease:

1. A posh executive office. One actor is the VIP, the other is looking for work.
2. A shelter for the homeless. One actor is a society person who has come to do good deeds, the other a chronic homeless person who wants to be left alone.

3. A campsite in the woods, at night. One actor is an outdoors person, the other has never left the big city.

As you worked, what did you discover about how your relationship to the environment affects everything you feel and do? Did you play stereotyped responses, or did you find interesting ways to cope with the circumstances? Note your observations in your log. The reciprocal relationships between environment and action and feeling is a fundamental part of integrated acting technique.

When

When can refer to time of day, time of year, specific events, and to historical time. When can tell you the period in which a play was written, and determine acting style. Because the when of a scene is often apparent if a stage is set, and lighting and costumes are in place, actors sometimes forget how the when must affect their comportment.

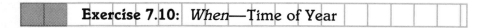

Exercise 7.9: *When*—Time of Day

Perform the following actions at 8 A.M., noon, midnight, and 3 A.M.

1. Go to the refrigerator to get something to eat.
2. Pour yourself an alcoholic drink.
3. Take two aspirin.
4. Get undressed.

Did you fully justify your actions for each time change? Did the time of day affect your action choices?

Exercise 7.10: *When*—Time of Year

Walk in the woods on:

1. The first day of spring
2. A late autumn day
3. A midwinter evening
4. A blistering hot summer afternoon

To sense the interaction between *when* and *where* use the same four times of the year and take your walk in the city, on a beach, inside your apartment. Did changing the *when* and *where* affect how you walked? What was altered? Note your observations in your log.

Studies have shown that people have personal emotional clocks. Suicides are more likely to occur during the week between Christmas and New Year's Eve, on birthdays, and in the early spring than at other times. With this in mind, perform the following exercise.

Exercise 7.11: *When*—Event Time

Eat your dinner alone at home:

1. After a difficult day at work
2. On New Year's Eve
3. After the departure of an obnoxious weekend house-guest
4. On your birthday

Be careful not to make the expected and obvious choices in this exercise. Instead of playing the depression of a lonely New Year's Eve, you might play the struggle against the depression. Choose interesting ways of evoking the occasion.

Could you choose an event and perform an action so we know what event time it is? Were you able to make interesting action choices?

Historical time affects all aspects of behavior. Not only are social customs and manners in evolution, but fashion changes alter the way we move and act. A woman in slacks behaves differently from one who is corsetted in a long skirt. When you act in plays whose historical time differs from your own, it is important to adjust the way you think, move, and act accordingly.

Exercise 7.12: *When*—Historical Time

Meet an attractive member of the opposite sex for the first time in:

1. Fifth century B.C. Athens
2. Medieval France
3. Restoration England
4. Versailles in 1660
5. Japan, 1800
6. Victorian England
7. The U.S.A., 1955
8. The U.S.A., 1969
9. The U.S.A., present
10. Stalinist U.S.S.R., 1939

Did you give full physical life to each time period? How did the meeting change? What factors affects your actions? Note your observations in your log. Can you think of other eras that would affect behavior?

What

What refers to what has happened up to the moment of your stage life, and what is happening as you begin to work. *What* is the dramatic circumstances under which you must operate that determine your objective. *What* defines your conflict. How you respond to what has happened and what is happening will depend on *who* and *where* you are.

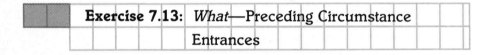

Exercise 7.13: *What*—Preceding Circumstance
Entrances

Enter your apartment:

1. Having just escaped from a mugger
2. Returning from your grandmother's funeral
3. After having been fired
4. After having won the Academy Award for best actor or actress

Add to these specific time of day, season, and weather conditions.
How did your entrance change? How did you physicalize the circumstances? What happened to your energy, respiration, and center? What does this tell you about making a stage entrance? Note your observations in your log.

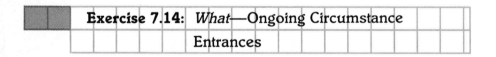

Exercise 7.14: *What*—Ongoing Circumstance
Entrances

Enter your apartment:

1. Upon finding the door unlocked and ajar
2. Hearing your parents arguing in the bedroom
3. Hearing your roommate with a lover in the bedroom
4. To discover your place has been ransacked
   What adjustment did you make for each new circumstance?

The given circumstances are part of an actor's homework on a part. Before each scene that you will do, you must find specific answers to the

Figure 7.2 Betty Buckley in *Carrie*, music by Michael Gore, lyrics by Dean Pitchford; book by Lawrence Cohen based on the novel by Stephen King; director, Terry Hands. Note how the body reveals the given circumstances. (Photo—Peter Cunningham.)

who, what, where, and *when.* These must become part of what you know about a character and a scene.

Integrating the Given Circumstances

You have discovered that *physicalizing* the given circumstances of a dramatic situation enriches and energizes your stage life. The audience receives more information vital to the life of the drama, and our sense of the dramatic situation is deepened. The more given circumstances you can live in your acting, the more interesting you will be on stage. We have just worked through isolating *who*, *what*, *where*, and *when*. The following exercises integrate several given circumstances.

Exercise 7.15: Given-Circumstance Integration— Musical Chairs

This exercise requires at least five people. Your *what* is a game of musical chairs. For each of the following *wheres* listed below, you must define your *who*. A member of the class can sing the music if there is no music available. Play musical chairs in:

1. a kindergarten class
2. a prison recreation room for lifers
3. a mental institution
4. a monastery or convent
5. a corporate party
6. a nursing home

Did you carefully define your *who?* For example, in number two, did you decide upon age, size, looks, what crime you committed, and how long you had been incarcerated? Did you give these choices physical life? It is important to learn to be as specific as possible!

Exercise 7.16: Given-Circumstance Integration— Happy Birthday

This is a solo exercise. We talked of how the *magic if* defines your partner in a scene as well as yourself. In this exercise, your partner is imaginary, but you must play as if he or she were there and were the *who* listed below. Set up a chair where you will place your imaginary other. Your *what* is to sing Happy Birthday. You must define your *where* in terms of the *whos* listed below. Sing Happy Birthday to:

1. Your great-grandmother on her one hundredth birthday
2. To a six-year-old boy dying of leukemia with six months to live
3. To the man or woman who just stole your boy or girlfriend from you
4. To yourself on your twenty-first birthday
5. To the person you love most in the world
6. To the teacher of a class you are failing

Did you actually see your imaginary other in the chair? Had you carefully defined your relationship and where you were? Did you know what you wanted to communicate?

Endowing the Given Circumstances with Emotional Meaning

In the exercise above, your primary focus was on integrating given circumstances. Significantly, you were also engaged in endowing the *who* with emotional meaning. We began this process in Exercise 6.5, "Discovering Your Partner." When we project our subjective emotions onto objects or people, we endow them with qualities that are not objectively present. The technique of **endowment** gives added depth and meaning to our stage life. We can make inanimate objects come alive and relationships palpable. The key to endowment is action and interaction. *Do not try to play feelings. Play the situation.* All these exercises require integrating the given circumstances to achieve a full sense of the dramatic situation.

Exercise 7.17: Endowing the *Where*

Set up a simple living room, using chairs, and a few common objects—a book, a pen, or photo—things that would be found around a room. You must enter the room and touch every piece of furniture and every object reflecting the following circumstances:

1. This is your mother's home. You are returning for the first time since her death two days before.
2. This is your childhood home. The family has sold it after twenty-five years and you will never see it again.
3. This is your home. You are married and you just saw your husband or wife kissing another man or woman.
4. This is a furnished apartment for rent "as is." You are a prospective lessee.
5. This is a neighbor's apartment. She is away and you came to water the plants and are snooping around.

Could you find a way of meaningfully touching everything in the room? Did you feel your thoughts working to justify your actions? Did your respiration alter?

Exercise 7.18: Endowing Objects

Make a pile of random objects present in the room—photos, cigarettes, books, sweaters, earrings, and so forth. Choose any object that is not yours and sit in a chair in the playing space. Choose an emotional context and meaning for the object that will justify your interaction. Create for this object a past—how you got it, where you were, what kind of day it was, create all the things that happened to give this object special meaning. Interact with the object so that you endow it with personal significance. Make choices that represent something of importance. For example, if you use a piece of jewelry, decide who gave it to you, what the occasion was, what its sentimental or material value is. Make these imaginary decisions and project them onto the object through your treatment of it. As you are not using anything that belongs to you, the emotional meaning will be a product of your imagination. When you have completed your interaction with your object, return it to its original place. Do not break your connection to the significance of the object until it is out of your hands.

If you have successfully completed this exercise, you have learned a valuable lesson about working with stage props. You can make the simplest act with a prop a meaningful one.

Exercise 7.19: Endowing the Other

This is a solo exercise. Sit at a sidewalk cafe and imagine you see:

1. An ex-lover with another man or woman
2. A famous celebrity whom you idolize
3. Your father with another woman
4. Someone you have been wanting to date for months
5. A friend to whom you owe $500.

How did you express your reactions to whom you were seeing? Did you let your thoughts and feelings run through your body?

Summary

The given circumstances justify all action on stage. Within every scene of a play exists a set of conditions that determine the behavior of a character. If the given circumstances are real and tangible to you, the power of the *magic if* can enable you to live fully within the dramatic situation. Through physicalizing the *who, what, when,* and *where* of the dramatic situation, you can give life and meaning to all that inhabits the stage.

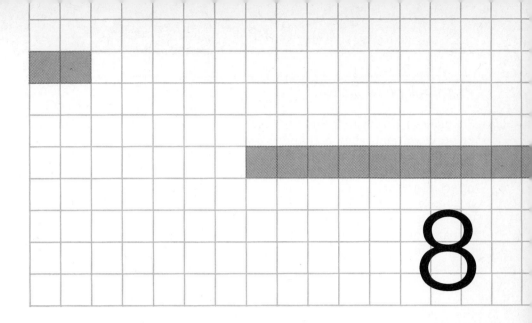

8

Action and Emotion

The bond between the body and the soul is indivisible. The life of one engenders the life of the other. . . . In every physical action, unless it is purely mechanical, there is concealed some inner action, some feelings. This is how the two levels of life in a part are created, the inner and the outer. They are intertwined. A common purpose brings them closer together and reinforces the unbreakable bond between them.

Constantin Stanislavski, *Creating a Role*

What we watch on the stage is action, action as it reflects emotions, thoughts, character, and situation. Yet for centuries, actors have focused on emotions—how to portray, evoke, and create them. At the end of the nineteenth century, psychologists began to apply scientific methods to the exploration of human emotion. Many turned away from an introspective, philosophical approach to human behavior toward a pragmatic and empirical study. In the years following Darwin's discoveries, emotions were viewed as the by-product of our physical life as it interacts with the environment. Out of these new intellectual currents emerged Stanislavski's concept of ***psychophysical action***.

Psychophysical Action

Stanislavski discovered that the evocative connection between action and emotion worked when action was performed as a result of the given circumstances in a play to affect a change in the dramatic situation. Purposeful action aimed at fulfilling a character's goals appeared to be the most direct route to the emotions. He termed this technique *psychophysical action*, later abbreviated to *physical action*. Each role can be seen as a series of physical actions that when linked together provide the portrait of a character's behavior under the specific circumstances of a play. An actor can create psychophysical actions by returning to the *magic if* and asking— "What would I do if I were this character with these objectives in this situation?

This shift in emphasis toward a physical base for feelings liberated the actor from the quest of his elusive emotions, and put the focus instead on purposeful action. Unlike emotions, actions can be produced at will, and are repeatable and controllable. The possibility of consistent performance was finally at hand.

Stanislavski's thinking was influenced by new ideas advanced in the areas of physiology and psychology at the turn of the century. The great Russian physiologist Ivan Pavlov had discovered that physical stimuli could provoke an unconscious response in animals. In the 1890 work *Principles of Psychology*, William James underscored the vital connections between our physical and emotional life, stating that emotions arise as a result of our physical interaction with the environment and are understood through our physical sensations. Feelings are then expressed and evoked by sound and movement. Following these concepts, Stanislavski believed an actor who reacts physically to the conditions of the dramatic environment undergoes an ensuing emotional change.

Exercise 8.1: Feeling an Action—Border Patrol

Work with a partner. One of you is a border guard, the other is attempting to cross the border illegally. Draw an imaginary demarcation line on the floor in chalk. Find a strong action that will enable you to fulfill your objective of either protecting or crossing the border. You must really want to achieve your goal. See who fulfills the objective. If one of you is much bigger or stronger than the other, be careful not to hurt each other.

As you worked, did you discover that action toward an objective creates an emotional connection with the situation? Breath is immediately engaged with the body, and you may have even found yourself releasing sound. Purposeful action involves all of you.

Action Choices and Character

Implicit in Stanislavski's understanding of behavior as a psychophysical process is the portrayal of character through action. If you are to play the role of Claudius in *Hamlet,* you must not try to *be* a king, but to *behave* as a king would behave in Claudius's situation. We perceive what kind of person a character is through behavior, through the way a character interacts with the dramatic situation. Action is the key to both character and emotion.

Let's look at the scene between Treplev and his mother in Act III of *The Seagull* for an example of psychophysical action. Treplev, recovering from a suicide attempt, asks his mother to change his head bandage in an effort to force her to be involved with him maternally. The nurturing role is an awkward one for Arkadina, having been a self-centered, absentee parent, involved with her career—hence their conflict. During the scene they each perform actions involving the bandage that reveal both their conflict and objectives as well as their character. Forced to change the dressing, an actress playing the role might choose to attempt the maternal act but fumble and hesitate because of her incapacity to love. Another choice would be to work overattentively, adding kisses, strokes and other superficial tenderness to cover up her inability to mother. In either case, the choice of physical actions reveals the psychological content of the scene as well as the inner workings of the character and an actor's interpretation of the role. When their attempt at loving interaction explodes into a violent argument, Treplev tears off the bandage his mother placed and throws it to the floor, rejecting his mother's half-hearted attempts at caring. This action reflects their entire relationship and conflict. (See Figures 8.1a–b.)

Every actor must learn to create a series of logical and justified actions that link his or her character to the given circumstances of the play. These actions begin from the moment of your first entrance and carry you through to your final exit. The composite of all that you do on stage is called a *score of actions.* A sample score of actions for Arkadina in the first section of this scene from *The Seagull* might be:

1. Takes medical kit out of cabinet
2. Removes bandage from Treplev's head
3. Strokes Treplev's head
4. Kisses wound
5. Puts on fresh bandage
6. Showers Treplev with kisses

An actor following this simple list of actions would find her behavior rooted in the logic of the scene, creating an immediate connection to the dramatic situation. When these actions are linked to the inner thoughts of a character, their meaning becomes specific. The repetition of internally justified actions can evoke the feelings of the character in the circum-

Figure 8.1a–b Jeff Oppenheim and Michaele Lettire in the Hunter College production of *The Sea Gull* by Anton Chekhov. Study the action choices of the actors as the scene moves from love to rage.

stances. If the emotions do not immediately arise, the actor is still doing his or her fundamental job—behaving in a way appropriate to the character in the specific given circumstances. Future chapters will examine the factors that influence an actor's choice of physical actions.

Rehearsal becomes a period of experimentation where, through trial and error, you hunt for the action that best achieves your character's objectives within the given circumstances. Simultaneously, you seek inside for justification of your actions through the given circumstances of the play. When you have found the right action and inner justification, you will feel a sense of total integration, of becoming one with the character in the dramatic situation. You will know when this happens. It is an unmistakable feeling.

The ability to find the right action is linked to the freedom of your body and voice. If you are tense or inhibited, you will block the path to your emotions through muscular tension. You must be accessible to yourself. Our physical and vocal work in Part I prepared you to let the psychophysical response take place.

Creating Belief

Your thoughts should always be directed toward justifying action within the given circumstances. This creates the purposeful behavior that links action to our emotional life. Thinking about the given circumstances as you act or speak enables you to reinforce the power of the *magic if* and personalize the dramatic situation. There may be times when you are working to create additional circumstances to justify your behavior. This inspires belief in the imaginary world of your character and gives purpose to all that you do. Action performed with conviction has emotion as its natural by-product. Your thoughts are the catalyst in the psychophysical technique.

Never focus on producing an emotion. Keep your thoughts on the given circumstances. When I think about opening night I don't think about how anxious I am. What I do think about is all the people in the audience, the scene I'm still having difficulty with, the fellow actor I'm not comfortable with, and so forth. I think about the given circumstances of opening night and these concrete images make my heart race and hands sweat. Notice that these physical responses evoke the feeling of anxiety. My focus is not on my emotions, yet the feeling comes.

Act II, scene 2, of *Agnes of God* provides a good example of how this channeling of your thoughts onto the given circumstances works. Here Agnes relives the night the baby was born, actually re-creating the pain of labor. To play this scene, an actor's thoughts should not be on "feeling" the pain, but on the concrete images the scene provides as it retraces the events of that night. The writing itself supports this idea, going step by step through Agnes's activities that evening in order to evoke her pain.

Exercise 8.2 Thinking Through Physical Actions

Take a short section of a scene on which you are working. After analyzing the given circumstances, work out a series of actions your character might perform within the situation of the scene. Justify in your mind each choice you make. Perform the series of actions, thinking clearly about why you the character are behaving in this specific way. If you need to, invent more *magic ifs* to justify your behavior. Repeat the series of actions several times, keeping the line of inner action alive in your mind. With each repetition, you should find an increasing connection to the feelings of your character. Your thoughts, justifying your actions, become the basis for the subtext of your part.

Voice Is Action

Speech is action when words are uttered with purpose and conviction. If you fill your words with purpose and meaning that reflect the given circumstances, then all that you say, every sound that you make becomes an action toward your objective and will reveal who you are. If you look back to our work on voice, you will recall how sound often elicited and expressed feeling. It is important to keep the vocal channel open so you can let the full power of your vocal action be felt. Certain sounds in words can express particular emotions more directly, so it is important to connect the sound of a word to your objective. Often you will hear directors or acting teachers say, "It's all in the words." They mean that you must find that emotional link between objective, action, character, and language.

Exercise 8.3: Language as Psychophysical Action

For each of the following expressions, create an imaginary situation that would justify the words as action towards an objective. Repeat each five times, really focusing on the meaning of the words, and the sounds that best express your goal:

1. Don't touch me!
2. Love me.
3. Hey, you!

Repeat the same exercise, adding a strong physical action every time you say each expression.

Did you find that using words as action could evoke an emotion? What happened when you added a physical action? Did the emotion intensify?

Apply this same technique to the lines in your scene. Make the words work for you.

Action, Movement, and Gesture

Not all movement is a psychophysical action. Action, movement, and gesture are different kinetic experiences. **Action** for the theatre presupposes two key points: (1) It must be justified—preceded by thought and choice; (2) it is directed to act upon someone or something to effect change.

Movement refers to the manner in which we change position or place. While an actor needs movement training to develop grace, flexibility, strength, and coordination, movement for the actor is at the service of action. You may need movement to carry out an action, but movement that is not task-oriented is not action.

Gesture is a kinetic experience involving movement that is performed not to cause change but to express emotion, attitude, disposition, or emphasis. You may choose to give a character a series of nervous habits, or idiosyncratic movements, but if they reflect a state of mind without acting upon an object, they are not actions, but **mannerisms** or gesture. This area of unconscious behavior of a character, which you consciously choose as an actor, is important for its expression of personality. Further discussion of gesture will appear in the chapter on characterization.

Movement and mannerism must not be confused with psychophysical action, which is the driving force in the drama and works to advance your character's objectives and further the plot. Aimless movement reveals neither character nor choice, often occurs without you even realizing it is taking place, and does not belong on stage.

Indicating Versus Experiencing Emotion

According to the technique of psychophysical action, your primary concern when you are on stage is what you must *do*, not the creation of emotion. To act sad, happy, upset, angry, in love, or any other such emotion is misplaced focus. We call this "playing a quality," and it inevitably leads to the behavioral cliché. Actors who try to demonstrate an emotion instead of playing an action are said to be **indicating.** Indicating means you are showing a feeling without experiencing it. It leads to the pumping up of emotion for external display without any inner justification.

If you have ever been in a situation where you did not experience what you thought were appropriate feelings and tried to feign an emotional response, you have actually experienced what it feels like to indicate. You know the feelings are not there, but you try to force some semblance of them externally through facial mugging, voice, and gesture in order to achieve an effect. In the scene from *The Seagull* we examined earlier, if an actor playing Treplev were to scream and rant to portray the externals of his anger without letting his rage come as a natural result of the circumstances (his mother's lack of love and support) that stimulate it, he would be indicating an emotion. This focus on "playing angry" takes the actor away from what Treplev is really trying to *do*—to get his mother's love and respect. This artificial straining for emotion appears on stage as overacting.

Relax as you perform your score of actions instead of forcing feelings. If you are working hard to produce emotion, you are wasting energy that could be put to better use in action. It is also the dead give-away that you are not viscerally experiencing the effects of the dramatic situation. Working for effects or results short-circuits the actor's process.

To avoid falling into this trap, you must never think in terms of adjectives and nouns but, instead, define every moment of your stage life in terms of playing an action verb. You will learn how to create a logical series of stage actions in the chapters ahead.

It is hard for a beginning actor to believe that we do not concern ourselves with emotions in performance. The significance of this premise will become clear through our work. The following exercise underscores this point.

Exercise 8.4: Playing Qualities Versus Actions

Try acting the following emotions. Be in turn:

1. happy
2. frustrated
3. angry

What did you do to play these "qualities"? Did you really feel the emotions they expressed or did you indicate the feelings externally? You may have discovered that you need something to be happy, frustrated, or angry about, and something specific to *do* about it. You cannot simply "be" in a vacuum. You need to create sets of circumstances that would justify your feeling happy, frustrated, or angry and perform specific actions under these circumstances.

Study the pairs below. The first is a "quality," the second is an action. Play each in turn.

1. Being hungry versus to hunt for something to eat.
2. Being depressed versus to look for a way to kill yourself.
3. Being tired versus to fight to stay awake.

Did you find that playing a quality led you to indicate an emotional state through externals? What happened when you played an action?

Being is a passive concept. If you are playing "being" sad, angry, or frustrated, your energy is directed inward toward your emotional center instead of outward toward acting in the dramatic situation. Remember that all stage energy must be directed toward the theatrical space. Action is fundamental to the stage, and playing "being" a quality depletes the dynamism of the dramatic situation.

This focus on action and task-oriented behavior on stage displaces your attention from your self-consciousness and personal feelings and concerns onto what you must do within the world of the play. It enables you to free yourself from inhibitions and fears to work freely within the dramatic situation.

Action Before Emotion or Emotion Before Action?

Often students say, "If I'm not feeling it, how can I do it?" or "I didn't feel it strongly enough to justify action, so I didn't do anything." The pitfall of the emotion before action approach is obvious: If you wait for the feeling before you act, what do you do on stage until it comes, or if it never shows up? You cannot say to the audience, "Sorry, I didn't feel anything so I decided not to act." You must *do* something on stage, and that something must be to behave in a manner appropriate to who you are in the dramatic situation.

If you are emotionally dry, then perform natural behavior within the given circumstances, letting your choices be guided by the *magic if*. Always return to the basic question: "What would I do *if* I were this character in this situation?" The audience will accept this logical behavior more easily than a strained performance in search of feelings. Often, actors will tell you that they didn't feel truly emotionally connected during a performance, yet the audience will think they have witnessed a brilliant effort. How can this happen?

We can be moved by paintings, sculpture, and photographs, where the external signs of feeling are enough to stir an empathetic chord. People in paintings and sculpture are not "living the part," but they are expressing the appropriate behavior within the context of a dramatic situation and we can be moved.

Conversely, it is possible for an actor to really feel an emotion, to indulge feelings completely, and for the audience to be untouched by the display. If the emotions become the actor's focus without relating them to the circumstances and character prescribed by the play, the audience may have no clue how to empathize. The actor will appear merely emotionally self-indulgent. Emotion alone cannot guarantee an effective performance.

Many times actors are surprised to find that as they go through the motions of the physical actions, the feelings eventually arrive through the work. Or, faint emotions intensify through expressive action. Recent psychological studies have shown that expressed emotions are felt more strongly than those we suppress. The very act of giving vent to our emotions enables them to live. If you think of a time that you have choked back tears and compare that to the emotional intensity of the feelings at a time when you have let yourself sob openly, you may note that the suppression actually stifles the feeling as our body tenses to control it.

Stanislavski's great contribution is the development of a controllable and reliable technique. Very few of us have so open a channel to our feelings that we can call them forth at will, and emotions that arise are not always subject to control. The result is that the more you call for your emotions, the more you may come up empty. Psychophysical actions provide actors with something to *do* if the emotions do not immediately appear.

This should not be construed to mean that the goal of the technique of physical actions is a completely externalized performance. Nothing could be further from the fact. Emotional connection to the dramatic character and situation is the desired end; however, it is not the technical focus of the actor. The system of physical actions believes that emotions are often more readily induced by indirect means.

Summary

Action is the central focus of the actor. Although an actor's performance must be emotionally charged, those feelings must never be played directly, but evoked through internal and external action. An actor must act, and you cannot perform an emotion.

The actions you choose connect you emotionally to the dramatic situation. They energize your performance, transfuse dialogue, define your character, and give meaning and form to dramatic material. Action winds like a spiraling thread through all the techniques you will learn. You will discover how to make strong and creative action choices as you work through the lessons ahead.

9

Objectives and Actions

Desire is the motive for action. Therefore, the fundamental thing which an actor must learn is to wish.
Eugene Vachtangov, "Preparing for the Role"

In our work on given circumstances, you may have noticed that we omitted the journalistic fifth *w*—the *why* of our actions. Why we do what we do is the motor behind our acting. The *why* is our *objective*, sometimes called intention or purpose. The *who, what, where,* and *when* of the given circumstances determine the *why*. Action is the *how*—the means of achieving your objective.

Strong and meaningful objectives are essential to the success of your acting. You must always have a good reason to be on stage, and attaining your objective must always be the center of your focus. If you let your attention wander from your objective, your acting will lose clarity, energy, and interest. Therefore, it is important to understand how to formulate your objective in a way that commands all your attention and resources.

Objectives and Action Verbs

Because all objectives demand action if they are to be fulfilled, objectives are best expressed through *action verbs.* You must avoid intransitive verbs that express a state of being. Objectives formulated with "I am" usually require an adjective or noun to end the sentence and lead you back into the trap of playing qualities and feigning emotion. Seek instead verbs that imply a clear action.

Some verbs are more powerful springboards to action than others. Part of an actor's job is learning to express objectives in the strongest terms with the most compelling verbs. Implicit in the statement of objective is a sense of urgency that enhances theatrical excitement.

Objectives should answer the question "What do I want?" and should express your primary need or desire in a scene. Remember, the objective must be of importance to your character. Inherent in the formulation of the objective is the suggestion that action will fulfill your purpose. Let's take a simple situation. You are in the bedroom and see and smell smoke coming from the living room. You can say that your objective is *to leave the house.* Or you may strengthen the statement by saying your objective is *to get out of the house.* You can increase the power of your objective if you say it is *to flee the fire.* Or strengthen it even further by saying it is *to escape* the fire. Note how each verb increased the energy required of your actions on stage. Each objective could have begun with "I want" and expressed in terms of a verb and object. It is not enough to say your objective is *to escape. To escape* is not specific enough and would lead to generalized action on stage. *To escape the fire* implies a series of actions that determine your behavior.

If an objective is obtained, there should be an ensuing change in the dramatic situation. Objectives that are formulated with clear action verbs and include an object of the verb can engage you in action that will alter the given circumstances and force a response in other characters.

Let's apply this principle to Hamlet's objective in the scene where the players enact the murder of his father. To choose *to watch Claudius's reaction* or *to let Claudius see that he knows* would use too passive a verb and not compel an action from Claudius. The objective stated actively with an object of the verb—*to force Claudius to admit his guilt*—animates Hamlet's behavior while provoking a response in Claudius.

Exercise 9.1: Objectives with Action Verbs

For each of the following situations write statements of objectives that answer the question "what do I want to do," using strong action verbs and a specific object of the verb:

1. You have received a letter from the registrar saying you are being expelled from college for bad grades. You need an A in one class to stay in school.

2. Your boy or girlfriend, with whom you are madly in love, has said he or she does not want to see you anymore. You do not accept this decision.
3. You see a good friend standing in a sixth floor window about to jump to his or her death.
4. You are a passenger in a car with a drunk driver.

Were you able to create strong statements of objectives? Do you have an object of your objective? Do your objectives inspire action?

Many broader objectives can be broken down into a series of more specific moment-to-moment objectives. The more specific the verb you use, the more direction and focus in your acting. The more strongly your statement of objective expresses what action you must take to achieve your goal, the more energized you will be on stage. The more specifically you direct your active verb toward its object, the greater your effect on the dramatic situation. The following exercise underscores how your mental postulating of purpose will influence what you do.

Exercise 9.2: Making Objectives Specific

Using the situation in Number 2 of Exercise 9.1, let's formulate a strong objective. First we should embellish the given circumstances to justify making strong choices. You are in your apartment. Your boy or girlfriend of two years, whom you were planning to marry this summer, has told you he or she is in love with someone else and doesn't want to see you anymore. Set the situation up for an improvisation. First play the general objective "to keep him or her from leaving." Note how you felt and what you did.

This time, play the moment-to-moment objectives "to beg him or her not to leave," and "to seduce him or her into staying." Did this strengthen your stage actions? Did making the verbs more specific change how directed your actions were? Did you feel a stronger sense of purpose with the objectives *to seduce* and *to beg* than with the more general statement *to keep him or her from leaving*? Note your response in your journal.

Your choice of objective is a reflection of character and circumstance. Not every person in the above situation would have elected to seduce a lover in order to keep him. Different personalities may have opted to elicit pity, or throw a punch. How you characterize your objective depends on who you are and what the other given circumstances are. Had your lover told you he or she was leaving while you were out to dinner in a restaurant, you might not have chosen the objective *to seduce*. Think of all the different ways Mama deals with Jessie's threatened suicide in *'Night Mother*.

These intimate choices—from offering cocoa to getting a manicure are possible because they are at home in a familial situation.

It is important to analyze and think specifically about what a character would do in a specific situation. It underscores the need for an actor to do thinking homework before working on a scene. In Part III we will apply this principle more specifically to text.

Objectives and Obstacles

Objectives make two assumptions: First, that I am on stage because I am motivated to act for a purpose by the given circumstances. Second, that within the dramatic situation, my objective will meet with obstacles to fulfillment. This struggle provides the essential energy of the theatre.

The relationship between objective and obstacle increases the feeling of urgency and is crucial to achieving an exciting stage presence. Obstacles may be physical, situational impediments, or they may be personal, as when another character thwarts your achieving your purpose.

In Exercise 9.2, the obstacle was the personal opposition of the lover who wanted to leave the relationship. If you tried to seduce him or her and the immediate reaction was, "O.K., you win. I'll make love to you and stay," there would be no scene, no dramatic situation. The fact that the other character in your scene has an opposing objective creates the obstacle and is the source of the conflict that drives the dramatic situation. Good playwrights usually provide strong obstacles. Romeo and Juliet are thwarted in their love by the opposition of their feuding parents. In A Raisin in the Sun, Walter's desire to fulfill his dreams of owning a business meet the obstacles of a lack of money, the absence of emotional and financial support from his wife and mother, and a society that robs a black man of his manhood. Look at all the obstacles thwarting Hamlet's objective to avenge his father's murder; there are internal doubts, situational conflicts, and emotional blocks.

There will, however, be times when you will need to provide additional obstacles to intensify your sense of purpose. Let's return to the smoke-filled room for an example of a situational obstacle. Your objective is to escape the fire. If you go to the door, open it and leave, there is no obstacle to your objective, and little drama on stage. But if you go to the door to discover that it has been bolted shut from the outside, that you are trapped, now your objective has met with an obstacle within the situation. You must now look for alternative means of achieving your objective. Try to find another exit. As you do, add the obstacle that the smoke has grown so dense, you cannot see to find your way, and you are choking. With these obstacles, try to find a way out. If we watched you try to escape under these circumstances, with these obstacles as part of your circumstances, your situation has become increasingly dramatic, and your stage energy must intensify if you are to overcome the obstacles.

Using the following list of given circumstances and objectives, create the obstacles that will infuse your stage presence with energy.

1. You are being followed home late at night. Escape your pursuer.
2. You are late for your flight for your first trip to Europe and have misplaced your passport and tickets. Find them.
3. You are a thief robbing an apartment when the tenants return. Evade them.
4. You have committed a murder and are washing blood stains out of a rug. Remove the evidence.

   Were you able to find several obstacles, situational and personal, that enhanced your struggle to achieve your objective for each situation?

Actions as Tactical Adjustments

If your actions are the means of achieving your objectives, then as obstacles impede victory, you must change your course of action to overcome each new obstacle. This requires seeing your actions as tactics in the pursuit of your objective. New obstacles alter the given circumstances, which, in turn, delimit the range of possible action. Each change of action in function of a change in circumstances is called an *adjustment.*

You are always in search of the most expedient means of achieving your objective. We decide to alter our tactics based upon the feedback we receive after each action. If our actions seem to be ineffective, we must think strategically and change our tactical actions accordingly.

It is important to think in terms of dynamic actions that give life and energy to your acting. Although speech and thought are important forms of action, strong physical choices, when possible, infuse a performance with vitality.

Choosing Tactical Actions

You are constantly engaged in the process of choosing *tactical actions* as a part of daily living. If you examine your interactions with other people during the course of a day, you will be astonished how often you are weighing the effectiveness of one course of action or another to get you what you want. The more important your objective, the more consideration you give to the tactics you will use to achieve it. We do not like to think of ourselves as premeditated manipulators in our interpersonal relations, but it is nonetheless true.

Figure 9.1 Kenneth Welsh and Kathy Bates in Terence McNally's *Frankie and Johnny in the Clair de Lune,* directed by Paul Benedict. Observe Kenneth Walsh's strong action toward his objective. (Photo—Peter Cunningham.)

The choices we make define who we are. When an actor chooses specific action, it automatically defines character, for the audience has only what we say and do on stage as means of judging who we are. You must carefully select your tactical actions to reflect the nature of your character.

Exercise 9.4: Observing Tactical Behavior

Observe your behavior for twenty-four hours. Note in your journal how often you engaged in tactical maneuvers to get what you wanted. Note how the relative importance of your moment-to-moment objectives affected the amount of energy you expended on strategic thinking and tactical action. Can you delineate your process of developing tactical action?

The process of choosing tactical action is much the same in the dramatic situation as it is in everyday living. Often, we are thinking so quickly that we do not recognize the steps in the decision-making procedure. But as actors, it is important to be aware of your working process in order to effectively apply it to text analysis in Part III. The steps enumerated below outline how to choose tactical action within the dramatic situation.

1. Decide if your objective is constant.
2. Identify changes in the given circumstances.
3. Ascertain the nature of the obstacles to your objective.
4. If your obstacle is situational, decide the best way around the constraints.
5. If your obstacle is another person, decide how best to exert your influence.
6. Weigh the action options available to you within the circumstances. (Remember, your choice must make sense in the context of your character and the dramatic situation.)
7. Make a strong choice of action that you believe will lead you to obtaining your objective.

These seven points emphasize an actor's need to think quickly and make choices.

Exercise 9.5: Objectives and Tactical Actions

This exercise requires two people. Actor one will pursue the objective, and actor two must choose an opposing objective, justify it, and resist as long as possible to provide the obstacle. For each of the following objectives, choose at least three different tactical actions to achieve your goal. Actor two must assess how each action choice of your partner makes you feel and react when your partner affects you. Sense when your tactics are getting results and when they are failing, and alter your tactical actions accordingly. Be careful not to talk your way to your goal. Each of the following objectives leaves room for physical action choices.

1. Get your partner to do an exercise workout.
2. Get your partner to dance with you.
3. Get your partner to sing the national anthem.
4. Get your partner to give you a kiss.

How well did you fare at finding new tactics? Did you feel yourself working through the decision-making process? Did you notice how quickly you can react with new tactics? Did you feel you had a wide range of choices open to you at all times? Note your impressions in your journal. Was the relationship between objectives and tactical actions clear?

Inner Action and Justification

The process of adjusting objectives and actions and making choices is **inner action.** It enables you to justify your stage behavior. When you did Exercise 9.5, you were engaging in inner action every time you assessed your partner's feedback. An actor who is thinking appears to be active, even when immobile. The audience is aware of the ongoing inner life and can perceive mental energy.

Beginning actors often feel that they cannot think of any action and stand on stage uttering lines from a static and unenergized physical and mental state. You must take as a given that options exist for you at all times if your stage presence is to reflect inner action. Remember, you always have the option to choose not to act, as long as you chose to do nothing as the result of an *active* thought process, and the choice not to act is an action that helps achieve your objective. Even the choice to do nothing must be justified. The existence of alternative choices of action is crucial to the life of the dramatic situation. When a character has run out of options, the drama is over. You must never act with a sense of an inevitable outcome. Even when you are intellectually aware of the end of a play or scene, you must make your action choices with belief in your ability to effect a result.

The process of internal action is continual and ongoing. You have an intention, you act to fulfill it, you assess your feedback, and react with a new tactical action, assess your feedback anew, and react again. Think back to the circular diagram of energy flow in Chapter 3. There, we traced the physical energy flow constantly present on stage. We have added to our understanding of unbroken physical energy the dimension of unbroken psychological energy as understood through objective and action.

To keep the energy flowing it is important to go through the choice-making process anew each time you perform a scene. This means you must at all cost avoid simply repeating your actions mechanically and must actually take in feedback, assess your options, and make a choice as if you were living each moment for the first time. Every time you perform a part, you must enter the character's consciousness and thought processes. This keeps the inner action of a scene alive.

Although you are constantly receiving feedback and making choices, the process is not a lengthy one. We learn to weigh information and make decisions on a split-second basis in life, and such speedy reaction time is transferred to the stage. There are moments in the dramatic situation that you may choose to prolong the decision-making process because it aids your objective. The tempo of the deliberation process should be in keeping with the nature of your character and the demands of the play. We will discuss tempo in relation to dramatic structure in Chapters 10 and 11. The success of your acting will rely on your ability to create a dynamic balance of internal and external action.

Exercise 9.6: Inner Action and Justification

Listed below are two series of five unrelated actions. Perform them in sequence, creating a logical relationship among them by justifying them through inner action.

1. Kick off your shoes.
2. Open a letter.
3. Read a book.
4. Look out the window.
5. Clap your hands.

1. Hit the wall.
2. Crumple a sheet of paper.
3. Yawn.
4. Throw your coat down.
5. Make a phone call.

Were you able to create a dramatic context for these actions through inner action? Did your thoughts give your actions a purpose?

Almost any action is possible within the dramatic situation if you can justify it through the given circumstances and your objective. The following exercise is a real challenge to your imagination and powers of justification.

Exercise 9.7: Justifying Actions

The following is a list of actions:

1. Do ten jumping jacks.
2. Beat your chest like Tarzan letting out his cry.
3. Do five sit-ups.
4. Waltz.
5. Sing two arpeggios.
6. Whistle "Dixie."
7. Take off your shoes and socks.
8. Open and close a book.
9. Comb your hair.
10. Take off your belt.
11. Sing "Whistle a Happy Tune."
12. Toss keys up and down.
13. Hop around the room on one foot.
14. Run in place for twenty seconds.
15. Stand on a chair.
16. Say "lalalalalalala."

Many of the above actions would seem unusual, unexpected, or bizarre in certain situations. You and your partner must each choose four different actions from this list and justify them as you improvise one of the following objectives and circumstances. The actions should be made to appear natural within the context of the scene. Make sure you have memorized the four actions you must use before you begin the improv. Try to choose four actions that give variety in their physical and vocal demands. As you master this exercise, you may wish to add new ideas to this list.

1. You are in the student cafeteria. One of you wants to borrow the notes from a class to study for an exam. The other refuses.
2. You are at a party. One of you wants to get the other to dance. The other one is uninterested.
3. You are roommates. One of you wants the other to leave so you can be alone with your date. The other refuses to go.
4. You are roommates. One of you wants the other to pay the month's rent he or she is behind. The other refuses.

Were you able to make these actions work in the dramatic context? This exercise should demonstrate how zany and unexpected actions can be justified through your imagination and inner action.

Never again should you feel at a complete loss for action. This exercise teaches you to justify strong action choices under fire. If you successfully completed this exercise, you felt the energy infusion from inner action and strong external action choices working simultaneously.

Making Interesting Choices

Seeing the options available to us as actors is part of learning to act. Choices abound within the dramatic situation, but you need the imagination, intelligence, and daring to find them, and a voice and body capable of carrying them out. It is hard to choose to be menacing if your voice is locked into head resonance; or to decide to leap from Juliet's balcony if you are stiff and inflexible. We worked so hard in Part I to free your physical and vocal powers in order to expand your range of choice of action. Your body must be at the service of your imagination, but without directives from a free and creative mind, even a trained voice and body will lack excitement and interest on stage. This is the key to the integrated process for the actor. As you learn to think creatively, your body and emotions must follow.

Some of us have difficulty making choices in life, and this is only exacerbated when we are under the pressure of a theatrical experience. But making interesting and intelligent choices is perhaps the strongest mark of a fine actor. The action choices you make define a character and leave your personal imprint on a role. What separates Laurence Olivier's work from the run-of-the-mill actor is the daring, provocative, and exciting choices he makes for every character he plays. He avoids the hackneyed, the expected. His choices are never safe; they are always risky in their creative leap. Yet for all this, they always conform to the logic of the given circumstances: They are plausible, but unusual; coherent, yet they expand interpretive possibilities.

How do we learn to make such choices? Clearly part is pure talent and instinct. But you can improve your choice potential by liberating your imagination, freeing your body and voice to expand creative range, and learning to trust and take risks. When we make choices, we must think in terms of the interesting, strange, or unexpected possibilities within the given circumstances.

Exercise 9.8: Making Exciting Choices

Let's return to the situation of Exercise 8.2. The given circumstances remain the same. You are in your apartment where your boy or girlfriend of two years tells you he or she is in love with someone else and does not want to see you anymore. With the objective "to force him or her to stay," improvise the scene, making at least one tactical action choice that can be characterized under each of the following categories: unexpected, bizarre, and daring. Make sure your actions are justified.

Were you able to find such actions within the logic of the given circumstances? Notice how such choices defined your character. The stronger choices should have added vigor and excitement to your acting.

Adjusting Actions Under Fire

Learning to adapt your actions expediently to changing circumstances gives performance vitality. It may also get you out of a jam on stage. It is a skill which can save you if another actor forgets a line, or a prop malfunctions, or if you are confronted with any number of production mishaps. As long as you are actively thinking in character, you can adjust to the unexpected without missing a beat. Part of the excitement of the theatre is that it is live, and the unforeseen may occur. I will never forget a production of *Uncle Vanya*, at the Circle in the Square, when Julie Christie's long dress got caught on a nail on the step as she made her entrance. The sound of the tear rang through the house, and she was hooked to the nail. Unable to pursue her original objective, she made a quick decision to adjust her actions to the new circumstances. She bent down, unhooked her dress from the nail, assessed the damage done by the tear, and sighed, "and it was my favorite dress." She overcame this unexpected obstacle by maintaining character, making quick choices within the new circumstances, and returning to pursue her original objective.

Integrating Technique

The exercises in this section are geared to synthesize what you have
learned about given circumstances with objectives and actions, while
using optimum concentration and communication.

Improvisations often go awry because of a lack of focus. Dramatic
intensity and energy fall off and the exercise can literally fizzle out. You
may have experienced this in some of your earlier work. Now you are
ready to take control of your improvisations. As you work, remember the
following key points:

1. Go for your objective. Don't let yourself get sidetracked or introduce
   extraneous material.
2. Make every action count. Don't waste time and energy on empty activities. Make sure everything you do is an action toward your objective.
   If the other actor or the audience takes you off your objective, then *your*
   concentration has failed.
3. Choose your actions tactically, taking in all that your partner does.
4. Do not indicate or play to the audience. Keep your focus within the dramatic situation.
5. Don't be a critic; be an actor. Do not pass judgment on your work. It is
   impossible to have total concentration on two things at once. To be a
   critic, you have to step out of the stage reality and that means you have
   lost focus.

Exercise 9.9: Action and Objective Interactions with Environment

To concretize the relationship between the *where* and behavior, pursue the
same objective in four different environments, choosing actions according
to the *where.* You decide on the *who,* keeping the relationship consistent in
each environment. Make the environment an active component of the
scene.

A. Get your partner to loan you money in:

1. a posh French restaurant
2. the outdoor observation deck of the Eiffel Tower
3. a nursery school
4. a hospital room

B. Seduce your partner:

1. at the beach
2. in church

3. at the office
4. at a singles' bar

    C. Make your partner leave:

1. your home
2. a restaurant
3. a street corner
4. a bank

    Did you find that the actions changed in each environment although the objective and the relationship was constant? How did you use the given circumstances when you weighed your action choices? Did you experience the vital interplay between given circumstance and action?

Exercise 9.10: Discovering Objectives

This exercise teaches concentration, communication, actions, and objectives within the given circumstances. In this exercise, your instructor or another actor will whisper objectives to you and your partner so that you are unaware of the objective of the other actor. You will be given a specific *where* and will pursue your objectives while trying to discover your relationship to your partner and his or her objective. Do not walk in and state your objective right off or the purpose of the exercise is defeated. Try to define your relationship and objectives through your choice of actions. The examples given below are to inspire other choices.

1. Actor A wants to have a baby. Actor B wants to end the relationship because he or she is in love with someone else.
2. Actor A wants a salary raise. Actor B wants to fire actor A.

    Were you able to determine your partner's objectives through the interaction between you? Did you feel the increased concentration necessary to read your partner's intent?

Exercise 9.11: Defining Text Through Action and Objective

Memorize the following dialogue. Do not alter one word. Play the text with each set of circumstances listed below, choosing an objective and a strong physical action for each circumstance. Let your objectives, actions, and circumstances justify the meaning of the words.

Actor 1: Hi!
Actor 2: Hello.
Actor 1: How are you?
Actor 2: Fine, and how are you?
Actor 1: Not bad.
Actor 2: How was your weekend?
Actor 1: Fine. How was yours?
Actor 2: O.K. Did you have fun?
Actor 1: Sure. How about you?
Actor 2: Yeah. Lots of fun.
Actor 1: Good. Well, good-bye.
Actor 2: Bye.

1. Meet your boy or girlfriend who you believe spent the weekend with your best friend.
2. Meet a friend who had a party Saturday night and didn't invite you.
3. See a professor for whom you had a paper due but did not write.
4. Greet a friend who has recently recovered from a suicide attempt.
5. Welcome your spouse home from "a business trip," when you suspect he or she is seeing another person.

The success of this exercise depends on your level of concentration and communication, for you will be defining your relationship to your partner as you work. When performed successfully, this exercise confirms what you have learned—that the nature of the dramatic situation directs your thoughts; your thoughts give meaning to words; your objectives give them energy; your actions give them life.

Summary

Every character on stage must have a reason for being there—an objective. If your focus wanders from your objective, your acting will lack clarity and intensity. You are constantly involved in the process of choosing and executing actions that enable you to achieve your objectives and overcome obstacles. This means you must always know what you want and what is in the way of your attaining it. Every moment on stage is kept alive through the inner action of taking in and choosing tactical action. This process of internal justification makes a thinking actor. The choices you make must reflect the nature of your character and the logic of the given circumstances. Keeping the process of objective-choice-action energized is vital for a coherent and exciting performance.

PART III

Understanding the Script

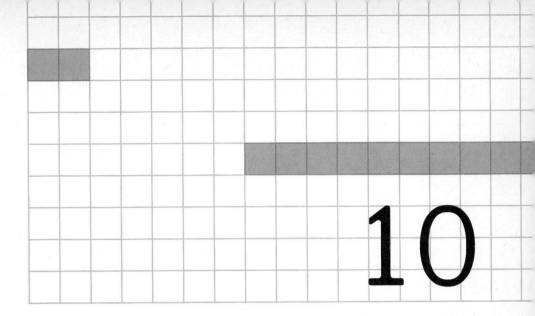

The Elements of Dramatic Analysis

... *the result of an artistic analysis is feeling.*
Constantin Stanislavski, *Creating a Role*

The actor creates the embodiment of the playwright's idea. Your ability to penetrate a script's inner meaning and make a visceral connection with the text is vital to successful performance. An actor must learn how to think about a play. The work in this chapter prepares you to act. Many of the exercises ahead require analysis and writing, so your desire to perform may be frustrated by this material. Acting students, above all else, want to be on stage acting, and this is as it should be. But you must recognize that all you will eventually *do* on stage depends on learning how to effectively read a play.

You are about to begin a voyage into the life of the drama. The lessons ahead will give you mastery over your material. An enlightened actor works with confidence. Once you have learned to read a play for performance, you can take the creative risks that are the mark of a fine artist.

The Process of Interpretation

Your initial encounter with a play usually evokes a direct emotional response. You may find a play personally meaningful and relate easily to the situation and characters. These feelings are immediate and visceral and provide a vital connection to a part upon which to build your technical work. But few actors can create a logical and coherent role, especially a complex one, using only their immediate intuition as a guide. Just as acting is an integrated process, interpretation also requires a synthesis of thought and feeling with each informing and inspiring the other reciprocally. When your understanding of a play deepens, the bond to the emotional life of a character becomes increasingly profound. This happens in all human relationships. As you grow to understand someone, your connection to his or her inner life strengthens, and inevitably your ability to share thoughts and feelings with this person increases. This is also true in our relationships with dramatic characters.

Interpreting a play is a complex process. From our first emotional encounter with the text, we enter planes of intellectual analysis, to emerge with the play alive within us. Ultimately, the play becomes so much a part of us that we can make choices of actions and objectives as a natural and spontaneous effort. Stanislavski described this profound connection to the play as entering "the threshold of the subconscious." True inspiration can occur only when this connection is made.

An actor's choices for a character must support the central idea inherent in the dramatic action. The decisions you make will be determined by your understanding of the script; if you circumvent the analytic process you will be susceptible to doubts and uncertainties about creative choices. Such hesitation makes your acting tentative and ultimately unconvincing. Your "sense of faith" in what you do on stage affects your "sense of truth." Your intellectual homework affirms your belief and frees you to take risks and make the daring and inspired acting choices we have discussed. Your conscious, detailed examination of a play liberates the creative energy of the unconscious.

Understanding the text requires the ability to penetrate the drama on several levels of analysis:

1. Your immediate visceral response to the first reading
2. The external plane—story and plot
3. Literary plane—theme, style, language
4. Dramatic situation—the given circumstances
5. Psychological understanding of the characters needs and objectives
6. Physical choices for action
7. Personal involvement and inner connection to the play
8. Aesthetic and production values (often the director's choice)

The chapters that follow will give you the tools for exploring the play.

Although these levels of analysis are examined individually, remember, an actor must eventually integrate the results of this process into one cohesive whole.

The Story

The full telling of events and facts in a play makes up the ***story*** of the drama. The actor is responsible for knowing all the facts of the story, even those that take place before the play begins. If some crucial piece of information is omitted by the playwright, the actor must fill it in so it conforms to the logic of the given circumstances.

Read the whole play: *In a good drama, the playwright weaves an intricate web of relationships; remove one piece and the entire structure collapses.* To read only the scene on which you are working, or only those in which your character appears gives a distorted impression. This point cannot be underscored enough. If you select your scene from an anthology, you are responsible for obtaining and reading the play containing the scene you have chosen.

Learning how to read a play for the simple facts—the given circumstances—is the first level of entry into the world of your character. In a play, the author speaks only through the dialogue so every word must be seen as a source of significant data. As you read, appraise the facts from the point of view of your character. The personalization process can begin in the first reading.

Often actors in a scene together find that they have not drawn the same conclusions about the events in the story. They have different ideas of when they met, what their relationship is, what has happened between them and the other characters, even what has happened to their own character. These areas of factual dispute must be resolved early in the rehearsal process or actors will be working within different logical frameworks.

To prove how easy it is to read the facts of a story differently, ask two actors who are working on a scene together to tell their individual versions of the story of the play. You will be amazed to find how many areas of disagreement there are as to actual events and their relative importance. It is important to agree on the basic facts of the story before you proceed with rehearsals.

Exercise 10.1: Tell the Story

Read the play on which you are working carefully. Write down the story, including all the data that you believe is significant to you as an actor. The story should define your relationships and significant events that have shaped your current situation. Compare your version of the story to that of your scene partner. What were the areas of overlap? Did you disagree on significant information? Were these differences perceptual or factual? Go back to the play to check your facts to see who is right. What did you discover about your ability to read a play closely for information?

Plot

Plot is created by the playwright's selected arrangement of the events of the story. When the narrative is given dramatic structure, the story has a plot. To turn a story into a play requires organizing events in the story around a central idea embodying dramatic action. A playwright may decide to omit certain events, begin late in the narrative, tell the story from the perspective of a particular character, or highlight certain facts for thematic purposes. Each choice is a step toward the creation of plot. The plot is unique to an individual play, although the same story may appear in several works. For instance, we have three different extant Greek tragedies all written around the the story of Electra's and Orestes' revenge for the murder of their father. Yet the plays of Aeschylus, Sophocles, and Euripides dealing with this same story are remarkably different. One element that individualizes each version is plot. The events are structured differently, the focus on character shifts, and ultimately the meaning of the play is changed through plot.

Understanding the relationship between story and plot is vital for the actor. You need to know the story so that you can get your facts straight. But plot reveals the author's point of view. By analyzing how the events in the story were chosen and selected, you can approach the author's desired thematic content and gain insight into the central struggle of the drama.

Plot Structure

Plot is structured to portray the essential elements of the dramatic situation—action, conflict, and obstacle. Plot must derive its energy from these driving forces.

Although there are various kinds of plot structure, most plots share the common elements of action, conflict, and the resulting tension. The place in the story where the drama begins is called the *point of attack*. The opening of the drama provides the *exposition* of those parts of the story that have occurred prior to the play. Some incident, often called the *inciting force*, triggers the central conflict and its ensuing obstacles. In traditional plots, complications and obstacles take characters through a series of achievements and defeats on the road to their objectives leading to a major *crisis*—a decisive turning point in the plot. This is followed by the **climax,** the point of highest emotional intensity in the play. Following the climax, the complications and obstacles resolve in a *denouement*. The overall shape of the plot is seen as the arc of ***dramatic action.*** Because the tensions build until the climax, we refer to this as the rising action. The falling action, which takes us to the end of the play, is usually shorter and resolves the entanglements of the play.

Aristotle described this kind of play structure in his description of *Oedipus Rex* in *The Poetics,* so we have come to call this Aristotelian, or climactic strucutre. The following diagram illustrates this:

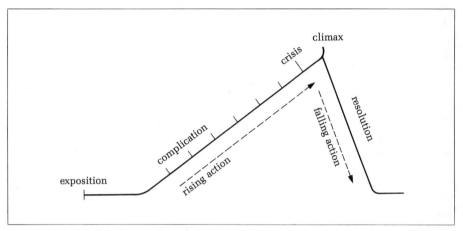

Figure 10.1 Aristotelian, or Climactic, Plot Structure.

Variations on Aristotle's structure have occurred over the centuries, but the fundamental relationship of exposition, complication, climax and resolution dominates. Energy builds throughout the rising action, through the intensifying conflict, until it explodes at the climax. The resolution is marked by a dissipation in energy intensity. The actor must work within this structure to shape a role.

It is interesting to note that the very pattern of normal respiration—inhalation, retention, and exhalation—reflects the fundamental shape of the climactic plot with rising and falling action, building and releasing tension. This underscores how close dramatic structure is to a basic life force. As you work, you will discover a visceral conneciton to this primitive energy inherent in the drama.

During certain eras, a form of plot called epic structure dominated. Epic structure is characterized by an early point of attack in the story and a proliferation of characters and inciting incidents. Shakespeare's plays are an example of epic form. Whereas Aristotelian structure is compressed, heightening tension, epic structure is expansive. The events in an episodic plot are not necessarily related through cause and effect and often drive home a play's central meaning through parallel plots and contrasting elements. Epic drama achieves its effect through cumulative tension. Aristotelian drama works through a straight line of rising tension. Yet within the epic structure, conflict and obstacle are still the energizing force, and often small scenes are held together with Aristotelian form.

Many modern plays are written with a circular structure. They lack a climax and resolution, for the character is engaged in a struggle against a condition or situation in the face of which he is impotent. The play takes us through a series of struggles against the human condition, only to be led back to the beginning, for the struggle is irrational and unending. Characters in such plays often lack psychological pasts and personal motivation; they are existential, defining themselves only through the moment. *Waiting for Godot* is an example of this form. Although these plays dramatize certain realities of the human condition, they pose many difficulties for the actor. Nonpsychological characters present special demands and should be avoided in your early scene work. As your technique advances you can address the problems presented by these plays.

No matter what the structure of the play, you must shape your performance around the basic architecture of the text. The arc of the plot of the play itself is manifested through your breath pattern. As a play moves toward its climax, tempo tends to quicken. Actors are carried by this momentum, and the rhythm and tempo of breath intensify and quicken accordingly. In plays without a strong climax and resolution, the changes are more subtle. In either case, the actor's body is organically connected to the very architecture of a play, and the breath is an actor's lifeline to the script.

Exercise 10.2: Analyzing Plot Structure

Using the play from which the scene you are preparing is taken, diagram the structure of the play. Include:

1. The exposition
2. The inciting event
3. The complication
4. The moment of crisis
5. The climax
6. The resolution (denouement), if it occurs.

Identify the point in the play to which each term refers. Note if your play does not contain all of these elements and explain how it is structured.

Superobjective and Dramatic Action

As characters struggle toward some goal against obstacles, the play's dramatic action has a central purpose or idea. This purpose is called the *superobjective* or **spine,** of a play, so named because it provides the super-structure for the characters' individual objectives and actions. The super-objective is formulated as a function of the drama's driving conflict. In the words of David Mamet: "The play is a quest for a solution."[1] If we take Mamet's image a step further, we see that a play is a problem-solving situation, and the dramatic action works to resolve a play's central conflict. According to Stanislavski:

> *The superobjective is the quintessence of the play. The through line of action is the leitmotif which runs through the entire work. Together they guide the creativeness and strivings of the actor.*[2]

Superobjective and through-action are to a play what objectives and actions are to a character. Conflict and complication energize the dramatic action in much the same way obstacles intensify a character's objectives and actions. A play's central struggle motivates the action of a drama and is the source of energy for all the characters.

Let's turn to *Oedipus Rex* for an example. When the play begins, Thebes is beseiged by a terrible plague which is killing its people and polluting the land. The superobjective of the play is: "to save the city, to drive the pollution from the land." This search for a means to save the city drives the action of the play forward. It motivates all the characters to act as they do. Although individual characters' objectives may vary from the superobjective, they are all formulated as a function of the dramatic action. When Oedipus learns from Creon that the source of the plague is the unpunished murder of Laius, Oedipus takes on the objective "to find the murderer," but this objective is only meaningful in terms of the central driving action of the play toward the goal—"to save the city."

Notice that the superobjective is formulated with a strong action verb and object, just as you learned to formulate actions and objectives in Chapter 9. This action verb formulation serves the same energizing function for the play as it does for the actor. As you work to determine a superobjective, ask yourself how your statement provides a purpose for the dramatic action. This means identifying the central conflict in the play and how the dramatic action works to resolve it.

Identifying a superobjective for a play is often a difficult task. Your initial conclusion may change as your understanding of the play deepens through the rehearsal process. But it is important to have some operative concept of the superobjective, even if you later modify it. Without this, your choices may lack an internal logic. If you change your first statement of superobjective, you must trace the ramifications of such a shift down to the smallest character objective.

---

[1]David Mamet, *Writing in Restaurants* (New York: Viking Penguin, 1986), p. 8.
[2]Constantin Stanislavski, *Creating a Role* (New York: Theatre Arts Books, 1983), p. 79.

Character and Dramatic Action

Your character's *dramatic function* is to further the through-action of the play, so all that you choose to do on stage, each objective and action must result from a clear sense of your character's relationship to the superobjective of the play. Plot and action elucidate each other. You must see your character in relation to the whole play as a generator of action.

Just as a play has a superobjective and through-action, so does each character in the drama. This is the goal or desire that drives the character throughout the play. Your character's superobjective, sometimes called the *motivating desire,* determines all that he or she will do, so the choice you make will have ramifications in every moment of each scene. You cannot choose a superobjective for your character that does not fall within the central meaning and action of the play or your performance will be unrelated to the whole. Most characters' objectives serve to either advance or hinder the realization of the play's superobjective, the one providing obstacles for the other, giving rise to the central conflict in the play. Your definition of your character's superobjective determines the choice of physical actions through which your character reveals the plot.

Character's superobjectives are the results of the conflicts that drive their actions. Most often conflict is between characters with opposing personal goals who provide obstacles for each other. Conflict can find its roots within the individual working out a personal dilemma as in *Death of a Salesman* or *Cat on a Hot Tin Roof.* Characters in farce and melodrama usually find their initial energy from a conflict with the situation. Conflict can be generated from an individual at odds with society. Brecht's *Galileo,* Ionesco's *Rhinoceros,* or Bolt's *A Man for All Seasons* are examples. In complex plays the central conflict can cause repercussions on other levels. Social conflict usually results in personal conflicts with representatives of opposing social forces as well as inner emotional conlfict as the hero struggles with a choice of action. *Hamet* is such a complex play because every level of conflict is present.

Your choice of motivating conflict gives a distinct interpretation to the play. If you choose to play the inciting conflict in *Hamlet* as a sociopolitical one—Hamlet's superobjective becomes "to regain the throne." The play will be acted quite differently from the choice of Hamlet's Oedipal conflict as the inciting force.

A clear statement of your superobjective guides you through each smaller objective in the play. Just as you formulated objectives, the superobjective is formulated with "I want" followed by a strong action verb that draws you into the dramatic action. The set of actions your character makes throughout a play is your *through-line of action* or *through-action.* These should all be directed toward fulfilling your superobjective if the pattern of action is to be logical and coherent. Stanislavski graphically illustrated the importance of linking your action choices to the super-objective in the following diagram:[3]

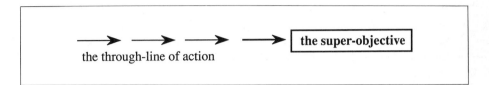

Each division in the through-line can be seen as representing smaller scene objectives and actions. These concepts will be discussed in greater detail in the next chapter. Stanislavski warned that if an actor has not properly analyzed the superobjective, illogical objectives and actions may be chosen along the way, creating a confusing performance. He diagramed the results of working without understanding text as follows:[4]

Always steer your character's actions along a personal superobjective that parallels the central action of the play.

The ability to define the superobjective and through-action of your character is a crucial part of your acting process. When you are preparing scenes for acting class, you are responsible for this kind of analysis. In productions, the director will have made decisions about the nature of the superobjective or spine and may give you guidance in formulating your character's superobjective accordingly.

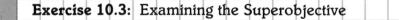

Exercise 10.3: Examining the Superobjective

Using the play on which you are currently working:

1. Formulate a carefully worded statement of the superobjective of the play, making sure to use a strong action verb in your statement. Ask yourself if what you wrote motivates the action of the drama effectively.

[3]Cosntantin Stanislavski, *An Actor Prepares* (Harmondsworth: Penguin Books, 1967), pp. 252–254.

[4]Ibid., pp. 252–254.

2. Develop a strong statement of your character's superobjective. Does it express your character's driving desire? Make sure to use a verb that will propel your character into action and that represents the purpose toward which your character is working through the play. Your through-line objective should help you determine your scene objectives in the next chapter. If you have difficulty determining the logical relationship between them, you may have to reexamine your choice of super-objective.

3. Discuss the relationship between your character's superobjective and the superobjective of the play.

Theme

The **theme** is the central idea of the play. It is what the play means. The theme may be the very reason you like a play and choose to work on it. Theme and superobjective are different but related terms. Theme is often expressed as a social or philosophical concept. The superobjective states this central idea in a form that is meaningful to the characters and playable by actors. The dramatic action embodies the theme on stage.

The theme of *The Sea Gull* might be expressed as a sociological comment on the decadence and self-indulgence of provincial life, or as a philosophical exploration of the inevitable solitude and alienation of individuals. The actor, however, needs a more specific and energizing statement of the force behind the dramatic action. The superobjective, actively stated as *to search for love and fulfillment,* can provide an impulse that inspires actions and guides the shaping of a role, while elucidating the theme. The superobjective provides a logical bridge between idea and action.

Theme is a subjective judgment. Great and complex plays can be interpreted in many ways. *Oedipus Rex, The Bacchae, Hamlet, Waiting for Godot* are examples of plays that have been interpreted in widely varying manners. *Oedipus Rex* has been seen as a play about destiny, or about man's relationship to the gods, or about the weakness of one man's character. The ability to be viewed in varying perspectives is what enables a play to live for centuries, with each new generation finding a significance relevant to contemporary concerns. Perhaps the most important rule in making a statement of theme is this: The theme must be consistent with the content of the play and be inherent in the dramatic action.

It is important to have a deep understanding of the nature of the play and its period. Often much light is shed on various levels of meaning within a play if you have a good grounding in theatre history and general culture. For example, understanding how the ancient Greeks viewed their gods is crucial to an intelligent interpretation of Greek tragedy. Actors well educated in the arts and humanities are better able to probe deeply into the inner life of a play and are less apt to make choices that distort a play. This does not mean that you must interpret a play exactly the way it was done in its original period. But it is important to avoid interpretations that go against the basic fabric of the text. Your interpretation should not contradict the logic inherent in a play's content.

When you are in a production, the interpretation of the play upon which the performance is based will be the decision of the director. It is important to accept and understand the director's interpretation because you will be responsible for making your performance support the concept that the production is putting forth.

Exercise 10.4: Determining a Theme

Carefully read the play on which you are currently working. Can you make a one sentence statement that concisely expresses the central idea of the play as you see it? Is your theme justified by all the events in the play? Did information about the author or the period in which the play was written help you to determine thematic content? Why is this theme significant to you? Is it the reason you want to do a scene from this play? Does the superobjective support the thematic content?

Style

The manner in which a play presents its story, plot, and theme is its **style.** Just as painting may run the gamut from photographic naturalism to total abstraction, theatre too has its range of expressive possibilities. Although theatre always maintains the reference point of the human actor, costumes, masks, and makeup can transform the omnipresent human element into phantasmagoria or abstract forms.

We usually define theatrical styles according to the way they portray reality on the stage. Some styles try to duplicate the real world as closely as possible within the limits of theatrical conventions, to give the illusion of real life on stage. The extreme of this approach is called *naturalism.* The use of carefully selected elements of everyday life is called *realism.* Often these styles are called representational because they attempt to represent reality on stage.

Naturalism and realism in acting have only existed for a little over one hundred years. In earlier eras, the theatre was not concerned with providing illusions of reality. The use of masks, song, dance, and stereotyped gestures in the classical period, the empty Elizabethan stage, the long declamatory speeches of neoclassicism and romanticism, the addressing of dialogue directly to the audience, among other accepted stage conventions, precluded any illusion of real life. These styles are sometimes called *presentational* because of the open recognition of their theatricality.

As beginning actors, most of the scenes you will do will be drawn from the realistic repertory. But it is important to note that the style of a play has a direct effect on what actors are required to do. Although it is impossible in the context of a basic acting text to adequately study the subject of style, I do want to underscore that what will be accepted as "truth" on stage is a subjective judgment and varies according to the style of the material. The degree to which you can or cannot acknowledge the audience, the broadness of gesture, the quality of movement, the very nature of the words you speak, all are determined by the style of a play and its production.

Style is often demonstrated most clearly through the language of a play. Although language can be examined from the point of view of a period, an author, or a character, there are some sweeping styles that set off certain moments in theatre history. In certain periods plays were written in a verse form that imposed a rhythmic pattern on the dialogue. This requires that an actor learn to shape actions and feelings to fit the metrical structure of the play. Often the actor is aided in this by good playwrights, who mold their poetry so that words expressing the most powerful emotions land on stressed syllables. Poetic material is often full of larger-than-life images that need to be supported by an actor's internal imaging process. These plays require advanced technical training for the actor, and you should be sure to understand the demands of this kind of material before you attempt it.

Genre

Every playwright reflects a point of view on life through dramatic *genre*—the category of drama in which the writer's vision is given form. We often see a basic division between comedy and serious drama, but in fact, many other genres exist within these divisions—farce, melodrama, tragedy, for example—and other forms that mix elements from all of these. Genre may be determined by the prevalent forms in a given era or by the personal predilections of a writer.

It is important for you as an actor to be clear on the genre of a play on which you are working, or else your interpretation of character may run against the fabric of the drama. This requires careful analysis and determinations about the author's attitude toward the subject within the context of the social values at the time the play was written. If you play a tragedy as a farce you risk destroying the essential meaning and feeling of the play and creating a distorted performance.

It is important to remember that your character does not know if he or she is in a comedy or tragedy. To the character, the dramatic situation is always real, as is the conflict. Beginning acting students sometimes make the mistake of not internalizing the given circumstances in a comedy because they are playing for the laugh. A character in a comedy who takes

a fall does not find it funny. An actor must respond to the given circumstances with equal truth in comedy or serious drama. The audience may
find a situation humorous precisely because the character does not. The
audience is allowed objectivity on the human condition through comedy,
but such distance is not given to the character. You cannot play a comic
character with emotional detachment. You must feel the pain and take
your predicament seriously. Objectives must be pursued with strong
actions no matter what the genre of the play. However, genre may affect
the style of movement, voice, and speech you may choose for your
characterization.

Exercise 10.5: Style, Language, and Genre

For the play you are currently studying, analyze:

1. The style—explain how you analyzed the play to determine style.
2. The nature of language—what demands does the language of your play
   place on the actor?
3. The genre—how did you define the genre? Why do you think the
   playwright made this choice to best communicate the theme?

   For each point above, consider how your analysis will affect your
acting choices. What adjustments will you make to best express the
aesthetic values of the text?

Tempo and Rhythm

Tempo is the speed at which you act; *rhythm,* the duration of the accents
or stresses within the tempo. Just as every piece of music has a tempo and
rhythm that enhance certain interpretations, so does every play. The mood
of a play guides these determinations. Mood is often a way of giving expression to genre or style. Although there is some latitude within the choice of
tempo and rhythm, you cannot play a tragedy at break-neck speed or a
farce in slow motion; just as the opening of the *Moonlight Sonata* could not
be played at the tempo and rhythm of the *William Tell Overture* or vice
versa without destroying something fundamental to the nature of each
work.

   Although each play has an overriding tempo and rhythm that evokes
the appropriate mood for the piece, within this pace is an internal tempo
and rhythm that is geared to the structure of the plot. As a drama moves
toward its climax, tempo inevitably quickens, and rhythm reflects the
intensifying conflict. It is important for an actor to pace a performance
around the essential structure of the dramatic action, increasing tempo and

intensifying rhythm during the rising action of the plot. In Chapter 13, you will learn how to relate character rhythm and tempo to that of the plot.

Eventually, you will learn to play your score of actions according to the tempo and rhythm of your material. Until sensing the natural rhythm and tempo becomes an organic process, you must learn to control your acting so you won't be propelled into fast-forward through nervous energy, or slow down to indulge your emotions, or be paralyzed by other concerns. Gauge your pace to avoid an up-tempo exposition or dragging your heels at the climactic moment. Developing sensitivity to the appropriate rhythm and tempo of a play is something that comes with time and practice.

Exercise 10.6: Tempo and Rhythm

1. Beat out a rhythm and tempo that best expresses the general spirit of your play. The tempo and rhythm should reflect the mood created by the style, genre, and language.
2. Using your chart of plot structure, beat out a tempo and rhythm that reflect the arc of dramatic action within the play. How did you express the intensifying conflict? The resolution?
3. Using your respiration, let the pattern of your inhalation, retention, and exhalation express the overall mood of the play on which you are working. Your effort may run the gamut from light panting to deep, labored breathing.
4. Using your chart of plot structure again, breathe your way through the plot, tracing the tempo and intensity of the dramatic action from exposition to resolution through your breath. How did you breathe during the exposition? The rising action? The climax? The resolution?
5. Choose a method of locomotion—walk, run, skip, gallop, hop, and so forth—that best expresses the mood of your play. Propel yourself around the room using the spirit of the play as the animating force. Use the breath pattern you chose for Number 3 of this exercise to support your choice.
6. Now outline the arc of the dramatic action as you move around the room. Perhaps you build from an ever-quickening walk to a run at the climax, or use an ever-intensifying gallop. Do what feels like the most natural expression of the play's dramatic action. Keep the breath pattern as a natural complement to the action. When you feel your breath and movement organically connected, repeat this exercise, using a release of sound to express the dramatic action. Let the voice achieve full release at the climax. Sense the power and energy of the play running through your body.

If you were able to complete Number 6 with a complete energy release, you have come a long way toward an organic connection with the text.

The ultimate goal of play analysis for the actor is to find a visceral link between your body rhythms and the arc of dramatic action. The deeper your understanding of the life of the drama, the more organic your connection will be. Eventually, even your respiration and heartbeat will reflect the natural pattern of the play.

Summary

As an actor, you have an obligation to reveal the essential aesthetic values of a play through your performance. The choices you make for your character must be rooted in the logic of the text. Learning to analyze dramatic material for its structure, meaning, and style informs your creative impulses and enables you to define your characterization in terms of the fundamental line of dramatic action. Once you possess the tools for analysis you can enter the world of the play and make appropriate acting choices. The better your understanding of the play the more readily it will come alive within you. Effective play analysis enhances and liberates your acting while elucidating the text.

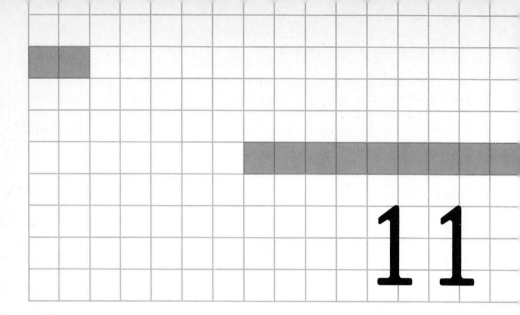

11

The Scene as Microcosm of the Play

Before chewing words I eat ideas. . . . I place my head in the respiration of the text, the rhythm of scenes, the lyric quality of interior movement.

Charles Dullin,
Memoirs and Notes of an Actor

As we have seen, every play has a design of action, a basic structure to which each segment of the text connects. Within this larger framework are smaller units whose cumulative action comprise the plot of the drama. Each unit of action in a well-crafted play should echo the structure, theme, and style of the play. Each division should drive the drama toward the superobjective and fit logically into the through-action of the play. This chapter will explore the relationship among the units of dramatic action.

Defining a Scene

The basic unit through which student actors explore their craft is the **scene.** A good scene is a microcosm of the play and your understanding of play analysis will help you to effectively dissect the anatomy of a scene.

The work we will do in this chapter assumes that you have worked through all the exercises in Chapter 10.

A scene is a unit of the dramatic action that serves to advance the through-action of a play. In plays with Aristotelian structure, each scene represents movement toward the eventual climax and resolution of the play. Each scene contains a scene objective that links the action of the scene logically to the superobjective of the play. A scene not only reflects the structure, style, and thematic material of the play but also ideally contains the essential elements of the drama—conflict, crisis, and dramatic tension.

Scene divisions are formulated in several ways. In classical drama, plays are divided by the author into large divisions—acts—and the acts are divided into smaller segments—scenes. Each division is made because of a change of place or characters. Within these formal structural scenes, there are often smaller subscenes that form a natural division of dramatic action within the larger one. The term *French scene* refers to a change in scene caused by the entrance or exit of a major character.

Your job as an actor is to learn to recognize the natural breakdown of dramatic content within a play. In many modern plays, there may be no change of place and the same characters may be present on stage for the entire play. Yet within this consistent structure there are organic divisions when the direction of the overall dramatic action of the play is altered or advanced in some way. In this case, the scene is defined by its emotional content expressed through a change in scene objective, and you need to learn to recognize such sections.

To formulate a scene objective, ask yourself why this scene is crucial to the play and how it reflects the central conflict of the plot? How does it serve the plot's dramatic action? Inherent in your answer will be the key to the scene's objective and the characters' goals. Understanding this process requires a firm grip on the through-action of the play and its superobjective, for a scene must contain a piece of action essential to the life of the drama. If you sense the play could climax and resolve without the scene you have delineated, then it is possible the section you have marked off does not represent a complete scene with a clear objective, or that the scene is missing a strong central conflict which makes it a weak choice for acting class.

Because the scene represents a complete unit of action, we can give it a title. This enables us to identify the scene and place it correctly in the context of dramatic action. You might, for example, identify a scene as the recognition scene, or the conquest, or the reconciliation, or the confrontation. These titles define the basic content and action of a scene and can usually be restated as an objective by turning the noun into a verb. Naming your scene helps to focus on its central action and purpose while aiding the determination of your objectives.

To recapitulate: A workable scene for acting class is a unit of the dramatic action possessing a clear central conflict and objective in relation to the superobjective of the play. The content is thus vital to the dramatic action. Its start and finish are often marked by the entrance or departure of a named character, or a change in action and objective of the scene or character.

Exercise 11.1: Scene Analysis

Using the scene on which you are currently working, answer the following questions:

1. On what basis did you decide on the beginning and ending of the scene?
2. State an objective for the scene. How does it relate to the superobjective you stated for the play?
3. Name your scene.
4. How does the scene advance or alter the dramatic action of the play?
5. Where would you place this scene in the overall plot structure of the play? How close is it to the climax? Is it the climactic scene? How does its position in the plot influence your acting choices?

Scene Structure and Conflict

Just as the play has an architecture of action that gives it form, each scene has a shape that reinforces its content and meaning. The energizing force of conflict drives the scene as it drives the play.

A scene's structure usually parallels that of the climactic plot with a rising and falling action. To chart the rising tension, ask yourself what are the opposing forces in your scene. What is the nature of the inciting conflict? Follow the progression of the conflict, how it intensifies and does or does not resolve. The point of highest intensity is the scene's climax. Scenes that are not the climactic scenes of the plot may have weak climaxes or may end in crisis; often there is no resolution within a scene, merely an easing of tension that enables the action to progress to the next scene. Once you have defined the structure of your scene you can learn to build the arc of dramatic action through your acting.

Exercise 11.2: Charting Scene Structure

Diagram the structure of the scene as you diagramed the structure of the plot. Note each obstacle that causes an escalation in tension. What did you discover? Does the scene have a rising and falling action? Does the scene structure reflect the larger plot structure? In what ways is the scene a microcosm of the play?

Exercise 11.3: Scene Tempo and Rhythm

With the text open before you, follow the action of the scene using the techniques of Exercise 10.6 by:

1. Beating out the tempo and rhythm of the scene's dramatic action.
2. Tracing the action of the scene through your respiration.
3. Physicalizing the scene through locomotion, moving around the room. Add breath, then sound.

Note what parallels you found between the scene and the play.

Determining Given Circumstances

As we found in Chapter 9, all objective and action choices must be appropriate to the given circumstances of the dramatic situation. Before you can rehearse a scene, you must be certain to have a clear understanding of the *who, where, what,* and *when* of your scene. The work we did in physicalizing the given circumstances can give life to the dramatic situation revealed in your scenes.

In Chapter 7, we examined how the *who* begins your search for your character. When you work on a scene, the *who* is rooted in the factual information provided about your character in the text of the play. You will learn to use this data base to build a role. Make sure you know *who* you are in great detail as well as the facts that make the other characters in the scene important to you. The questions suggested in the *who* section of Chapter 8 are a good orientation point. Search for the answers in the play. Take special note of physical descriptions provided by the author, as well as unique language patterns and vocabulary. A character like Shelley in *Moonchildren* using "like" or "wow" in every other sentence reveals a lot about her inner makeup. Scrutinize all that your character does. Remember, character is best expressed through action.

How characters relate can tell you much about who they are, so study your character's interactions carefully. Define the nature of your relationship to all those present on stage with you. This means that many of the questions you must ask about your own character you must also pose for those with whom you interact. This information is sometimes contained in author's descriptions, but most significant information is revealed through the dialogue and the dramatic action. Note what characters say about each other and how they say it. Decide how much of what is said about you is true. Most of the vital information for the *who* will be provided by the playwright, but when significant information is missing, you will be required to fill the gaps through your imagination. Your analysis of your character's dramatic function will tell you what facts you need to know to justify action. We will discuss how to write an imaginary character biography in Chapter 12, where the information you gather for the *who* will serve as the basis for characterization.

The *where* is often described by the playwright. Read all place descriptions carefully. It is not crucial to reproduce every physical aspect of the *where*. What is important is your ability to shape your behavior to conform to the sociopsychological limitations and mood of the *where*. The *where* also comprises geographical place. Manners in eighteenth-century France were quite different from those in America or China in the same period. Consider the nuances of behavior between the Northeast and South of the United States. The *where* creates part of the social context for your actions, so it is important to understand how the environment set forth by the playwright will affect your acting choices.

The historical *when* can be determined by the period in which the play was set or written and may affect your choice of acting style. A play set in ancient Greece will have different acting demands from one set in the present. Although most historical *whens* are determined by the author, often directors choose to place a play in a particular time period not specified by the playwright. Such specifications change the costumes and sets, as well as the standard of social comportment for your character. You should do research on the historical *when* to make your acting choices accurate. Something as simple as how to greet someone is subject to time period, social rank, and the specific *where*. Be sure you have gathered enough information about the period in which your scene is set to avoid anachronistic behavior.

Look back at the different *whens* we examined in Chapter 7. Make sure you have determined time of day, season, and event time. Each of these can effect behavior and influence your choice of action. If no specific data is given in the script, make logical choices.

The *what* means understanding the emotional content of the dramatic situation. To do this, you must place your scene in the context of the through-action of the play. Ascertaining the *what* requires understanding the preceding circumstances of your character as well as the ongoing situation in the scene to determine your character's objective. You need to decide where your character has been physically and emotionally in the moment preceding your entrance on stage and what the circumstances were. Read the play for any information given about your character's activity before the scene. A character may proclaim earlier in the play what his or her course of action will be, or you may be able to infer such data from the preceding scenes. Your character may in fact have been on stage engaged in some conflict prior to this scene. Whatever happened in the scene before will influence behavior in the next. Read such a preceding scene carefully to incorporate this information and all that it reveals about your character's objective into your physical presence on stage. Make sure your stage entrance expresses the *what*.

What do you do if the playwright has indicated few or no given circumstances? Although an author has not explicitly set the scene, you will discover that within the text, there are often many references to given circumstances that a close reading will reveal. Look at the opening scene of *Hamlet* as an example. All that we are given is the *where*. The text merely says: Elsinore. A platform before the castle. Within the first few lines of dialogue we have the following information revealed: Bernardo. "'Tis now struck twelve. Get thee to bed." We have discovered the *when*; it is midnight, a fact that will affect the mood when the ghost appears. Francisco. "For this relief much thanks. 'Tis bitter cold, and I am sick at heart." This line reveals not only the weather conditions but also how they correspond to the general emotional mood around the palace. This is a signal to an actor that the cold is an important given circumstance within the dramatic situation. Bernardo. "Have you had a quiet guard?" We now know *who* these characters are and *what* their purpose is in the scene. You can see from this example that the given circumstances are often camouflaged in the dialogue.

In plays written before the era of naturalism, it was quite common to have little descriptive information provided by the author other than a general reference to place. Many modern nonrealistic plays also provide meager descriptive data. You must read a play with a searching eye to unearth the information you need to play a part. If after a thorough examination of the play, you can't find specific given circumstances you feel are vital to justify your character's behavior, you must provide them for yourself. You must make certain decisions based on the information that is provided by the text. Every choice affects the meaning of a play. Take care not to make choices that may create difficulties for your interpretation of character.

Although we have spent much time concretizing the specifics of the given circumstances, note that they are not all equally significant for your character. Some have more immediate effect on the dramatic situation than others and you must focus on those circumstances that have direct bearing on the dramatic situation. To understand the relative importance of each given circumstance, ask yourself whether the nature of the play would be altered by a major change in any of the specifics. For example, the fact that Beth Henley's *Crimes of the Heart* is set in a small town in the South is as significant to the characters' objectives as Wendy Wasserstein's *Isn't It Romantic* being set in New York City. Something fundamental to those plays would be missing if you did not let the *where* affect your acting choices.

Exercise 11.4: Analyzing the Given Circumstances

For each scene on which you work, answer the following questions:

1. Who am I? Include age, occupation, economic, and educational background, physical description, sexual proclivity, emotional stability, feelings toward the self. List any other relevant data provided by the author.
2. Who is the other character in the scene? Answer all of the above questions as they apply to your partner's character.
3. What is the general relationship—friend, colleague, family member, and so forth? How do I feel about this character? How does he or she feel about me? How well do we know each other? What do we want from each other?
4. Where is the scene taking place? Be as specific as possible.
5. When is the scene taking place? Include time of day, year, day of the week, event, and historical time.
6. What was I doing before my entrance on stage? Under what given circumstances was I doing it? What is the ongoing stage action?

Exercise 11.5: Physicalizing the Given Circumstances

After you have answered all of the above questions, decide which are most important to the acting choices you will make in this scene. Write down the effect these specific circumstances will have on your behavior.

Using the exercises in Chapter 7 as a guide, work to physicalize those circumstances that are vital to the meaning of the play. Do at least one exercise for each specific and important *who, what, where,* and *when* in your scene.

Determining Objectives

Once you have identified the nature of the conflict and the given circumstances in a scene, you are ready to think about your character's scene objectives. Remember, not only must the objective be geared toward winning the immediate conflict in the scene, it must relate logically to the superobjective and through-line action of your character. Formulate your intention accordingly.

The following points can serve as guides in determining your objectives:

1. First and foremost, the objective must be relevant and meaningful to your character. A good choice of objective reveals how your character thinks.
2. Your objective should relate to the inner life of the play and should serve to advance the dramatic action. The objective must relate to your character's through-line and further the goal of your superobjective.
3. Your objective should inspire action, stimulate a response from other characters, and energize the scene.
4. When possible, your objective should reveal a creative and original way of viewing the dramatic situation.
5. The objective should be playable and truthful within the given circumstances.

Exercise 11.6: Determining Objectives

Using the scene conflict and given circumstances to guide your decision-making process, write a clear statement of your character's scene objective. The objective should furnish a direction for your character's behavior in the scene. Make sure your statement of objective is specific and contains a strong verb and specific object to propel you into action. Review the section "Objectives and Action Verbs" in Chapter 9 for guidance. Look back to your statement of superobjective in the preceding chapter. Does your scene objective keep your character's through-line action on track?

Beats and Moments

We have examined how each scene is dominated by an objective and action that is a unit of the larger superobjective and dramatic action. Within each scene are individual character's scene objectives, units of a character's superobjective. These in turn are broken down into smaller objectives that advance each character's overall goals within the scene. These smaller objectives and the actions performed to attain them comprise a segment of the scene called a *beat*. Bobby Lewis defines a beat as "the distance from the beginning to the end of an intention."[1] Each beat

---

[1]Robert Lewis, *Method or Madness* (New York: Samuel French Inc., 1958), p. 33.

contains an objective, an action, a conflict, and an obstacle. However small, every complete unit of a play contains a cycle of rising and falling action, directly analogous to the arc of the plot.

Each new beat and change of objective is a tactical adjustment to the obstacles confronting us in the dramatic situation. In the scene between Willy and Howard in *Death of a Salesman*, Willy's scene objective is "to get Howard to give him a job in town," which conforms to Willy's superobjective "to establish his self worth." Howard's objective is "to fire Willy." The conflict is clear. Willy tries to achieve his scene objective through a series of smaller objectives that represent changes in tactics toward accomplishing the scene objective. He first tries to persuade Howard that he's too old and tired to travel. He tries to get Howard to do it as a favor. When that fails, he reminds Howard of his long friendship with his father to elicit emotional sympathy and guilt. When that fails, he offers to work for next to nothing to persuade Howard it won't cost him much. When Howard won't give, he tries to explain his failure at selling on a change in the business world. Willy then tries to beg Howard, making it worth Howard's while by offering to work for even less. As Howard refuses to listen, Willy attempts to hold him to promises made by his father, lying about how successful he was twenty years before. He then gets aggressive and tries to bully Howard. Finally Howard tells him he's through. Willy's scene objective has failed. Although Willy's scene objective "to get a job in the home office" remained constant, he changed tactics and immediate objectives along the way. He asked a favor, elicited pity, provoked guilt, rationalized, begged, and bullied. Each tactical change en route to the scene objective represented a new beat in the scene.

Each beat can be broken down into a series of **moments.** A moment comprises a purposeful action toward the beat objective and your assessment of your success or failure at achieving it based on the response received from the situation or from another character. A moment is thus a cycle of *intention→realization→reaction*—that circle of energy flow and communication we have described in preceding chapters. As a result of your feedback in the moment, you may decide to stay in the beat or make a tactical adjustment moving to a new objective and new beat. As long as the intention remains unchanged you are still in the same beat although you may have moved through several moments. In the exercises we did on actions, obstacles, and tactics in Chapter 9 you learned to think through each moment and assess feedback in an improvised situation. Apply those techniques to determine beats and moments in the text.

Although each beat and moment are connected to your superobjective and through-line, when you act, it is the needs of the immediate moment that determine your course of action. The overarching concepts are there to keep your performance on course but are not part of your active consciousness, just as in life what you do at any given moment is usually a reaction to the immediate situation and not a result of pondering your life philosophy and goals. Who you are and what you want out of life are part of your internal sense of self and you need not weigh them before every choice of action. They have become part of your identity. As you work more and more on a role, you will not have to think about the superobjective; it will become an unconscious guide for your acting choices.

You will hear actors use the expression "to be in the moment"—this emphasizes the importance of staying alive and aware at all times on stage so that even the smallest unit of the script is responded to with centered energy and thought. Each action and objective must stimulate the next, generating our performance from the immediacy of the moment. Thus we build upon the basic idea of constant energy flow in the smallest unit to create the dramatic action of a play.

When you do your homework on a role you will work from macrocosm to microcosm, establishing the superobjective and through-action, then the smaller scene objectives, beat objectives, and moments. On stage, the process is reversed. In performance, your attention will be focused on the smallest unit—the immediate moment—as you build the action of a play from the smallest unit, guided almost unconsciously by all that you know about the larger through-action of your role.

Scoring the Beats

A *score of beats* serves as a map through your scene. It keeps you along the charted course of your through-action toward your superobjective. To score the beats in a scene, define your specific objective at every moment. You must ask yourself, "What am I trying to do? What do I want to accomplish now?" Every time the answer to these questions changes, you have begun a new beat. Do not be fooled by lines that are disguising subtext. Make sure your statement of beat objectives reveals what you are *really* trying to achieve, not what your line says you are doing. Learning to effectively score a scene avoids playing generalities and stereotypes while giving focus to your acting.

A portion of the scene between Willy and Howard is reproduced below and scored for Willy. Notice how each tactical change is marked, and how each new beat suggests a change in action. Can you score Howard's beat objectives?

Willy's Scene Objective: To get Howard to give him job in town

Howard

HOWARD: Say, aren't you supposed to be in Boston?

Willy

To find a way to ask for a transfer

WILLY: That's what I want to talk to you about, Howard. You got a minute? *He draws a chair in from the wing.*

HOWARD: What happened? What're you doing here?

WILLY: Well . . .

HOWARD: You didn't crack up again, did you?

WILLY: Oh, no. No . . .

HOWARD: Geez, you had me worried there for a minute. What's the trouble?

To get the job in town by reminding Howard of promises

WILLY: Well, tell you the truth, Howard. I've come to the decision that I'd rather not travel anymore.

HOWARD: Not travel! Well, what'll you do?

WILLY: Remember, Christmas time, when you had the party here? You said you'd try to think of some spot for me here in town.

HOWARD: With us?

WILLY: Well, sure.

HOWARD: Oh, yeah, yeah. I remember. Well, I couldn't think of anything for you, Willy.

To offer himself on the cheap

WILLY: I tell ya, Howard. The kids are all grown up, y'know. I don't need much anymore. If I could take home—well, sixty-five dollars a week, I could swing it.

HOWARD: Yeah, but Willy, see I—

WILLY: I tell ya why, Howard. Speaking frankly and between the two of us, y'know—I'm just a little tired.

Figure 11.1 Scoring the Beats.

To elicit sympathy

HOWARD: Oh, I could understand that, Willy. But you're a road man, Willy, and we do a road business. We've only got a half-dozen salesmen on the floor here.

To ask for a favor based on his friendship with Howard's father

WILLY: God knows, Howard, I never asked a favor of any man. But I was with the firm when your father used to carry you in here in his arms.

HOWARD: I know that, Willy, but—

WILLY: Your father came to me the day you were born and asked me what I thought of the name of Howard, may he rest in peace.

HOWARD: I appreciate that, Willy, but there just is no spot here for you. If I had a spot I'd slam you right in, but I just don't have a single solitary spot.

To beg Howard

He looks for his lighter. Willy has picked it up and gives it to him. Pause.

WILLY, *with increasing anger:*   Howard, all I need to set my table is fifty dollars a week.

HOWARD: But where am I going to put you, kid?

WILLY: Look, it isn't a question of whether I can sell merchandise, is it?

HOWARD: No, but it's a business, kid, and everybody's gotta pull his own weight.

WILLY, *desperately:*   Just let me tell you a story, Howard—

HOWARD: 'Cause you gotta admit, business is business.

To make excuses for his lack of

WILLY, *angrily:*   Business is definitely business, but just listen for a minute. You don't understand this. When I was a boy— eighteen, nineteen—I was already on the road. And there was a question in my mind as to

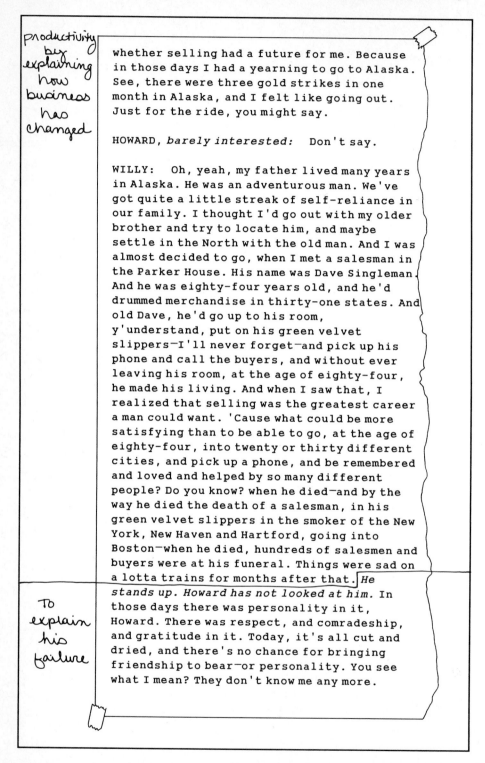

productivity by explaining how business has changed

whether selling had a future for me. Because in those days I had a yearning to go to Alaska. See, there were three gold strikes in one month in Alaska, and I felt like going out. Just for the ride, you might say.

HOWARD, *barely interested:*   Don't say.

WILLY: Oh, yeah, my father lived many years in Alaska. He was an adventurous man. We've got quite a little streak of self-reliance in our family. I thought I'd go out with my older brother and try to locate him, and maybe settle in the North with the old man. And I was almost decided to go, when I met a salesman in the Parker House. His name was Dave Singleman. And he was eighty-four years old, and he'd drummed merchandise in thirty-one states. And old Dave, he'd go up to his room, y'understand, put on his green velvet slippers—I'll never forget—and pick up his phone and call the buyers, and without ever leaving his room, at the age of eighty-four, he made his living. And when I saw that, I realized that selling was the greatest career a man could want. 'Cause what could be more satisfying than to be able to go, at the age of eighty-four, into twenty or thirty different cities, and pick up a phone, and be remembered and loved and helped by so many different people? Do you know? when he died—and by the way he died the death of a salesman, in his green velvet slippers in the smoker of the New York, New Haven and Hartford, going into Boston—when he died, hundreds of salesmen and buyers were at his funeral. Things were sad on a lotta trains for months after that. *He stands up. Howard has not looked at him.* In those days there was personality in it, Howard. There was respect, and comradeship, and gratitude in it. Today, it's all cut and dried, and there's no chance for bringing friendship to bear—or personality. You see what I mean? They don't know me any more.

To explain his failure

Figure 11.1 (*continued*)

HOWARD, *moving away, to the right:*   That's just the thing, Willy.

To plead by offering himself for even less

WILLY: If I had forty dollars a week—that's all I'd need. Forty dollars, Howard.

HOWARD: Kid, I can't take blood from a stone, I—

To appeal to Howard's conscience and evoke guilt

WILLY, *desperation is on him now:*   Howard, the year Al Smith was nominated, your father came to me and—

HOWARD, *starting to go off:*   I've got to see some people, kid.

WILLY, *stopping him:*   I'm talking about your father! There were promises made across this desk! You mustn't tell me you've got people to see—I put thirty-four years into this firm, Howard, and now I can't pay my insurance! You can't eat the orange and throw the peel away—a man is not a piece of fruit! *After a pause:* Now pay attention. Your father—in 1928 I had a big year. I averaged a hundred and seventy dollars a week in commissions.

To bully Howard

HOWARD, *impatiently:*   Now, Willy, you never averaged—

WILLY, *banging his hand on the desk:*   I averaged a hundred and seventy dollars a week in the year of 1928! And your father came to me—or rather, I was in the office here—it was right over this desk—and he put his hand on my shoulder—

HOWARD, *getting up:*   You'll have to excuse me, Willy, I gotta see some people. Pull yourself together. *Going out:* I'll be back in a little while.

To regain composure

On Howard's exit, the light on his chair grows very bright and strange.

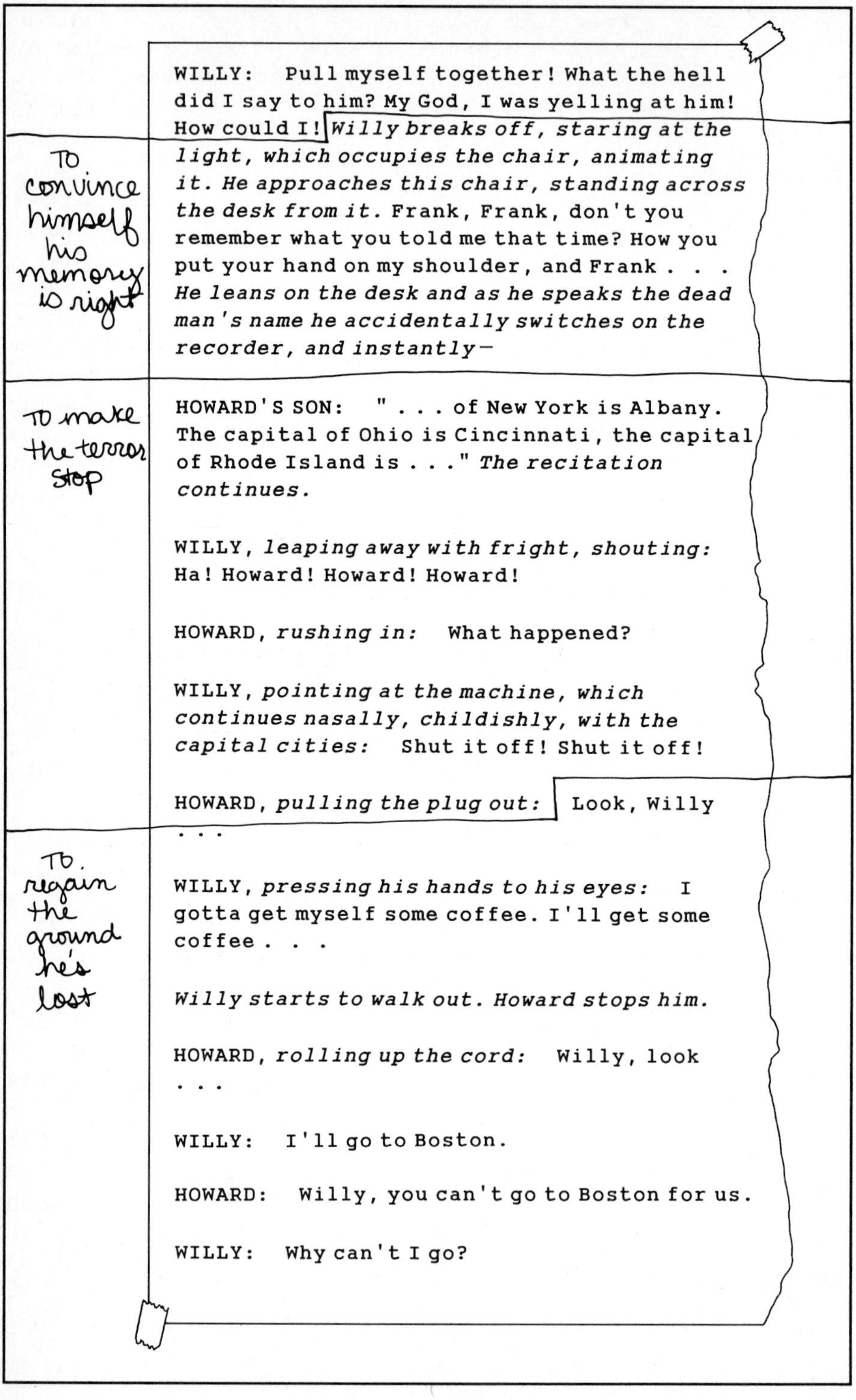

TO convince himself his memory is right

WILLY: Pull myself together! What the hell did I say to him? My God, I was yelling at him! How could I! *Willy breaks off, staring at the light, which occupies the chair, animating it. He approaches this chair, standing across the desk from it.* Frank, Frank, don't you remember what you told me that time? How you put your hand on my shoulder, and Frank . . . *He leans on the desk and as he speaks the dead man's name he accidentally switches on the recorder, and instantly—*

TO make the terror stop

HOWARD'S SON: " . . . of New York is Albany. The capital of Ohio is Cincinnati, the capital of Rhode Island is . . ." *The recitation continues.*

WILLY, *leaping away with fright, shouting:* Ha! Howard! Howard! Howard!

HOWARD, *rushing in:*   What happened?

WILLY, *pointing at the machine, which continues nasally, childishly, with the capital cities:*   Shut it off! Shut it off!

HOWARD, *pulling the plug out:*   Look, Willy . . .

TO regain the ground he's lost

WILLY, *pressing his hands to his eyes:*   I gotta get myself some coffee. I'll get some coffee . . .

Willy starts to walk out. Howard stops him.

HOWARD, *rolling up the cord:*   Willy, look . . .

WILLY: I'll go to Boston.

HOWARD: Willy, you can't go to Boston for us.

WILLY: Why can't I go?

Figure 11.1 (*continued*)

HOWARD: I don't want you to represent us.
I've been meaning to tell you for a long time
now.

WILLY: Howard, are you firing me?

HOWARD: I think you need a good long rest,
Willy.

WILLY: Howard—

HOWARD: And when you feel better, come back,
and we'll see if we can work something out.

WILLY: But I gotta earn money, Howard. I'm in
no position to—

*To cover
up the
truth
about
his
sons*

HOWARD: Where are your sons? Why don't your
sons give you a hand?

WILLY: They're working on a very big deal.

HOWARD: This is no time for false pride,
Willy. You go to your sons and you tell them
that you're tired. You've got two great boys,
haven't you?

WILLY: Oh, no question, no question, but in
the meantime . . .

HOWARD: Then that's that, heh?

*To
get
his
job
back*

WILLY: All right, I'll go to Boston
tomorrow.

HOWARD: No, no.

WILLY: I can't throw myself on my sons. I'm
not a cripple!

HOWARD: Look, kid, I'm busy this morning.

WILLY, *grasping Howard's arm:*   Howard,
you've got to let me go to Boston!

> HOWARD, *hard, keeping himself under control:*
> I've got a line of people to see this morning.
> Sit down, take five minutes, and pull yourself
> together, and then go home, will ya? I need the
> office, Willy. *He starts to go, turns,*
> *remembering the recorder, starts to push off*
> *the table holding the recorder.* Oh, yeah.
> Whenever you can this week, stop by and drop
> off the samples. You'll feel better, Willy,
> and then come back and we'll talk. Pull
> yourself together, kid, there's people
> outside.

Figure 11.1 (*continued*)

Exercise 11.7: Scoring the Beats

Paste the scene on which you are working onto a larger sheet of paper, creating a wide margin for the notes you will be making as we work. (Use the sample score of beats for guidance.)

Using the process demonstrated above, carefully read through the scene asking what your objective is on every line. When you discover a change in objective, draw a line *in pencil* across the text and margin to indicate the beginning of a new beat. Write the beat objective in the margin. Make sure you take subtext into account when you are determining your score of beats.

You may wish to rethink the beats as you rehearse a scene. For this reason, work in pencil so that you can make changes in your script as you gain new insights and still keep readable copy.

You may feel that it is confining to score every beat in a scene. You will learn that such a score is invaluable and keeps your acting focused. Verbalizing objectives forces you to really think through the logic of a scene. If you just play it by ear and don't write anything down, you may end up off course. Remember, the beats are not written in stone. Anytime you feel you want to make a change because of new discoveries you should feel free to do so.

Beats and Action

The score of beats is the basis for your score of actions. You have learned that actions are tactically aimed at achieving your objectives. As each beat objective changes, you must choose a new action directed toward achieving your intention. The underlying logic for your score of actions is determined by the subtext and objectives.

When we worked on actions improvisationally, you discovered that many choices of action are open to you in pursuing your objective, but some choices are better than others. When working with text, action choices are limited by the logic of the play. The following are ground rules for action choices in your scene work:

1. Actions must be purposeful and directed toward achieving your objective and winning a conflict.
2. Actions should be natural to your character in the dramatic situation. A choice that goes against the grain of your character's personality or is inappropriate to the given circumstances is confusing and exhibitionist.
3. Action should reveal character.
4. Actions should be dynamic and infuse your acting with energy.
5. Strong physical choices that conform to the logic of the given circumstances make a performance interesting to watch.
6. Action choices should be as creative and original as possible within the limits of character and circumstance.
7. Action choices should aid the flow of the dramatic action of the play. You cannot destroy a prop needed for a later scene or perform some physical action that puts you in an untenable position for the next beat of the play. Your choices should help the flow of energy on stage.

Exercise 11.8: Scoring the Actions

Return to your score of beats. Some beats will immediately provoke an idea for an action that you can try out in rehearsal. Under your beat objective write the tactical action you will use. For some beats, no action may come to mind until you are actually rehearsing the scene. Use the rehearsals as a period for experimenting with actions. As you set more and more of the actions write them in the margins under the beat objectives. When you have thoroughly worked a scene, your score of beats and actions becomes a blueprint for your acting. Eventually the score becomes integrated inside of you, and each beat naturally triggers the next.

Lines Are Spoken Action

The dialogue can be seen as a vocal action toward your objective. The success of this spoken action depends on how effectively your **line readings** reveal the content of your score of beats.

Each line reading must be accompanied by a strong inner image that corresponds to the feelings of your character at the moment and serves to justify the line. It is as if you are creating an inner personal text for a scene. These internal thought patterns must be expressed through your voice. Sometimes the author can suggest a line reading through punctuation. Most often, you create the meaning of dialogue through intonation, stressed sounds, rhythm, and pauses. As you manipulate these elements you can create subtle nuances of meaning. Every line is subject to a multitude of readings. Be careful not to get locked into a particular reading before you have explored other possibilities. The test of the effectiveness of a line reading is whether it brings you closer to achieving your objective. Remember that line readings are influenced by physical action. An effective reading coordinates voice and action at the body center.

Exercise 11.9: Line Readings

Work with your scene partner on this exercise. Choose a line of dialogue from your scene. Check your score of beats to be sure of your objective on the line. Try to achieve your objective through your line reading by using each of the following techniques, gauging your success by the feedback you receive from your partner:

1. Stress a word that you feel will communicate your intention to your partner.
2. Place a pause in an effective position.
3. Alter the intonation in your voice.
4. Change the rhythm and tempo of the line.
5. Modulate the volume.
6. Use a strong image to communicate your purpose.
7. Create an effective reading out of a combination of the elements that worked best.

Could you feel the differences between each reading? Were you able to use each technique effectively? Did you realize that some readings were inappropriate to the objective, circumstances or character? Why were some readings more effective than others? This exercise should point out how important it is to understand the power of vocal technique in achieving objectives.

A word of caution. In this exercise you created line readings by using techniques externally. This was designed to give you an awareness of the multitude of possible subtle shades of meaning. However, when you are in a scene, the line reading should grow organically out of the objectives and action.

Defining Beats

Since changes in beats reflect a change in objective and action, learning to clearly define these moments of transition through your acting is an important skill if the audience is to follow your through-line. Let's take the following scenario as a departure point for analysis:

> I am late for class and have mislaid the term paper I stayed up half the night writing. It is due today. I failed the midterm, and my professor has warned the class she will not accept late papers. I look for the paper and cannot find it and wonder if my roommate put it somewhere. While I am hunting, the telephone rings. I answer the phone. It is someone I have just met and to whom I am wildly attracted. I finish the phone call and resume my search growing more and more anxious and upset as I realize I may miss class. Clearing desks, tables, dressers, looking under and behind furniture, I find fifty dollars I mislaid two months before. Increasingly late, and increasingly frantic, I knock over a cup of coffee and wet the front of my pants and all my class notes. Cleaning the mess, I find the term paper had been hiding under the coffee cup with other class notes. I dry the paper, clean myself up as best as possible and leave.

The above scene is described as a score of action. It has a clear objective: *to find the term paper*. The conflict is situational, and I can trace the dramatic action as it rises to the crisis of the spilled coffee, climaxes as I find the paper, resolves as I clean up and get ready to leave. The given circumstances of the failed midterm and strict professor intensify my objective. It is an actor's job to mark the beats of the scene through inner action.

You will note that the through-line objective is often interrupted or suspended. When the telephone rings, my attention is temporarily diverted to the phone call. I have a series of thoughts—why does it have to ring now? Should I answer? No I won't! What if it's important—someone ill or a family emergency? I *decide* to answer the phone. At that point my objective is altered—*to find out who's calling*, or *to get rid of the caller*. I answer, but find the call is from someone I'm infatuated with and must decide whether to seduce or get on with my search. I *decide* my objective is *to seduce first, then explain my situation after I've made my desires clear*. Completing these new objectives, I return to the original purpose and try *to find the paper*. When I discover the fifty dollars, my reaction is more subdued than it would have been had I found it when I was not engaged in pursuing an important objective. I *take note* of the find but do not alter my objective because of it. I intensify the search, in my frantic haste spilling the coffee. The situation has reached crisis proportions. My objective changes to *cleaning up the mess and assessing the damage done to my notes as rapidly as possible*. When I discover the term paper in the pile, the scene has reached its climactic moment. The scene resolves as my objective changes to *cleaning the paper and my pants*. The final objective is *to get to class*.

Every time the through-line objective *to find the term paper* was temporarily suspended and replaced by various other objectives, we had an adjustment and a new *beat*. Each beat was marked by a change in my thoughts. Note, I do not simply change the action, but also change my objective as the result of an active mental decision-making process in which I assess the obstacle and new given circumstances to decide how best to proceed. Notice how many times in the simple scenario I stopped to think or make a decision. It is important to register this inner action for every new beat or you will appear to be performing a series of unrelated actions. The logical connection between beats on stage is provided by your inner action. Remember, the process of actively choosing an action must occur *every time* you rehearse or perform a scene or your acting will appear unmotivated.

In Chapter 4 we discussed the reciprocal relationship between respiration and emotion. Because each new beat alters your emotional state, your body physically registers these changes through a new breath. If you observe your own behavior in life, you will notice that you inhale everytime you change your course of action or alter your purpose. Recall a time when you were on your way out and realized you left something you needed behind. Did not this realization that obliges you to suspend your objective *to leave* for the objective *to get what I forgot* occur with a simultaneous inhalation? This taking in of air is an involuntary response that prepares the body for the energy expenditure necessary to achieve your life objectives.

On stage, such energy harnessing through respiration is vital for performance. When you have truly internalized a role and let it enter the realm of the creative unconscious, if you are centered, you will inhale spontaneously for each new beat. In the early rehearsals, if you are not taking this necessary breath, it is a sign that you are not thinking through your objectives, that you are not reacting to the feedback you are receiving on stage, that you are not truly living the moment. When this happens, not only does your acting appear mechanical, but it also lacks any internal logic. The beats will turn one into the other without definition, resulting in a confusing performance and an audience that cannot follow the through-line action.

Respiration immediately alters in response to emotional state. Each circle of communication, each intention→realization→reaction loop provides a moment to assess your success in achieving your objective. The feedback you receive is registered by the way you breathe.

Exercise 11.10: Respiration and Beat Definition

Situation: You are being pursued down a dark street at night. Perform the following actions with the objective *to escape a pursuer:* Using the room as the street, run around the room, really trying to elude your pursuer for a minute, then hide in a niche or doorway, hoping not to be seen. Perform the identical actions two times, noting how your respiratory pattern reflects each of the following outcomes:

1. Your pursuer discovers you in your hiding place.
2. Your pursuer does not see you, runs by, and you are safe.

What did you notice about your respiratory pattern? Did you note that you inhaled at the moment of discovery in the first outcome, and exhaled in relief at the second? Although you performed all the same actions, you registered the success and failure of your objective through the breath. The release of breath in the second outcome was a result of the situation resolving and creating a falling action. The inhalation in the first outcome reveals the scene has not resolved so respiratory tension is maintained.

Just as we charted the rising action of the play and scene through respiration and movement, we can trace each moment and beat through the pattern of breath and muscular energy. Each inhalation prepares you for a new beat and action.

This discussion of respiration and scene structure is not meant to send you into an artificially appliqued pattern of respiration as you work. It is information that offers you a barometer by which to gauge whether you have achieved your build (physicalization of the rising tension), marked your beats, and made sense of the general line of action of the scene. The respiratory changes should occur organically as a response to being in the moment. If they are not occurring, you must focus on thinking through your objectives and registering feedback. No respiratory change indicates that your communication loop is not continuous.

Building Beats into a Scene

The performance of a play reflects the cumulative effect of smaller action patterns. These are like rhythmic waves that give texture to a play. Each scene builds toward its crisis or climax through a progressive intensification of beats. When you are working on a scene, you build moments into a beat, and the beats into the rising action of the scene. Each beat must be played with clarity so that the audience can feel the rising tension and understand the logical connections between each moment and beat. You must learn to build to the crisis or climax of a scene, and eventually when you perform in a play, you will learn to measure the intensity of each scene as you build to the climax of the drama. Remember that scenes that do not contain the climax of the play cannot be played with an intensity that will overshadow the actual climactic moment of the script. Once you understand the arc of dramatic action, you can build the architecture of a play from microcosm to macrocosm.

The structure of a scene is expressed, just like the play's, through tempo and rhythm. This must result from an organic process. In our earlier discussion of stage energy, we learned that intensity of feeling is aroused through creating given circumstances that intensify the objective and necessitate strong actions. This inevitably alters tempo, volume, and muscular dynamics. Note how the Willy-Howard scene from *Death of a Salesman* quickens, echoing the building tension. You can also change tempo by giving more or less time to the process of inner action. You may choose to delay the decision-making process to underscore the importance of a particular choice to your character, to manipulate another character, or to create suspense. The tempo of inner action is usually a natural result of the dramatic action, quickening as conflict heightens and you near a crisis or climax.

As you perform the following exercise, try to achieve the **build** organically through inner action, intensifying your objective and action, rather than building externally through unjustified tempo and volume modification.

Exercise 11.11: Building Dramatic Tension

You and a partner will play the following dialogue below. The objectives are those literally set forth in the lines.

A. Shut up.
B. No.
A. Shut up.
B. No.
A. Shut up!
B. No.
A. Shut up!
B. No.
A. Shut up.
B. No.

1. Play this so that the tension rises to its highest point on the final exchange.
2. Play this so that the tension rises to its highest point on the next to the last exchange.
3. Add two more exchanges and repeat Variations 1 and 2, stretching the building tension to accommodate the additional lines.
4. Add two more exchanges and repeat as above.

Repeat this exercise with the lines: A. I want you. B. Do you? These lines are more subtle and will require a careful build.

Be careful not to start this exercise at too high an emotional pitch or you will have nowhere to go for your climax. Learning to control emotional intensity is important if you are to give your scenes shape and clarity.

Most dramatic writing has a build of tension inherent in its structure. You need only let yourself be carried by the content and rhythm of the material. The following exercise enables you to structure a scene around a song whose conflict and build are reinforced by the musical phrasing.

Exercise 11.12: Can You Top This?

Using the lyrics from Irving Berlin's famous song *Anything You Can Do I Can Do Better,* sing this song with a partner, underscoring the basic conflict through your objectives. Treat each verse as a beat. Build each verse into a rising action, intensifying the energy as you work.

Were you able to achieve a build on this song? Did you intensify through focusing on the conflict? Did the music help to achieve a build? Did you notice how the words that fell on the stressed notes helped heighten the conflict? How do you think building through song is different from building on dialogue?

Notice that the rhythmic pattern and elongated sounds of the music increase your ability to intensify expression. Apply this to dialogue, allowing stresses and elongated vowels to express your emotions when you need to achieve a build.

Summary

Every play is divided into units of dramatic action. Even the smallest unit represents a complete communication cycle of *intention→realization→reaction.* These cycles must be joined to create the architecture of a play. Your work for acting class will be based on the scene—a unit of action with a conflict, objective, and structure that connect it to the larger play. Your goal is to build each moment (a cycle of communication) into a beat (a unit of intention) and each beat into the dramatic action of the scene. To do this effectively, you need to score every beat and action into a logically developed dramatic action. You must integrate the natural rhythm and tempo of the scene with your respiratory process so you are organically linked to the text.

PART IV

The Integrated Process

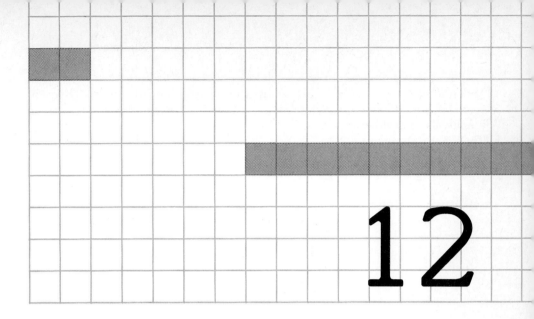

Analyzing a Character

When I confront the character I'm going to play, I must ask myself, "Who am I?"

Uta Hagen,
Respect for Acting

From the time people first put on masks and changed themselves into other beings, the power of transformation has been a potent mystery. If you have ever watched someone you know perform, then you have felt the awe of seeing a person metamorphosed into another being. This primitive magic that binds the actor to the shaman is at the heart of the theatre experience.

Creating a dramatic character is a complex process that integrates your intellectual, emotional, and physical technique. There is no magic recipe. This chapter and the one that follows work together to guide you through the development of a role. Although the work is divided into a chapter on analysis and a chapter on physical work, the process is interactive. The body responds spontaneously to all the thoughts and feelings you have about your role, while your sensations inform your mind and emotions. Although you begin exploring your character through rational analysis, your transformation is complete only when the character becomes an organic part of your being, when the irrational powers of the unconscious give life to this new persona.

To gain optimum benefit from this work, choose a character from a scene for which you have completed script analysis and use this same character for all of the exercises in this chapter and the next. This will enable you to have a complete picture of the dramatic persona and to relate analysis to performance.

Creating a Psychology of Character

Discovering the psychology of your character is a journey into the mind, heart, body, and soul of another being. You have already begun the process. Every choice you make from the first time you read a play brings you one step closer to the definition of character. All that you say and do to further your through-action and fulfill your dramatic function defines who you are. Through formulating a superobjective and scene objectives and choosing and performing actions within the given circumstances, you create a pattern of behavior that reveals character. As you constantly justify action choices, you actually think as your character. A character is not created apart from rehearsing the play but evolves gradually through the work. From your first contact with a play to your final performance, you begin a gestation period through which the dramatic character is born.

Character is a dynamic element of the play. Most good plays take their major characters on an emotional voyage in which they are altered in some way. Because a play compresses life, the transformations of character can be momentous within the emotionally charged dramatic situation. Character must be a living force that can act and be acted upon. To create this living being you need a complete psychological portrait.

Psychology explains behavior. As an actor, you are concerned with your character acting appropriately within the given circumstances of the drama. Your psychological portrait of character must justify your character's actions and dramatic function.

The roles we play as we live are all rooted in our personal psychology, but when we play a character, we create a new psychological being whose thoughts and behavior pattern are quite different from our own. Social psychologist Erving Goffman underscores that in life, "this mask represents the conception we have formed of ourselves—the role we are striving to live up to—this mask is our truer self."[1] The character mask is not your "truer self": it is an artistic creation, just as a painter is not the subject of every portrait he or she might paint. We create through ourselves, but we are not the subject of our creation. The character mask must not be confused with the real you.

If an actor believed that character portrayal revealed the true self, the deepest parts of the soul, the result would be total inhibition. As an actor, you must be free to create without fear of denuding the most intimate parts

[1]Erving Goffman, *The Presentation of Self in Everyday Life* (Garden City: Doubleday/Anchor Books, 1959), p. 19.

of your being. In fact, characterization must be seen as a liberation for the actor. Stanislavski affirmed this idea: "A characterization is the mask which hides the actor-individual. Protected by it, he can lay bare his soul down to the last intimate detail."[2] For this reason, it is important to work on characterization from your very first scene work. It enables you to take your "Self" off the line and to use your psyche and body as creative instruments of expression for a new being.

What distinguishes you from your character is the creation of a separate psychology—an aggregate of the emotions, traits, and behavior patterns that create an individual's identity. Ultimately, we want to create a process of thought and behavior that reflects this dramatic personality. The dramatic character is a result of the same factors that create all human psychology—a composite of our experiences, relationships, and environment in interaction with the society in which we live. Since much of this information is contained in the play, we must review the given circumstances to extract those facts that relate to the psychological development of our character.

Interpersonal Psychology

Determine what you know about your character's emotional history as defined by interpersonal relationships, life experiences, childhood events, family interaction, and love ties. Add to this a character's immediate socioeconomic milieu, analyzing class, occupation, religion, education, intelligence, and financial status, which all affect behavior. In this interaction between environment, relationships, and experiences lies the basis for understanding how the world sees your character and how your character views himself or herself in relation to the larger community. This is your character's personal psychology.

Social Psychology

Many of our life choices are influenced by conditions that lie outside of our intimate lives. Social, cultural, and historical psychology are often ignored elements in characterization, yet they are crucial to your understanding of character. Every era has a world view that affects the way individuals look at themselves and act. None of us acts in a social vacuum. The choices a character makes are determined by the period in which the play was written as well as the era in which the play is set. You must determine what elements of cultural and historical psychology are significant to your character. The characters' objectives in *A Raisin in the Sun* reflect the values of the period, just as Willy Loman makes choices based on a 1940s' American dream, and the women in the plays of Wendy Wasserstein are all confronting their lives in view of the new feminism. The vital clues to an under-

[2]Constantin Stanislavski, *Building a Character* (New York: Theatre Arts Books, 1985), p. 28.

standing of your character's behavior may lie in the social, cultural, and historical milieu. These elements must eventually be integrated with aspects of personal psychology.

The relative importance of social, cultural, historical, and personal psychology in a play depends primarily on the author's intended theme. In a play such as Baraka's *Dutchman*, written with a strong political message, more emphasis is placed on the social and cultural psychology of Clay and Lula than on their individual emotional pasts. When you act in *Dutchman*, *Slaveship*, or other plays with social and political themes, you should be more concerned with cultural and historical psychology than if you were working on a play by a writer like Neil Simon where the emphasis would clearly be on personal psychology. In many contemporary plays, like Ionesco's *The Bald Soprano*, characters appear without a personal past and are merely a function of the situation. In these plays, it is important to analyze the situational psychology to give meaning to your character's actions. Such plays present special problems and are perhaps better tackled after you have experience with more accessible psychological characters.

How a character thinks and feels is thus a result of a confluence of circumstances. These circumstances justify your characterization, and, in turn, justify your action choices.

Exercise 12.1: Interpersonal and Social Psychology

Using your play analysis from Chapters 9 and 11 to guide your responses, list the following for your character:

1. The personal events and relationships that have had psychological effects
2. The socioeconomic class and its effects on psychology and life goals
3. The cultural and historical psychology and its effect on your character and goals

Which of the above is most significant to the dramatic function of your character? How do these factors influence your character's superobjective?

Physical Psychology

In recent years, we have become increasingly aware of the relationship of personality to body language. Psychologists have studied this connection and now believe our mental condition affects not just our external comportment but even the health of our body cells. Reciprocally, our physical condition affects our feelings. Discovering the relationship between personality and body is a vital part of an actor's work.

Specific physical traits of your character are usually noted in an author's descriptive passages or in the dialogue. You must assume that such descriptions were purposefully placed by the playwright, so ask yourself why they were specifically mentioned? How do these physical qualities affect the personality of your character? Are they psychologically induced? It is important to arrange the information given about your character's physical appearance in order of its relevance to your dramatic function.

Some physical traits are not essential to effective character portrayal, while others are vital to the dramatic action. If Celimene, the coquette in *The Misanthrope*, were fat and unattractive, she could not perform her dramatic function. And what would Cyrano be without his nose? On the other hand, I remember Arthur Miller's discussing his original concept for Willy Loman: a small slight man with a large imposing wife. Yet the two great actors Lee J. Cobb and Mildred Dunnock, who played those roles in the historic original production, were exactly opposite types. Through the power of their acting they were able to communicate the qualities vital to those characters.

Miller has written how Dunnock appeared completely wrong for the part at the first audition. She returned the next day with more appropriate dress and well-placed padding, and came back for several days running with more and more character elements until she was completely transformed into the role. Her ability to create a character won her the part. Two things are clear from the Miller story: A good actor who understands the psychological essence of a character can be physically transformed; and not every element of physical type needs to be precisely replicated to create the essence of a character.

Creating the inner essence of a character supersedes externals. You must read physical descriptions of characters with a discerning eye, learning to judge what specifics are vital to your creation of the role and what reveals a general type that you can capture through your internal characterization. Paul Robeson, Laurence Olivier, and James Earl Jones have all played Othello with convincing passion. While it is essential for Othello to be black to fulfill his dramatic function, it is not the grease-paint that transforms a white actor into Othello. Olivier puts it so well: "I had to be black. I had to feel black down to my soul. I had to look out from a black man's world."[3] Without that inner sense of the character, makeup would have been like icing on a nonexistent cake.

Psychology and physiognomy are engaged in a dynamic interaction. We reveal our personalities in every aspect of our physical demeanor and conversely are psychologically affected by our physical handicaps and endowments. To determine which physical traits are essential to your character, determine whether they have psychological ramifications. Richard III, Laura in *The Glass Menagerie*, and John Merrick in *The Elephant Man* are characters for whom it is impossible to separate the physical and

---

[3]Laurence Olivier, *On Acting* (New York: Simon and Schuster, 1986), p. 153.

Figure 12.1 Patti Cohenour and Michael Crawford in *The Phantom of the Opera*, music by Andrew Lloyd Webber; lyrics by Charles Hart; book by Richard Stilgoe; director, Harold Prince. Here is a strong example of the relationship between physical traits and psychological character. Study this picture for strong action toward an objective. Note the physical eloquence of Michael Crawford down to his fingertips. (Photo—Peter Cunningham.)

psychological aspects of personality so closely interwoven in their dramas. These characters are all burdened with striking physical handicaps, but more subtle traits can also be of consequence especially if your character finds them important.

It is often the smallest physical details that define a character. Blanche's fading beauty in *A Streetcar Named Desire* and the description of Lenny McGrath's round face and figure in *Crimes of the Heart* tell us much about each woman's psychology. Finding the just balance between the psychological and the physical is the key to effective portrayal of these characters. Ignore this interaction and you will find yourself playing a stereotype.

Exercise 12.2: Psychophysical Character

Most of us have had a minor physical blemish like a pimple that caused great grief. Prepare for a big date with someone you really like with an ugly black mole in the middle of your forehead. Really see it there. Comb your hair, fix your clothes—that mole is always there. Take your time to really feel the effect on your personality of this small trait. How does it affect how you feel about yourself? How are your emotions about the date changed by this single little problem?

Prepare for the same date knowing you are a physical knock-out— perfect face and a more perfect body. How does knowing you are fabulous-looking affect your sense of self? Does your entire character change?

Now imagine you were born with some horrible physical deformity. Your spine is twisted, every joint is slightly turned out of place, your fingers are spaced in a clawlike rigidity, one leg must be dragged behind the other. Walking is an enormous effort, your body is in a state of constant pain. Walk around the room, twisting your body as far as possible into strained positions for several minutes until the position feels organic. As you walk, note the stress on your respiration and muscles to sustain this posture. Prepare for the same date.

You should observe that certain feelings started to come as a natural result of the strain on your body even before you began to prepare for the date. A level of frustration may have set in, a desire to break out of the physical limitations. Perhaps anger, resignation, or defeat. But when you began to prepare for the date, your inner psychology emerged in relation to the physical self. What did you think as you readied yourself for someone attractive? Did you feel a new sense of who you are? Because of the severity of the physical problem, your sense of the character may have been intensified. Each emotional reaction reflected personality.

More subtle traits do not always cause more subtle effects. Because the relationship between psychology and physiology is reciprocal, the reaction to a small physical blemish can be intense for certain personalities. Repeat the exercise with the mole as someone with an inferiority complex, obsessed with perfection, who has never been loved. Note that character is reflected in the interaction between physical traits and personal psychology.

Exercise 12.3: Determining Physical Character Traits

Analyze what physical traits mentioned in the text can enhance your characterization. Next consider what physical traits you can invent as a vehicle for the expression of character. Remember, these can be tiny things that are significant because of how they are subjectively regarded by your character. Sometimes a well-chosen physical trait can trigger a characterization.

Using all that you know about your character's psychology, imagine a physical being for this person based on these traits. Really allow your imagination free reign, exploring in your mind's eye every aspect of this other being. Be specific as you flesh out this portrait. You have seen the impact of tiny physical traits so detail everything down to the turn of the feet and the state of the fingernails. This physical portrait will fuel your work. Write a complete character description in your log.

As you indulge your imaginary portrait, you may already feel small changes occurring just in response to the mental picture and intellectual homework you have done on your part. This is the start of integration. The body responds to thought, feeling, and image, so we need only build upon this natural response to physicalize character.

Once you have completed your physical description, you should have a detailed external and internal portrait of your character. Ask yourself how this character is different from you physically, emotionally, socially, and culturally. List these characteristics. No matter how close you may feel to your character, your character cannot be a carbon copy of you unless every aspect of his or her life is identical to yours. Even where there are close parallels, some divergence occurs and it is important to underscore these traits. These are the areas in which you have to grow into your character.

Writing a Character Biography

When you have identified the physical, personal, and social psychology of your character, it is helpful to write a brief character biography in which you integrate these elements into a complete picture of the life of the personality you are portraying. In this biography demonstrate how the personal, social, and physical aspects of your character interact. Look back at the data you accumulated in Exercises 12.1 and 12.3. This is the place to explore how past events provide psychological motivation for behavior and objectives. As you write, you may find that some vital information you need to flesh out a portrait that can justify your character's superobjective is missing. You may create this information based on the logic of the play.

When writing a character biography avoid getting carried away with superfluous detail. Ask yourself the relative importance of the facts you are compiling. Only information that ultimately helps to create your character in terms of its dramatic function is really important. It may be totally insignificant to determine whether Linda Loman did well in school as a child. In terms of her dramatic function that is not crucial information. Whether Willy, Biff, and Hap were good students is directly relevant to their psychological motivation and dramatic function. The play gives us specific information about the boys, but we may want to create information about Willy's school experience to justify the intensity of his reaction to Bernard's success and his disappointment in his own sons.

The test of the significance of data is whether or not it will affect the choices your character makes in the course of the play. If it is not germane to your character's active decision-making process, then it is irrelevant to the dramatic function. The test of a good character biography is that it psychologically justifies your character's superobjective.

The following is a sample character biography for Meg MaGrath from *Crimes of the Heart*. All the information is either directly revealed in the dialogue by Meg and other characters or inferred from the dramatic action. The facts were drawn from various scenes in the play and assembled in a logical order. The biography is written in a voice that approximates Meg's.

> *I am Meg MaGrath. In my twenty-seven years I have never really accomplished much. I had goals and dreams of becoming a singing star— thought my natural sex appeal would do it—but my hopes are all shattered.*
>
> *When I was eleven years old, my father abandoned us. I blame him for my mother hanging herself that year. I found her hanging in the basement. I struggled to strike that sight from my memory. In the small southern town where we live, it was a local scandal. My two sisters and I went to live with our tyrannical, misogynist grandfather who always let us know the shame he felt mother had brought upon the family. After mother's suicide, I used to go over to the library and look at pictures of people with horrible deforming diseases. I'd stare and stare until I felt numb to how awful it was. I had to prove that I wasn't weak and could take pain.*
>
> *In high school, I wasn't much of a student. I slept around a lot, but never had a real boyfriend. Caring too much would be a sign of weakness, and anyhow, my father taught me not to put much trust in men. Doc Porter had it real bad for me. I guess I did for him too, but it scared me. The night of hurricane Camille, I baited Doc into staying with me and not heeding the storm warnings. I found the danger exciting, a real turn on. I didn't mean for it to turn out badly. When Doc was injured in the roof collapse I was sorry, but I couldn't stay. I was afraid I'd begun to care too much.*

I left for California to make my career as a singer, but it never amounted to anything. I ended up working odd jobs to make ends meet, living on the edge. I drink and smoke too much; I like tempting death, a little of my mother in me. Then it all got to be too much. Everything I was running from caught up with me. I felt like I was choking, couldn't sing a note, couldn't get a sound out. I just had a breakdown and ended up in the L.A. County Psychiatric Ward.

Although I've never cared about much other than myself, I do love my sisters and I've come home because they need me.

From this biography, much becomes clear about Meg's psychology. We can begin to understand her needs and can formulate a statement of her motivating desire—her superobjective. Using the lessons on script analysis, her objectives can be stated in relation to the dramatic action and spine of the play.

The following analysis illustrates how understanding a character's psychology can lead you through the steps from superobjective to scoring the beats of a scene. The scene between Meg and Doc is used as a case study.

Crimes of the Heart

Superobjective: To break the stranglehold of the past ingrained in each character's self-image caused by mother's suicide and represented by the repressive values of grandfather and small-town society.

Scene: Meg and Doc
Each sister must confront the essential past relationship of her life in order to find release. Within the structure of the play, this scene is Meg's chance to free herself.

The language acts to reveal thematic and psychological content. The image of choking is repeated by Meg. The evidence of this psychological strangulation is that she can no longer sing. This evokes the image of her mother's suicide by hanging. Meg and Doc talk of the hurricane. The powerful image of the storm is both internal and external. Their stormy emotional relationship and the storm of their passion are metaphorically evoked by the hurricane. The through-action leads toward the peace they are both seeking, found in the image of the moon that closes this scene.

Scene objective: To heal past wounds and expiate guilt.

Meg's superobjective: To overcome her early trauma by learning to care and feel.

Doc's superobjective: To regain his manhood by getting Meg out of his system.

Meg's scene objective: To relieve her guilt and prove she can care and feel.

Doc's scene objective: To come to terms with the past by discovering her feelings and why she left him.

Note how each objective is rooted in the portrait of Meg that emerges in her character biography. The smaller objectives flow logically from the superobjective. Use this information to score the beats for the scene between Doc and Meg provided below. The beats are marked by a horizontal line. See if you can determine a logical series of beat objectives.

As you work to define the beats, note how the pouring and downing of drinks defines the emotional units of the scene. This is an important indication of how physical action can clarify meaning and provide a rhythm for a scene. Each drink, of course, furthers the scene objective, bringing them closer to finding release from the events of the past.

Meg   *Doc*

There is a knock at the back door. She starts. She brushes her hair out of her face and goes to answer the door. It is Doc.

DOC: Hello, Meggy.

MEG: Well, Doc. Well, it's Doc.

DOC, *after a pause:* You're home, Meggy.

MEG: Yeah, I've come home. I've come on home to see about Babe.

DOC: And how's Babe?

MEG: Oh, fine. Well, fair. She's fair.

Doc nods.

MEG: Hey, do you want a drink?

DOC: Whatcha got?

MEG: Bourbon.

DOC: Oh, don't tell me Lenny's stocking bourbon.

Figure 12.2 Scoring the Scene.

MEG: Well, no. I've been to the store. *She gets him a glass and pours them each a drink. They click glasses.*

MEG: So, how's your wife?

DOC: She's fine.

MEG: I hear ya got two kids.

DOC: Yeah. Yeah, I got two kids.

MEG: A boy and a girl.

DOC: That's right, Meggy, a boy and a girl.

MEG: That's what you always said you wanted, wasn't it? A boy and a girl.

DOC: Is that what I said?

MEG: I don't know. I thought it's what you said.

They finish their drinks in silence.

DOC: Whose cot?

MEG: Lenny's. She's taken to sleeping in the kitchen.

DOC: Ah. Where is Lenny?

MEG: She's in the upstairs room. I made her cry. Babe's up there seeing to her.

DOC: How'd you make her cry?

MEG: I don't know. Eating her birthday candy; talking on about her boyfriend from Memphis. I don't know. I'm upset about it. She's got a lot on her. Why can't I keep my mouth shut?

Figure 12.1 (*continued*)

DOC: I don't know, Meggy. Maybe it's because
you don't want to.

MEG: Maybe.

They smile at each other. Meg pours each of
them another drink.

DOC: Well, it's been a long time.

MEG: It has been a long time.

DOC: Let's see—when was the last time we saw
each other?

MEG: I can't quite recall.

DOC: Wasn't it in Biloxi?

MEG: Ah, Biloxi. I believe so.

DOC: And wasn't there a—a hurricane going on
at the time?

MEG: Was there?

DOC: Yes, there was; one hell of a hurricane.
Camille, I believe they called it. Hurricane
Camille.

MEG: Yes, now I remember. It was a beautiful
hurricane.

DOC: We had a time down there. We had quite a
time. Drinking vodka, eating oysters on the
half shell, dancing all night long. And the
wind was blowing.

MEG: Oh, God, was it blowing.

DOC: Goddamn, was it blowing.

MEG: There never has been such a wind
blowing.

DOC: Oh, God, Meggy. Oh, God.

MEG: I know, Doc. It was my fault to leave you. I was crazy. I thought I was choking. I felt choked!

DOC: I felt like a fool.

MEG: No.

DOC: I just kept on wondering why.

MEG: I don't know why . . . 'Cause I didn't want to care. I don't know. I did care, though. I did.

Doc, *after a pause:*   Ah, hell. *He pours them both another drink.* Are you still singing those sad songs?

MEG: No.

DOC: Why not?

MEG: I don't know, Doc. Things got worse for me. After a while, I just couldn't sing anymore. I tell you, I had one hell of a time over Christmas.

DOC: What do you mean?

MEG: I went nuts. I went insane. Ended up in L.A. County Hospital. Psychiatric ward.

DOC: Hell. Ah, hell, Meggy. What happened?

MEG: I don't really know. I couldn't sing anymore, so I lost my job. And I had a bad toothache. I had this incredibly painful toothache. For days I had it, but I wouldn't do anything about it. I just stayed inside my apartment. All I could do was sit around in chairs, chewing on my fingers. Then one afternoon I ran screaming out of the apartment

Figure 12.1 (*continued*)

with all my money and jewelry and valuables,
and tried to stuff it all into one of those
March of Dimes collection boxes. That was when
they nabbed me. Sad story. Meg goes mad.

Doc stares at her for a long moment. *He pours
them both another drink.*

Doc, *after quite a pause:*   There's a moon out.

MEG: Is there?

DOC: Wanna go take a ride in my truck and look
out at the moon?

MEG: I don't know, Doc. I don't wanna start
up. It'll be too hard if we start up.

DOC: Who says we're gonna start up? We're
just gonna look at the moon. For one night just
you and me are gonna go for a ride in the
country and look out at the moon.

MEG: One night?

DOC: Right.

MEG: Look out at the moon?

DOC: You got it.

MEG: Well . . . all right. *She gets up.*

DOC: Better take your coat. *He helps her into
her coat.* And the bottle. *He takes the bottle.
Meg picks up the glasses.* Forget the glasses.

MEG, *laughing:*   Yeah—forget the glasses.
Forget the goddamn glasses.

*Meg shuts off the kitchen lights, leaving the
kitchen with only a dim light over the kitchen
sink. Meg and Doc leave. After a moment, Babe
comes down the stairs in her slip.*

Exercise 12.4: Writing a Character Biography

Write a character biography in the first person to begin the process of identification with your character. Include events in the formative years of your character that could exert influence in the present and that justify your character's behavior in the play. Make sure you include all the pertinent physical, personal, social, cultural, and historical data. Note each time you feel vital information is missing and create the necessary facts. For each piece of fabricated information, justify your decision.

In the light of all the new information you have gathered, rethink your character's superobjective in the play. Have you modified your original statement in any way to reflect your new psychological insights?

Living through Your Character's Psychology

Now that you have defined the personal, social, and physical psychology of your character, you must learn to let your thought processes be filtered through this new individual's psychological makeup. The series of incomplete sentences in the following exercise are used by psychiatrists to assess personality disorders. A patient's spontaneous responses reveal the nature of the individual's psychology. If you have really understood your character's psychology, your response should give a portrait of this personality.

Exercise 12.5: Character Sentence Completion

Answering as your character, complete the following sentences in as spontaneous and uninhibited a manner as possible:

1. I am happiest when . . .
2. I daydream about . . .
3. My mind . . .
4. If I had my way . . .
5. I don't understand why . . .
6. What I could do is . . .
7. My first reaction to him or her was (use your scene partner in character) . . .
8. Being scared makes me . . .
9. Sometimes I think that I . . .
10. I have a feeling that part of me . . .
11. I love my parents/child/spouse/lover [whichever applies] but . . .
12. A person's family . . .

13. No one could help so . . .
14. If I were in charge . . .
15. I get angry when . . .
16. People perceive me as . . .
17. I hate . . .
18. People wouldn't like it if . . .
19. I am afraid I . . .
20. I know . . .
21. I really am . . .
22. A person can't be happy unless . . .

Write the completed sentences down. Read your character's responses to these questions carefully. Do they reveal your character's psychological makeup? Did you learn anything about your character? How do these responses help you to determine appropriate objectives and actions for your scenes?

Repeat this exercise, answering as yourself. How much did you reveal about yourself through your responses? Compare your personal reactions with those of your character. This defines areas where you need to work to understand your character's inner life.

At this early stage, you may have had to give a good deal of thought to your character's completions. It will be interesting to repeat this exercise after you have finished the physical work in the next chapter.

The Psychological Past as Action in the Present

Although we have spent much time focusing on the events in the past that have shaped your character's psychology, these are significant to an actor only in terms of how they affect behavior in the present. When you are on stage, your concern is not to relive the past, but to act in the present. *Work on the psychological past is homework, not stage work.* Your focus in performance must be on your character's immediate desires and actions.

Exercise 12.6: Psychological Past as Action in the Present

Each situation below describes a past event and a situation in the present. Keep your focus on action as you perform the following stage entrances, using only breath, sound, and movement:

1. You have a fear of heights since you fell out of a window as a child. Enter the World Trade Center Observation Deck.
2. You are a recently recovered alcoholic. Enter a party where everyone is drunk and offering you a drink.

3. You were a physically abused child. Enter a classroom where the teacher has a reputation of being a strict disciplinarian and take your seat.
4. You have a fear of water, having almost drowned as a child. Enter a sailboat for a pleasure cruise.

Did you focus on your needs in the present or on indicating the past? For example, in the first situation, did you try to indicate your fear, reliving your childhood experience—or did you try to cope with it, control it, cover it up, or overcome it? What did you actually *do?* What action choices did you make? Were you able to find the physical effects of these events from a character's past in the present? Did you feel the changes in your breathing, in the placement of center? Note your responses to this exercise in your logs.

Through this work, you may have discovered that you have negative feelings about your character that block inner connection to the role. Never be judgmental or fearful of your character. You must penetrate the soul of the villain as you would the victim. Once you have created a psychology through objective analysis, you must enter your character and see the world through his or her eyes. The character biography enables you to understand what motivates your character to behave as he or she does. Understanding permits empathy. As long as you stand in judgment of your character, the character can never stand inside of you. Sir Laurence Olivier underscores the importance of truly loving your character: "Love is . . . the exaltation of understanding. Now understanding is the absolute *must* in our work, and the means whereby we can inform. Love is the means whereby we can bring that information home."[4]

Summary

Before we can give physical life to a character we need to create a psychological portrait that justifies our behavior. Astute script analysis enables you to cull the information you need to motivate your character's dramatic function and superobjective. Personal, social, and physical psychology merge in the writing of a character biography where the motivating desires of this persona become clear. As your understanding of your character grows, empathy deepens until you can step inside your character's emotions.

[4]Laurence Olivier, On Acting (New York: Simon & Schuster, 1986), pp. 376–377.

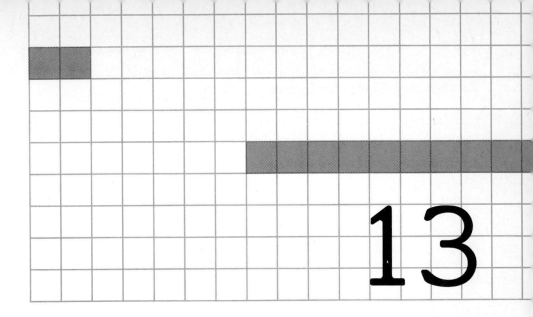

Physicalizing Character

The actor must always ask himself: In spite of my sincerity, is
my character truly sincere?

Jean-Louis Barrault,
Nouvelles réflexions sur le théâtre

Characterization requires externalization of inner truth. Your body must give expression to the character's psychology, or else you will be shaping every role around yourself. *Physicalizing* a character is a reciprocal process: Internal changes occur in response to external ones, and our inner images evoke physical expression.

We are about to begin a series of exercises that develop physical characterization. It is important that your external characterization does not overwhelm your internal work. Each physical choice must be justified or you can slide into a caricature. Because the emphasis here is on physical work, I wish to underscore that character is often built on a series of tiny, almost imperceptible adjustments that enable you to slip into a role. It is the cumulative effect of these small changes that create a character. Your work in the exercises that follow may be of the subtlest nature.

Establishing Character Center

Characterization puts your physical technique to the test. You must now maintain your personal centered state while giving expression to a dramatic character whose center is rarely efficiently placed. You must keep your energy flow unblocked despite the demands of a character under the stress of the dramatic situation. You need to think of your center as the energy source for your character and keep an open channel of expression and uninterrupted flow. Begin all work from a neutral, ready state.

The first step in the process of physical characterization is to determine a character's center. Begin by asking if your character is dominated by his or her intellectual, physical, sexual, or emotional life. The response to this question gives you some keys to proper center placement. If your character is primarily a sexual being, the center may be placed low in the pelvis. If the main energy is intellectual, the center may be in the head. Emotional beings center in the gut, and earthy ones in the pelvis.

Shades of character can be obtained by thinking even more specifically. Perhaps the head center is in the mouth, nose, or eyes; the chest center in the heart, sternum, or liver; the lower pelvic center in the genitals or anus. Center can also be influenced by age and health, so consider these elements. Sometimes character center is more complicated. An emotional being may be headstrong and stubborn and lead with the head. An intellectual may be at war with sexual energy, creating conflicting centers. A character may be psychotic and have no stable center. This requires working with multiple images and giving the lead to the one in action in a particular scene. Meg in *Crimes of the Heart* is an example of a character with conflicting centers. She would appear to be centered in the pelvis, given her sexual promiscuity, but her inability to care and feel, her sense that she is choking, might force the center into the neck and create internal physical conflict.

Center must be responsive to the given circumstances of the text. In some cases a character may be so altered during the course of a play that the original center is changed. Center and respiration may shift as a result of the natural build of a scene. Conflict disturbs the center, and a character may struggle to maintain a stable center when the action intensifies. You should be aware of such transformations and reflect them in your placement of center.

Your character center can be enhanced by imaging certain feelings around it that correspond to your character's personality. The genital center may be hot and fiery, the nose center sharp and pointed, the heart warm and glowing. These images help fill your character portrayal. There is no one correct image for any character. The choice is personal and reflects what inspires you as an actor. The Hamlets of Laurence Olivier, Richard Burton, and Derek Jacobi are different because each actor makes these choices on the basis of personally meaningful images.

Although there is no one correct center image, there are patently incorrect choices. Linda Loman and Laura Wingfield are not centered in the genitals any more than Blanche and Stanley in *A Streetcar Named Desire* are centered in the head. Those choices would simply contradict the content of the play. On the other hand, some plays are open to vastly differing interpretations and the choice of character center may determine the total meaning of the production. If you place Hamlet's center in the genitals you have immediately created a sexually motivated character, which leads to a Freudian interpretation of the play. This may or may not be a desired end. You should think through the entire play to make certain the ramifications of the choice for character center keep within the general concept. The center must reflect your understanding of your character's dramatic function within the through-action of the play.

Figure 13.1 Ed Dixon and Jennifer Butt in *Les Miserables* by Alain Boubil and Claude-Michel Schonberg; based on the novel by Victor Hugo; directed and adapted by Trevor Nunn and John Caird. Observe how the actors have defined their characters through their physical choices. (Photo—Peter Cunningham.)

Exercise 13.1: Creating a Character Center

Analzye your character to determine what part of this person motivates action. Choose an appropriate center based on your psychological portrait. Create an image for the center. Starting from a personally centered state with proper respiration, send the breath into your character's center, letting it fill with the animating power of the breath. Imagine this new center is growing and becoming a dominating force over your being. Feel the power flowing from your own center into the newfound character center. Take your time, letting these images course through the body. Focus all your energy into this new center.

After several minutes of directing the energy flow into the character center, you should have felt a change in your total being. Can you express what you felt? Did these new sensations feel appropriate to your character? If you did not feel this sensation, then you did not totally focus on the new center. Try again. If the feelings came but felt inappropriate to your character, then it is possible that your image and center placement were incorrect. Experiment with other choices until you have found a center that connects you viscerally to your character. Recognizing a correct center integrates intuition, analysis, and sensation.

Character Energy

In Chapter 3 we explored the relationship of energy to character. As you may recall, each individual gives off an energy field that reflects personality. The strength of this radiation depends upon whether a character is passive or active. This energy will affect the way you think, act, walk, move, and speak. In fact, no aspect of a character's existence is unaffected by personal energy level.

It is important to decide whether you are playing a passive or active character. Are you acted upon, or do you forge action? Answer this question in terms of your character's relationship to the dramatic action of the play. Does the weight of the world come down on your character, or does your character push out against the world? Reread the section "Character and Energy" in Chapter 3 and repeat Exercise 3.17 for the specific character on which you are currently working. Make sure the energy choice you have made conforms to your character's dramatic function. Let this energy radiate from your character's center.

When you feel confident in your energy choice, choose a color that best reflects your character, perhaps the color you imagine your character wearing. Repeat Exercise 3.18 for this specific character.

Character Rhythm and Tempo

Closely linked to energy is character rhythm and tempo. Rhythm and tempo can reveal a character's attitude toward life and toward self and affect the energy field. Finding this internal pattern can connect you viscerally to a part. Each personality has a corresponding rhythm and tempo, and you must discover the one that belongs to your character. Clues to character rhythm are often found in the lines. Read the dialogue carefully for any specific rhythmic pattern.

Tempo can be a function of intelligence. Characters who are slow to process information take more time for each cycle of communication and reaction, slowing down beats and dramatic action. Tempo is often directly related to energy level; passive characters work on a slower speed than more active ones. Body type affects speed; heavy characters are slower than lithe ones. Rhythm is a similar indicator of personality. Highly neurotic characters often work in syncopated or erratic rhythms; strong characters may have driving repeated rhythms.

While rhythm and tempo are expressions of personality, essential aspects of a character's dramatic situation are often established by the time lapse between perception and action. The speed with which a character responds to a moment of confrontation with choice reveals the level of internal conflict, and the nature of the obstacles, so character tempo requires dramatic analysis.

Exercise 13.2: Character Energy, Tempo, and Rhythm

Consider carefully your character's energy field. Send this level of energy out from the character center. As you work, sense a tempo and rhythm of movement that feel natural to your character.

Perform the following simple movements with the center, tempo, rhythm, and energy of your character.

1. Brush your hair.
2. Eat breakfast.
3. Put on your coat.
4. Do an exercise workout.

Could you feel how each activity reflected the choices you have made for your character?

Characters with contrasting rhythm and tempo can create conflict or heighten a preexisting one. Explore the relationship between conflict and character rhythm and tempo in the following exercise.

Exercise 13.3: Conflict through Character Rhythm and Tempo

Work with a partner. Actor 1 will be on a rapid tempo, Actor 2 is lethargic. Actor 1 arrives to pick up Actor 2 for an evening at the theatre. Actor 2 is not ready and it is growing increasingly late. Improvise the scene. The conflict can be intensified if you change the nature of the given circumstances. What if you are about to be married, 200 guests are waiting, and Actor 2 is not ready? Neil Simon's *Plaza Suite* builds upon such a juxtaposition.

Did conflict arise from each character's tempo? How can you use rhythm and tempo to heighten the conflict in your scene?

In Chapters 10 and 11, we discussed tempo and rhythm as a function of the arc of dramatic action. The dramatic situation may impose a tempo and rhythm that forms a counterpoint to the natural rhythm and tempo of your character. Often this contradiction heightens the dramatic tension. It is difficult to hold your character rhythms when the dramatic action is working at a different pace. Use these situations to create an internal struggle.

Exercise 13.4: Contrasting Rhythm and Tempo Variation

Perform four simple activities required of your character in your scene with the appropriate character center, energy, rhythm, and tempo.

Determine whether the tempo and rhythm of the dramatic situation in the scene contradicts or reinforces that of your character. Perform the same actions with special attention to the relationship of your character's rhythm and tempo to that of the scene. Remember to take into account the natural build of your scene.

Did the juxtaposition of character rhythm and tempo with that of the scene heighten tensions or create an internal struggle?

Figure 13.2 Ellen Greene in *Little Shop of Horrors* by Howard Ashman and Alan Menken, directed by Howard Ashman. Note how the actress has adjusted center and alignment to portray character. (Photo—Peter Cunningham.)

Character Alignment and Walk

Posture is a reflection of character. The placement of center alters our center of gravity and affects the alignment of the spine. The subtlest adjustment of the vertebrae will send different messages about your character. Our alignment in turn influences our walk as we tend to lead from our centers as we move. Add energy, rhythm, and tempo and a complete portrait begins to emerge.

Exercise 13.5: Character Alignment and Walk

Repeat Exercise 13.1. When you feel a strong sense of center, slowly adjust the spine so that the image of center determines the alignment. Let the energy from the character center flow through the body as you make all the vertebral adjustments to give play to the character center. Be aware of areas of tension that block the energy flow. Do they belong to you or the character? Work through any tension that may be your own. When you feel your alignment reflects your character, let the feelings flow through the body. This placement is your character's centered position.

Maintaining this new alignment, start to walk, leading from the body center. Let your sense of character infuse the walk. Does this feel appropriate to your character?

Add to the walk all that you have learned about your character's energy, tempo, and rhythm. You should now have a walk that makes a statement about who this character is.

Voice and Character

Our voices reveal much about who we are. Think about judgments you have made about people simply by hearing their voices over the telephone. We make assumptions about age, manners, intelligence, class, education, and personality just by what we hear. Vocal placement is a direct function of character center. We tend to resonate in a locus that reveals the dominating element of our personalities. Head centers resonate high in the body, pelvic centers lower down. The tonal quality of the voice directly reflects personality. Contradiction between physical and vocal center usually indicates internal or external conflict.

Similarly, our speech pattern echoes the natural character rhythm and tempo. Energy field is often evidenced in volume. Intonation indicates mood and personality. Diction directly reveals education and socioeconomic class, and articulation, while connected to diction, can often reveal aspects of personality from laziness to obsession with perfection. Some of these elements are revealed in the dialogue, but when they are not given by the playwright, you must choose appropriate speech for your character.

Accent can place a character in a geographic location or give relevant information about his or her past. It is also an area that traps young actors into playing stereotypes. If you try an accent out on your first reading, you will be playing a generalized accent without any relationship to those traits that individualize your character. *No accent should be attempted until you have found the resonating center, vocal energy, and speech rhythm and tempo.*

Exercise 13.6: Giving a Character a Voice

Center your character as you did in Exercise 12.6. Send the breath into your center and on the exhalation release a "ha" sound. Feed the image of the sound coming from the character center. Let the sound reflect your character's energy level. Release a series of "ha" sounds at the speed of your character's tempo and according to your character's rhythm.

When you feel you have made this connection, state your superobjective starting with "I want," in words natural to your character, using the tempo, rhythm, and resonator that reflect your character's center. When you feel connected, add your character's articulation and diction. Repeat or reformulate the superobjective until you feel deeply connected to your character's primary need and desire. Now recite your first line of dialogue with a clear objective, maintaining the character's resonator, energy, rhythm, tempo, and articulation. Try saying a few more lines, maintaining the connection between voice and feeling.

When you feel you have truly mastered the vocal characteristics of your character, this is the point to add a specific regional accent. (This assumes that you have completed a psychological analysis and worked through centering, alignment, energy, rhythm, and tempo exercises.) Continue working through your character's dialogue until the vocal pattern feels natural and organic.

Try speaking while using your character's walk. Do the body and voice feel integrated? Repeat your opening line, focusing clearly on your objective and adding a strong action. Do you feel more connected to your character than you did before? Have you succeeded in linking psychology, the body, and speech? Note the changes you felt each step of the way in your log.

Characteristic Gesture

People reflect personality through smaller movements that have become unconscious habits. These are characteristic gestures used primarily to reveal character. Just as action that is unrelated to the superobjective is illogical and confusing, gesture that does not enhance a psychological portrait is extraneous and distracting. When you choose characteristic gestures, you must ask if they reveal aspects of your character that serve its dramatic function.

Characteristic gesture can be commonplace like nail biting, pacing, playing with hair, or cracking knuckles. Others are a bit more original. I remember a lighting designer who always cleaned his nails with a hunting knife at production meetings, an unusual and revealing characteristic. You can imagine how this poised knife affected his interactions with others. To give a character this kind of gesture is a sample of a strong choice that could directly relate to his dramatic function. Your acting benefits when you find strong but believable gestures; repeat the hackneyed and you risk playing the stereotype.

Whether unusual or mundane, all of these gestures reveal character and can enliven your psychological portrait. I say this with a word of caution. Inexperienced actors can overplay characteristic gestures, using them so much that the scene becomes a scene about the gesture and not about the central action. Characteristic gesture must be used sparingly to enhance a character portrayal and must grow out of a thorough psychological study of character. When they occur, they should relate organically to the ongoing dramatic action.

Sometimes, when an actor has done all the homework on a part, a characteristic gesture starts to happen spontaneously and unconsciously during rehearsals. When you become one with a role you eventually start assuming these kinds of movement patterns. This, of course, is ideal because gesture becomes an organic part of a role.

Exercise 13.7: Characteristic Gesture

Examine your written character analysis from the last chapter. Can you think of a gesture that would reveal these aspects of this individual's psychology? Try to come up with something that will not appear hackneyed and expresses creative thinking on your part. Have any gestures unconsciously set in?

Dressing a Character

The expression "clothes make the man" is not without truth. The clothes we wear say a great deal about who we are or who we wish to be, and in turn influence the way we are perceived by others. Clothes not only reflect your sense of self but can influence how you feel. You need only remember how good you felt the last time you wore a favorite piece of clothing to understand how dress influences emotions. Costume provides the actor with a means of physicalizing character and offers another avenue to a character's inner life. In production work, the costume designer and director will clothe your character. For acting class this is your responsibility. Costume elements can trigger a characterization so select with care.

Clothes influence behavior. Few of us act the same way in a bathing suit as we would in formal dress. Women alter the way they sit and move when they change from pants to a dress and often a whole new persona emerges. Some young men, accustomed to wearing sneakers, jeans, and a sweatshirt feel imprisoned when forced into shoes, suit, and tie. Clothes also can emphasize certain physical traits: a low-cut blouse can emphasize cleavage and draw attention to seductive qualities; a tight T-shirt can show off a man's musculature; loose clothing can hide excess weight; the layered look can make you appear heavier. Clothes can also reflect socioeconomic class and the period and style of a play. Because we dress for the occasion, clothes interact with the *when* and *where* of the given circumstances as well as the *who*.

Costume is thus a wonderful way of both getting in touch with your character and of externalizing the internal qualities you have defined. It can alter your physical appearance—make you look heavier, thinner, sexier, stronger, clumsier, or more graceful. *However, the miracle of costume transformation is only attained if you have simultaneously worked on center, rhythm, tempo, alignment, and walk. You must provide the inner character that makes a costume work!* The sexiest dress will not make you seductive unless you move like a sexy woman. In fact, a provocative gown on an actor who feels and acts unattractive will appear comic.

Figure 13.3 David Dukes and B. D. Wong in David Henry Hwang's *M. Butterfly*, directed by John Dexter. Observe how B. D. Wong has transformed himself into a woman, enhancing his physical and psychological characterization through costume. David Dukes's body reveals his dejected state in his prison cell. (Photo—Peter Cunningham.)

Figure 13.4 David Dukes transforms himself in *M. Butterfly*'s dramatic finale. (Photo—Peter Cunningham.)

Not only are the specific articles of clothing and how they fit important, but the color you choose can make a strong statement about your character. Refer back to your work on color as character energy in Chapter 3. The color that best represents your character's energy field should be carried over into costume choices as well.

Costume choices that are vital to the expression of character should be used in rehearsal as early as possible. I will never forget a talented student who played the coquette Celimene in a scene from *The Misanthrope*. When she brought the scene to acting class, she was wearing the long skirt in which she had rehearsed. Yet her Celimene was leaden and moved with a heaviness that weighed down the rhythm of the verse in Richard Wilbur's delightful translation. The problem was evident. Under the long skirt she was wearing work boots that clomped along the stage with the sound and rhythm of a horse. We substituted ballet shoes for the boots and a new Celimene sprang to life. Something as simple as shoes can affect every aspect of a character—rhythms, movement, and interactions with all those on stage.

An additional note that is especially important to women. Hairdo and makeup are extensions of the total physical image. The sisters in *Crimes of the Heart* can each be defined by dress, hairdo, and amount of makeup. Or take the brothers in Sam Shepard's *True West* as an example. If Austin is unkempt at the beginning of the play and Lee well turned out, the entire action of the play is confused. These considerations affect the characters' interaction.

| | **Exercise 13.8:** Dressing a Character | | | | | | |

Consider all that you know about your character. Factor in the *where* and *when* of the scene and answer the following questions:

1. What physical traits do I wish to emphasize?
2. What aspects of personality can I reveal through costume?
3. What socioeconomic facts are vital to dress?
4. What aspects of my character's self-image should be expressed in costume?
5. What clothes best reflect my character's behavior in the scene?
6. How must costume reflect the period and style of the play?
7. Are there any articles of clothing specifically referred to in the scene?
8. Are there any required makeup and hairdo changes?
9. What color best expresses my character's energy?
10. How does my character feel about the clothes he or she is in?

On the basis of your answers to these questions, determine what an appropriate costume for your character would be. Write a complete costume description in your log. Which costume elements will you use in your scene?

Although you may not be able to obtain this ideal costume, the image you have can feed your characterization. Allow the costume elements to evoke an internal response.

Personal and Costume Props

We can express elements of character through the way we relate to certain objects. Props that are part of a costume or that are carried by a character can be effective expressions of personality and can connect you to your character. The importance of this often neglected element of characterization is underscored in these lines from the poem "The Props of Helen Weigel" by Bertolt Brecht:

> As the gardener for his nursery
> Chooses the fullest seeds and as the poet
> For his poem the right words, in this way
> She chose the objects that accompanied
> Her characters on the stage. The pewter spoon
> That Courage put in the buttonhole

Of her Mongolian jacket . . . the bronze urn
Of Antigone harboring dust. Impossible to confuse them. . . .[1]

A prop is a useful tool of characterization only if you, the actor, make it meaningful. If you do not connect to an object, it merely becomes an article of decoration. Props also take on significance because of how a particular character uses them. If a character carries a weapon, it can be held as a prized possession or as an object of contempt. Think how much we learn about a character from this interaction. Often a playwright provides you with a personal prop. The woman psychiatrist's Snoopy doll in Durang's *Beyond Therapy* is an example. Sometimes you can elect to give significance to a prop or costume piece such as the Mother Superior's crucifix in Pielmeier's *Agnes of God*. Small actions performed with props or as characteristic gesture are called ***business.***

An actor can creatively invent an object and endow it with significance by attaching certain feelings or memories to it. You might decide to give Mama in *A Raisin in the Sun* a picture of Big Walter and the dead baby. These would permit the character a variety of meaningful interactions. All choices of props must relate to a character's dramatic function. The object should never become a source of irrelevant stage business.

Exercise 13.9: Personal and Costume Props

To find a personal prop that permits an expression of character ask yourself the following questions:

1. Has the playwright noted any such prop in the script?
2. Is there a costume element that can have significance?
3. Can I create a prop through which my character can reveal psychological traits?

When you find such an object write down its significance in your log. Use Exercise 7.18, "Endowing Objects" to connect your character emotionally to the prop.

Personal props must be used with caution. You do not want your character so involved with a prop that he or she disconnects from the central action of the scene. The interactions should be brief and meaningful, and grow organically out of the dramatic action. Costume and prop accoutrements can enhance your characterization, but they should not be the basis of your work. The very selection of these items depends on the depth of your psychological understanding.

[1]Bertolt Brecht, *Écrits sur le théâtre* (Paris: L'arche, 1963), p. 228.

Summary

Physicalizing a character is predicated on an understanding of the psychological motivations of the dramatic persona. Take care to justify the physical characterization internally. Rooting all that you do in a secure character center, you slowly add the physical elements that give life to your portrait. Energy, alignment, voice, and walk turn your concept into a tangible reality. Each gesture, costume element, and prop reveals some significant aspect of this being. Subtlety and nuance can give finesse to your work. Developing a character requires the effective integration of all you have learned about acting technique. Astute analysis and a body and voice that can express your character's inner life are essential. Each choice you make must relate to the logic of the whole play. Effective characterization ultimately rests on your ability to let this new identity become an organic part of your own being, a second nature.

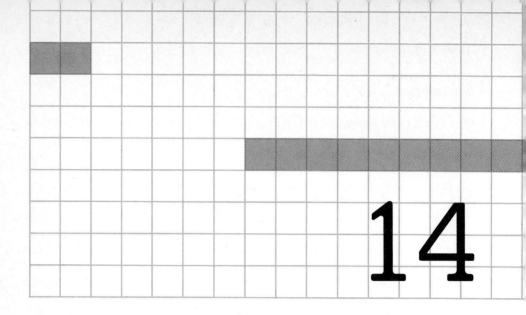

The Rehearsal Process

> *... this is not magic but work, my friends.*
> Bertolt Brecht, "The Curtain"

The rehearsal process integrates script analysis, physical and psychological technique, and characterization through patient, careful, and systematic work. Although performance situations may differ, the actor's focus during rehearsals remains fundamentally the same. Once you have understood the steps in this process, you will be able to adapt the principles to the necessities of each new situation.

The Undirected Scene

Scenes prepared for acting class are subject to the method of each teacher. The emphasis placed on achieving a finished product may vary, but you should never work for results. Always work through the steps in your creative process. The scene must develop organically through integrated technique. Some instructors like to see a scene several times to check on each step. Others prefer students to go as far as they can on their own toward a completed scene. In either case, the elements of the rehearsal process remain the same:

1. Analysis and determination of the superobjective

2. Personalization and determining scene and beat objectives
3. Scoring the beats
4. Learning lines
5. Experimentation with actions
6. Justifying adjustments
7. Blocking
8. Developing characterization
9. Propping
10. Set and costume elements

Because acting is an integrated process, these elements overlap. Some develop simultaneously. From your first reading, your imagination sets to work thinking of action, characterization, prop, costume, and set elements. Although you don't bring everything to your first rehearsal, much is already in the works as part of your creative process. Every choice you make along the way adds to the depth of your character. Selection of prop, set, and costume elements often evolves through rehearsals. The final score of beats and actions is full of unexpected new ideas. Rehearsal is a period of growth and discovery on every level.

It is important not to rush any step in the process. Follow the logical development of the work. Although there is no set pace or time for anything to happen, here are a few important guidelines:

1. Read the play and have a preliminary analysis and understanding before your first rehearsal.
2. Personalize and have a basic score of beats before you start choosing actions and tactics.
3. Don't set blocking until you are "off book."
4. Integrate character elements as you work.

A scene requires at least five hours of rehearsal before presentation unless your teacher asks to see it at an early stage in the work. When possible, meet for several shorter rehearsals rather than one or two marathons. It is good to leave time between rehearsals so your unconscious can set to work on the scene. Integration takes time. When possible, it is helpful to set a specific task on which to focus for each rehearsal. Personalization, developing actions, physicalizing given circumstances, developing characterization, and blocking would be a good breakdown for five one-hour rehearsals for acting class. Remember that results are cumulative: You continue personalizing while exploring actions; you develop actions while physicalizing the given circumstances; characterization grows from your first choice of objective and action; and blocking reflects the interaction of all your earlier work.

Choosing Appropriate Material

You are responsible for scene selection, role distribution and analysis. The biggest favor you can do for yourself is to pick a good scene. This is not an arbitrary judgment. There are ways of assessing the value of a scene. While it is important that a play appeals to you, liking a scene is not enough to justify doing it. First, you must know why you like the scene, *then you must see what makes it a good scene to act.* Putting this into words obliges you to make dramatic value judgments.

Your teacher may give specific criteria for scene selection and may have a particular approach in mind. In that case, whatever instructions are given by the instructor supersede the directions given here. In the absence of any such guidance, these enumerated points can steer you.

1. Avoid choosing lengthy scenes for your first effort, or it will be difficult to work in depth on the entire scene. As a general rule, the best scenes for class are about three to six pages long.
2. Be sure the scene is a complete unit of action. This means identifying a strong central conflict and arc of action. Ask yourself if the characters have clearly drawn objectives that meet with obstacles.
3. The characters' objectives should be strong and meaningful to them. If the characters don't have something on the line, the scene will not have dramatic interest.
4. The scene should be active. This does not mean the characters are running around, but that the conflict is active. Avoid scenes that are merely expository, where characters talk about the past. Scenes that have the possibility of action allow you to make creative action choices and to physicalize character.
5. The dialogue should be natural and speakable within the constraints of the style of the play.
6. The characters should be well drawn and interesting to you.
7. Don't pick a scene that requires complicated editing or cutting. Good scenes have an internal logic. If you slice lines out of various places in the text, the dramatic action and build may be adversely affected.

A general word of guidance. Your first material should be straightforward, with a clear conflict, meaningful objectives, approachable characters, and minimal style demands. As your technique grows, you may choose increasingly complex scenes. Hone your basic technique before you plunge into ambiguous materials, distorted characters, and heavily stylized plays. There are so many good scenes around that meet the above criteria that there is really no reason to make compromises in the quality of the material you choose.

Defining Mutual Responsibility

Your scene partner may be assigned to you, or you may be asked to find someone to work with in the class. It is important to see this as a collaborative effort from the start. You should immediately decide on a strategy for finding a scene and sharing this responsibility.

Part of successful teamwork is a joint effort to find mutually convenient rehearsal time and space. Punctuality to all rehearsals is the mark of shared respect. Most important, you should set certain goals and adhere to them. Decide when you will have the play read and analyzed, the character and scene analyzed, when you will be off book, and ready to block. When only one actor has met deadlines, resentment can set in, so try to respect commitments.

A rehearsal is a work period, so temperament has no place at a rehearsal. We all have bad days, and actors are no exception. Unfortunately, because we work with our feelings so much, actors sometimes feel that emotional displays are permissible behavior. In fact, this is the very reason that we must keep personal feelings in check. It is taboo to mix personal emotions with the work. It confuses and upsets your partners and can wreck trust and wreak havoc with the creative process.

When you have had a bad day, see this as a test of your ability to focus and concentrate. Temporarily shut out other issues and focus on your character's reality. You may discover new things in the scene precisely because of the mood you're in. Use your emotions constructively in the scene, not self-indulgently.

The real key is mutual respect. Give as much thought to your partner's needs as to your own and you will surely have a creative relationship from which you both will benefit. A good partnership makes the work easier and the satisfaction greater.

Prerehearsal Analysis

Before your first rehearsal, you are responsible for a preliminary play and scene analysis. If you have completed the exercises in Chapters 10 and 11, you are ready to work. This means you have read the entire play, studied the story and plot, and understood the dramatic action and your character's dramatic function. You should have a statement of the superobjective of the play and of your character's through-line objective.

You can now examine the specifics of your scene as they relate to the play. Analyze the objectives and given circumstances. Some basic character study automatically begins. By the time of your first meeting with your partner, you should have completed this level of analysis.

The first rehearsal is a time for comparing notes with your partner to make sure you agree on the story, the nature of the relationship you share, and the given circumstances of the scene. You should be ready to discuss objectives at this point. If you have not given the material any thought, you are not ready to work!

Rehearsal as Experiment and Exploration

From the first reading of a play, the process of experiment and exploration has begun. You probably already imagined many possibilities for your scene before you even met with your partner. Each new mental image is a discovery. As rehearsals progress you will continue this internal exploration process while simultaneously experimenting with ways of giving it external life. Rehearsals are as exciting and enjoyable as they are hard work.

Rehearsal Warm-Up

Before every rehearsal you should be sure to warm-up. Refer to Chapter 5 to construct an adequate series of exercises. The warm-up is not just preparatory to physical work. The fact that you are sitting in chairs and not standing on your feet does not reduce the necessity. Remember, tension blocks the flow of feelings and energy. If you have not released inhibitory muscle spasms, the entire communication process can break down. *All acting work must proceed from a centered state!* A tense actor is an invulnerable actor.

Warm up with your partner. This can start the communication channel going. Trade breath and sounds as you ready the voice. Try to make contact as you work. This puts you in the right frame of mind for sharing and trusting.

Personalizing a Scene

The first step in working on a scene with your partner is personalization. Seek a personal connection to your character's dramatic situation so that you can respond as if all that were happening were real. Part of personalizing a scene is determining the subtext of dialogue. What does your character really want at every moment?

View the initial read-through with your partner as a time of discovery. Sit in chairs facing each other in a relaxed but energized, centered position. Make eye contact and trade breaths before you begin while going over the given circumstances in your head. Try not to impose any prejudgments on your material. Read the scene, exploring the meaning of your lines and carefully assessing and reacting to your partner's feedback. The goal of the first reading is communication—to listen, take in, respond. Make sure you are open to adjustments and don't get locked into any early line readings.

The first reading is best accomplished seated. Do not start moving and choosing actions until you have explored the content of the scene. As you read, probe your character's objectives on every line. Ask yourself what the subtext is. As you become surer of your purpose, try to make the line work to achieve it. Each line must be given as feedback to whatever your partner gave you on the line before, creating a spiraling cycle of communication. As you say your lines find inner images that justify your words. With each new read-through, you should find a new and deeper internal connection and justification for your lines.

The most important part of this process is to be an active receiver, to really listen to what your partner is communicating and to keep your responses spontaneous and honest. In this honest exchange lies the basis of personalization. The first reading will be quite slow because you need to leave time to assess what you receive. You are just learning to think as your character so the response time is not up to speed. This is to be expected. Don't rush the reading. Patience and care is required.

Keep eye contact with your partner during the reading. I realize this is difficult at a time when you are as yet unfamiliar with the text, so pause after each phrase or sentence to see how your partner is reacting. Maintain as much direct eye contact as possible. If you never look up from the script during a reading, you are acting in a vacuum, not on the basis of cycles of communication. This results in arbitrary line readings.

As a result of the personalization process, you may decide to rethink your play analysis. You may have a new sense of who this person is and what his or her superobjective is. The scene objective must be adjusted accordingly. Major changes in understanding should be discussed with your partner. You cannot alter the given circumstances without mutual agreement.

Some discoveries you may wish to keep private for use in your characterization or in gaining your objective. Discerning how much to talk about with your partner is a sensitive process. Some actors like to discuss every discovery; others like to savor them inside. You must be sensitive to which kind of actor your partner is. If someone is reticent, do not force discussion. On the other hand, sense when a partner is in need of a sounding board to clarify ideas. Sometimes discussions end with one actor trying to direct the other. This inevitably creates resentment. If you feel your partner isn't giving you enough or that you want a certain action repeated, put it in terms of your acting needs: "I really felt connected when you did X," or "I'm having difficulty relating to my objectives; could you help me by trying Y?" Ask for help; don't give directions.

After several slow read-throughs to establish communication with your partner, you will feel that you have established a fundamental personalization of the scene. As you become increasingly certain of your objectives, you will feel a need to act to achieve them. This will mark the beginning of a search for effective action. It is inadvisable to leave a seated position until the internal need to act is strong. Once this happens, you can be sure some level of personalization has occurred.

Intensifying Objectives, Discovering Action

As a consequence of the work on personalization, you will strengthen your objectives and develop actions, all the while intensifying your internal justification. The first level of active experimentation is devoted to discovering effective actions toward your goals.

Each scene run-through now becomes a search for effective action. Try out new tactics. Feel free to experiment with interesting ideas. You cannot tell whether something will work until you have done it. Above all, go with your impulses and don't censor yourself. Rehearsal is a time to take chances. Be sure to carefully assess the feedback each new tactic produces from your partner. If it brings you closer to your objective, take note; you may wish to develop this particular action. As you make your choices, remember to keep them in line with the character and given circumstances. These are the only limits on your creativity. Stronger actions may require stronger internal justification, so formulate objectives and circumstances accordingly.

After rehearsal, it is important to review the script, checking your score of beats and noting in the margins successful actions that you may wish to keep. At this point you may also feel that your original beat notations are in need of revision.

Use the time between rehearsals to think of new things to try. Review the script and notice how differently you read it now than you did on your first encounter. Plan the things you need to work on for the next rehearsal.

Exploring the Given Circumstances

Review your list of given circumstances. Use several run-throughs of the scene to physicalize the *where* and *when*. Make certain you really place the scene for the audience. Decide if there are any elements in the environment that you must react to or that pose special problems or obstacles for your character and work to express this.

Ask yourself what elements you can use from the physical surroundings to achieve your objective. Invent actions that incorporate these elements. At this point, you may think of specific props in the *when* and *where* that can be used toward your objective or to establish character. Try to obtain these items for the next rehearsal.

This is the time to examine any physical adjustments you need to make. If your character has any physical impediments, these should be worked actively at this time. Costume elements that affect the action should appear.

Learning Lines

There are many different opinions on this subject. I have one cardinal rule: *Never memorize lines before your first rehearsal!* You may wonder why this is so strongly underscored. Is it not wonderful to come to the first rehearsal so well prepared? The answer is quite simply, "No!" At the first reading, you are discovering what lines mean—what the subtext really is. If you memorize lines before you have had communication with your partner, you may be locked into a subtextless line reading that has nothing to do with moment-to-moment objectives—the actual content of the scene—and your lines will be divorced from feedback from the other actor.

Lines are learned easily once you have a completed score of beats. If you know what you want at every moment in the scene, you will remember the line as a function of your objective. At the very least, you will be able to paraphrase it because it will be contextually meaningful to you. This is one of the reasons keeping a score of beats is so important. Once the score of beats reflects a clear sense of the dramatic action, the sooner you are off book, the better, so you can freely explore action and physical characterization.

The edict against memorizing lines for the first rehearsal does not mean that you never have to put any effort into the process. After that initial meeting, you are expected to put some time into your score and learning lines. The process is simply more organic and much easier when you know what you're really saying. Once you and your partner decide that by such and such a rehearsal you will be off book, you have a responsibility to meet that commitment and no excuses are really acceptable.

If you are having trouble with the lines in a particular section of the scene, the odds are you have not carefully scored the beats for that segment. Go to your score and review your analytic process. Once you have reviewed the script with the idea of following the logic of the dramatic action, learning lines will be less of a problem.

A word on paraphrasing. While this is helpful in early rehearsals because it keeps the scene moving, some actors get hooked on paraphrasing all through the rehearsal process. When you are working on a full-scale production, long-term paraphrasing throws off the tempo and rhythm of the play's language, while your fellow actors, waiting for cue lines that are never quite what they expect, often are hesitant in action and speech. Constant paraphrasers sometimes get to the point that they can't remember which line is theirs, and which was the playwright's. Be sure you return to the script for accuracy.

Blocking

Blocking is the term used to describe the process by which stage action and movement is developed and set. Until recent times, it was common for directors to block a play on paper and then spend rehearsals teaching the movement patterns to the actors. While some directors still work this way, rehearsals are more usually used to experiment with action and movement as an organic process flowing from objectives, actions, given circumstances, and characterization. Although directors still determine what the ultimate blocking of a play will be, actors are active participants in the process. Learning to make action choices and justify movement is a vital part of your job.

Once you have personalized the scene you are ready to experiment with blocking. However, nothing can be fixed until you are off book because the script in hand limits your choices and affects rhythm and tempo. Once you know your lines, you are ready to set blocking. Build upon the actions noted in your score, adding necessary movement and character business.

Read the script to determine any business or movement necessary to the scene's action. For example, you may be required to end up at a window at a specific line to justify commenting on the view. This means you must find some way of justifying your move to the window. You cannot simply walk to the window because you have to be there without any inner reason. You will have to invent one. Perhaps you go to the window to get away from another character with whom you are in conflict, or because you are warm and need air, or to change the subject because you've entered a new beat and altered your objective. These are all possible justifications for the cross. Once you create the inner justification for the action, the simple movement "cross to the window" becomes purposeful action.

Beware of actions that are continued through several beat changes. Actions usually change for every beat and moment. If you are continuing the same action without any adjustment whatsoever, the audience will not register a change of beat. Perhaps during an entire scene in which you are having an increasingly heated argument, you are hammering nails into bookshelves. That is your activity, but it is not your action. With each new beat the action of the hammering changes. You may hammer at a different tempo as your emotions build. You may intensify the strength of your hammering. You may alter the position of your body. Although the activity of hammering is continued, you have actually changed the action several times by making small adjustments that reflect the building tension of the beats. This enables the audience to understand the logic of the beats.

As your characterization deepens, you may wish to add character business to your blocking. This should be kept to a minimum. Try to express character through the action and movement patterns that flow organically from the dramatic action. Interrupting the flow of a scene to insert character "schtick" can upset the tempo and rhythm of a scene. However, sometimes an effective piece of business can justify future actions.

A word of caution about scenes that are violent. If an actor is afraid of getting hurt, it is hard to be free and creative. Scenes that contain physical aggression must be carefully choreographed so that actors are safe. Work out the blocking slowly and precisely so that both actors know exactly what is going to happen on each line. When the blocking is fixed, gradually bring the scene up to speed, repeating the blocking accurately. Once the blocking is set, neither actor should make any changes without alerting the other to a new idea and slowly working it through. The intensity of the violence is achieved through how actors react internally. If you behave as if you were hurt, the audience will believe it. Similar care should be exercised in sexually explicit scenes. Work out the blocking carefully so that neither actor feels violated.

Beginning actors often feel timid about action choices. Fear of doing something that won't work or sometimes just simple inhibition keeps actors standing around looking static and unenergized. Hopefully the exercises in Chapter 9 broke down some of those blocks. Learn to go with your impulses at the moment. If you have done all your homework, trust your instincts and experiment with action.

Actions and Stage Directions

Acting students always ask, "What do I do about stage directions written in the text?" If you ask a playwright to respond to this question, you will be told that they were written for a purpose with forethought and are intended to be followed. Few directors and actors would concur that stage directions should be followed categorically.

To gain perspective on this question, it is helpful to place it in historical context. Until the era of naturalism, stage directions other than "Exit" and "Enter" were rarely given. When playwrights became concerned with the accurate portrayal of reality on stage in the nineteenth century, they added elaborate set descriptions and stage directions to their plays. It is significant that when this practice began the modern stage director did not exist. There was no one to give a play conceptual unity except the playwright. Stage directions thus began in an era where the author was attempting to do the job of a director as well. Although all productions have a director today, the practice of writing stage directions has continued.

Stage directions can given valuable insight into the playwright's intent; however, the strict observance of an author's directions can result in several difficulties. If you simply follow stage directions slavishly, you may discover that your actions are not tactically linked to your objectives and are the result of an externally developed pattern. Further, every actor creates a unique chemistry with a role. You may come up with an action that is theatrically more effective than the one envisioned by the playwright. In places where playwrights have used adverbs and adjectives such as *increasingly desperate, discontented, aggressively, angrily, sweetly, lovingly,* actors can easily fall into the trap of playing of qualities and the cliché if they try to render the adjective or adverb described. Learn to use these kinds of directions to trigger your imagination and not for an external result.

Many stage directions require that you have reproduced the set description accurately in order to carry them out. Few scenes for acting class are that lavishly produced, and stage directions must be modified accordingly.

The best solution is to examine stage directions in your initial reading to clarify the author's intentions. Decide which directions are crucial to the dramatic action and which are result-oriented attempts by the author to direct the play. Work to incorporate the former into an organic pattern of action that flows from the score of beats and your interpretation of the scene.

Rehearsal Improvisations

Improvisation can trigger the personalization process, develop objectives, inspire action, and aid in the discovery of character. It is an invaluable technique when actors are having difficulty making the scene come alive. Improvisations use the characters and given circumstances of the scene, or circumstances analogous to those in the scene, but permit an actor to use his or her own words to deepen personalization. You can also improvise a scene not in the play to shed light on the scene on which you are working.

Once freed from concerns about lines, actors often find new connections to their characters. You can discover subtext and find behavior natural to the characters and the situation. Concentration and listening improves. The written scene is stripped down to the basic objectives and then used as an outline—a scenario for action. This focuses on the central conflict and obstacles and serves to energize the actors and the action.

When you improvise, it is important to keep a sense of your goals. An improvisation is not a free-for-all, it is a method of searching for understanding. Because an improv has a loose form, not everything discovered is applicable to the scene. Keep only what is relevant. After working improvisationally, the new insights and connections must be linked to the lines of the text as the playwright wrote them.

Improvisation is often used by acting coaches and directors to help actors relate to their characters and to each other. If beginning actors decide to improvise during rehearsal without supervision, you must be aware of what you need to get from the work. Because the improv highlights the conflict, it is possible for things to intensify to a dangerous level without a director or teacher present to set limits. Care must be taken to maintain control. Keep this in mind if you decide to improvise on your own.

Integrating Characterization

The elements of characterization must be gradually integrated during the rehearsal process. From your first reading, you are making decisions that will affect your characterization. Much of this early work toward building a character is homework. You do it without your partner before rehearsal. Even some initial experimentation with physical character can be done outside of shared rehearsal time.

The first read-throughs should be used to establish communication and personalization, not to work on character. Once the scene is personalized, you can bring in elements of your characterization. What comes in first will depend on how essential you feel a particular item is. Try starting with your physical characterization—center, voice, walk, energy, tempo, and rhythm—and add prop and costume elements later. This is not a categorical rule. Sometimes a prop like a cane can help you find center, walk, energy, rhythm, and tempo. In general, however, it is wise to root your character in the body before adding externals.

As you make more and more choices, bring in elements systematically. This gives you a chance to really feel what works, and provides your partner with an opportunity to adjust and react to each addition. Your character should be developing over the entire rehearsal period.

Setting the Scene

You should examine the needs of the dramatic action as well as what is required to create the *when* and *where* to determine set elements. The general rule for acting class is to use the minimum scenic elements necessary for the action to progress. A scene in a living room may require a sofa and chairs, perhaps a coffee table, but not necessarily every lamp, rug, ashtray, and piece of bric-a-brac unless some specific piece of dramatic action or stage business involves one of these items. Stick to what is essential and obtain those elements as soon as possible.

Sometimes the *when* and *where* are too complex to create for acting class. The Forest of Arden or a royal palace is best created by physicalizing it through your acting rather than creating a complete stage set. Sometimes one symbolic prop can set the scene. Use a coat stand for a tree; treat it accordingly and you're in the forest. Remember, the audience will see what you see, so let your imagination work scenic magic.

Propping a Scene

Props that are vital to the action of a scene should be brought to rehearsal. Work out business with the actual prop or something close to it in hand. At first you will feel awkward coordinating lines and business, but with practice this becomes a natural part of the scene.

Not all props have the same purpose. Props can serve:

1. necessary stage business
2. to advance the action
3. to give a sense of time and place
4. to be used with tactical action choices
5. to reveal character

When determining the props you need, ask yourself the relative importance of each item. Everything essential to the central action of the scene should be there, but don't waste time on insignificant items. **Make sure all props are safe.** A hazardous prop constrains your acting if you are worried about the danger of hurting another actor or yourself. If you can't find exactly what the scene calls for, substitute something that will serve the purpose. Do not try to fully stage a scene for acting class and get bogged down hunting for the precise prop called for in the stage directions. Use your creativity and imagination. An upside-down wastebasket has served as bongo drums for many run-throughs of Pinter's *The Lover*. If your scene takes place in a kitchen, a pot or bowl may be all you need to set the place. Don't try to create a kitchen and everything in it. A set full of things that are never used can be distracting, and unnecessary props can get in your way and impede the flow of movement.

Costuming a Scene

Look carefully at the costume description of your character and decide which elements are vital. In highly stylized or period pieces you may have to approximate the costume elements necessary to give you the feel of a character. For example, you may not be able to obtain a beautiful seventeenth-century lace gown, but a long skirt and pretty blouse can give you the general aura of your costume.

In addition, consider any costume elements that are necessary for the action of the scene. If a character must keep some important item in a pocket, make sure your costume has one. Read the script for any allusions to costumes in the dialogue. If there is a line that says, "Let me help you off with your coat," don't arrive in a T-shirt. Costume can also create the *where* and *when*. A flowered shawl can place a scene in Russia, a toga in ancient Rome.

Costuming for acting class can draw upon your creativity and engage teamwork. Many theatre departments have rehearsal costumes, so learn what's available. Accuracy in costuming is not the most important concern for acting class. Mood and feeling of dress are just as essential.

Late Rehearsal Check-Up

The rehearsal process is as exciting as it is complex. It is possible to lose track of your inner score of beats under the deluge of concerns about action, lines, character, props, set, and costume. If you feel that the scene has somehow gotten away from you, this is a good time to do a read-through in chairs, refocusing on communication with your partner and re-establishing the score of beats. You will be amazed how much can be learned from such a reading. It only takes about five minutes to run the scene this way, and the benefits derived are enormous. It is also a wonderful way to see how far you've come from that first searching read-through.

The first time you prepare a scene, you will feel a bit overwhelmed by the number of things you have to remember. The following checklists help keep track of all your responsibilities. If you have skipped anything, or feel uncertain of how well you really accomplished any of the steps, go back and rework that area.

Exercise 14.1: Prerehearsal Checklist

Analytic homework:

1. Have you read the whole play?
2. Do you have a grasp of the story?
3. Have you charted the plot?
4. Do you understand the play?
5. Are there any specific genre, style, or language demands?
6. Do you have a statement of the play's superobjective?
7. Do you understand your character's superobjective and dramatic function within the plot?
8. Have you established the scene conflict and do you have a scene objective for your character?
9. Have you analyzed the given circumstances of the scene? Do you know *who* you are; *who* your partner is; *where* you are; *when* it is; *what* is happening; *why* you are there; *what* you want, and *what* are your obstacles?
10. Have you created a psychological portrait of your character?

Exercise 14.2: Rehearsal Procedure Checklist

Rehearsal procedure:

1. Have you warmed up before rehearsals?
2. Have you personalized the scene?
3. Have you physically established the given circumstances?
4. Have you established a score of beats?
5. Have you experimented with physical action and line readings?
6. Have you learned your lines?
7. Have your brought in character elements?
8. Have you worked with props?
9. Have you brought in set and costume elements?
10. Have you blocked the scene?

Exercise 14.3: Energized Performance Checklist

Energized Performance

1. Are your objectives strong?
2. Is all your stage action purposeful?

3. Have you physicalized the environment?
4. Have you blocked the scene to use your playing space effectively?
5. Is your concentration and energy flow constant and directed?
6. Have you marked your beats?
7. Have you established the build of the scene?
8. Have you established character energy?
9. Have you physicalized your character?
10. Are you filling the theatrical space?

Preparing a Monologue

Monologues in acting class are usually given by an actor alone on stage. The character to whom you are speaking is absent, and you are left talking to an "imaginary other." In our discussion of rehearsal, we have underscored the importance of establishing the communication process with your partner in order to personalize a scene. In preparing a monologue, you must establish communication with someone who is not there. This means that a monologue provides an additional challenge for an actor—the creation of a partner, an imaginary *who*.

Just as you create your own character, you must create this *who*. See this person in every detail. Create a portrait of this *who* in your mind's eye. What does your imaginary other look like? Eye color, height, weight, clothes, demeanor, personality—all must be clearly drawn. Call upon your sense memory and endowment techniques. You have the skills you need to experience this character.

Once your have created your imaginary other, you must really share and communicate. You must pause and assess the imaginary feedback. You must see and feel every response you get as you speak or your words will appear empty. You must act as if the communication cycle were complete, playing both parts—one with your body and voice, one with your imagination. If the existence of this person is not real for you, your objective will have no meaning. This technique applies to telephone conversations that you have on stage as well. You must hear the other side of the conversation. Imagine what the other party is saying and weigh those responses before you say your next line.

Sometimes monologues are addressed directly to the audience. You are required to make eye contact and really feel you are talking to each individual in the theatre. Keep your mind on personalizing your needs and communicating your objective and you can reach every member of the audience.

A soliloquy is a monologue that takes the form of an internal dialogue. Because soliloquies usually occur when a character is in internal conflict, the soliloquy can be seen as one side of you talking to the other. When two sides of the same person are at war within, you need to define each side of the character's divided self. You need to know which one is talking and

Figure 14.1 Ed Asner in Garson Kanin's *Born Yesterday*. Observe the reaction to the imaginary voice on the phone. (Photo—Peter Cunningham.)

which is listening. Words said to the air cannot be said purposefully. Even if you are alone, you must still talk to someone. You need to hear the inner voices and respond to them.

Once you have determined the nature of your imaginary other and developed a communication channel, work on a monologue or soliloquy follows the same process as work on a character in a scene. Analysis, personalization, scoring the beats, searching for actions, developing character, and blocking all proceed in the same manner. One element is heightened—the need to fill the theatrical space solo. This emphasizes the importance of the centered and energized performance that is the natural foundation of our work.

Working with a Director

The relationship between actor and director is a personal one. Because its nature varies with the personalities involved, this discussion will only deal with the general expectations within the creative situation.

The director controls schedules and rehearsals and is the ultimate arbiter of the interpretation of the play and the final production values. These are givens that you must accept. The amount of input given by the actor will depend on individual situations. Most modern directors have great respect for well-trained actors and see the rehearsal process as a collaborative effort. In turn, many actors develop a healthy attitude toward the director's rule by defining their job in terms of the effective realization of the director's concept. The actor who says, "I pride myself in seeing how fully I can give the director what he or she wants," is one who can work well in varied situations. If you know your technique, you can continue to work constructively on your acting under any conditions. Just work through each step in the rehearsal process.

Although most actor-director relationships are creative and nurturing, it is possible to realize early on that your artistic differences with a director are so great that you cannot accept the interpretation of the play or any direction given. The best thing to do in such a case is to have a frank discussion with the director in which you will either find an arena for compromise or decide to leave the cast. You cannot stay in a production and defy the director or the esprit de corps will be ruined for everyone.

Sometimes directors will ask for qualities and results. You may hear comments like "play it angrier," "do it faster," or "I'd like you to look happy." You must always remember that your job is not just to deliver the results but to find an internal justification for them. If you're told to be angrier, find something in the scene to justify it. The same thing holds for stage directions. If you're requested to move stage right when X enters, then you need to find a reason you want to move away from X. The ability to justify direction is the test of a creative and thinking actor.

Although the director sets the tone, pace, goals, and interpretation, the steps in the rehearsal process remain the same. The first meeting is usually a round-table reading and discussion of the play in which the director imparts the overall vision, including a thematic analysis and statement of the superobjective for the production. Actors begin discussing individual character's superobjectives, a subject continued during smaller scene rehearsals. Slowly the play moves through personalization, action exploration, to blocking. You will gradually develop your character as you work. Visual elements appear along the way and are all present for the first time during a technical dress rehearsal. The stage manager will keep a score of beats and actions for the play, but you are expected to have a score for your character which you must study and learn as blocking is set. If you have learned to take an undirected scene from reading to performance, you should have little difficulty adapting to working with a director.

Summary

We have explored the basic principles of acting technique, but this is only the beginning. To continue in the theatre requires more training: honing the skills you have, learning new ones, keeping your voice and body in condition, incorporating everyday experience into your range of creative expression. You have found the freedom to act, and now you must maintain it.

You have experienced acting technique as an organic process in which thought and feeling are expressed through physical energy. This has demanded discipline and hard work. Look back through your journals and trace your path of personal growth and insight. Remember those first difficult steps of self-assessment and how you chipped away at the inhibitions limiting your expression. And never, never forget the moment that everything started to come together, when you experienced for the first time the magic—there is no other word—that only an actor can feel and exude.

To act is to play. To play we must be free. To be free we need understanding and faith. These are the lessons of this book. You have come a long way in our work together. Now enjoy feeling free to act!

Glossary of Theatrical Terms

action Purposeful activity directed toward achieving an objective.

adjustment A change in action or objective in relation to a change in given circumstances.

affective memory The recalling of details surrounding an event in an actor's life to reawaken personal emotions.

alignment Balanced arrangement of the skeletal structure that permits efficient counteraction to the force of gravity.

articulation The shaping of sound into speech.

beat A unit of dramatic action reflecting a single objective.

blocking The pattern of movement on the stage.

build The physicalization of the rising dramatic action.

business Small actions with props or as characteristic gesture.

center The point of convergence of the muscular, respiratory, emotional, and intellectual impulses within the body.

centering The integration of respiratory, muscular, emotional, and intellectual impulses into a single source.

climax The point of highest intensity in the dramatic action.

conflict Tension between opposing forces in the dramatic situation.

constructive rest position A relatively stressless position of the body in which physical weights are counterbalanced.

costume props Costume accessories used by the actor for stage business.

downstage The area of a proscenium stage closest to the audience.

dramatic action The movement of a play toward its superobjective.

dramatic function The relationship of a character to the through-action of a play.

emotional recall See *affective memory.*

endowment The projection of emotional values onto people, places, or things.

250

genre   A type or category of drama such as comedy, tragedy, farce, and so forth.

gesture   Movement associated with a character's psychology.

given circumstances   The conditions—the *who, what, where* and *when*—of the dramatic situation.

hand props   Objects handled by the actor on stage.

improvisation   The enacting of a dramatic situation in which actors are free to create text and action.

indication   The external display of an emotion without inner justification.

inner action   The actor's process of thought through which actions and objectives are justified within the dramatic situation.

intention   See *objective*.

justification   The reason for a character's behavior.

kinesthetic awareness   The perception of the relationship between our muscles and bones. The sense of our body in space.

line reading   A spoken action expressed through the inflection, tone, rhythm, or tempo of a line in order to achieve an objective.

listening   The process through which an actor reacts to other characters as if hearing their lines and meaning for the first time.

magic *if*   The ability to act as "if" the imaginary dramatic circumstances were real.

mannerism   A gesture reflecting the psychology of character.

moment   The smallest section of dramatic action reflecting a complete cycle of communication.

movement   The displacement of the body through space.

motivation   The psychological reason for a character's desires and objectives.

neutral   A ready state of the body that prepares the actor for action and reaction. A physical state free of personal psychology that serves as a base for characterization.

objective   The goal or purpose of a character at any moment in the dramatic situation that drives the action. What a character wants.

obstacle   What is in the way of objectives and actions.

personal prop   Props that are carried by a particular character.

personalization   The process of making the dramatic situation personally meaningful to an actor.

physicalization   The expression of the dramatic situation through the body and voice.

plot   The arrangement of events and the development of the dramatic action in a play.

point of attention   What the actor is focusing on.

properties, or props   Objects used for dressing the stage or for stage business by the actor.

psychophysical action   Purposeful action that enables an actor to connect to the emotional content of the drama.

psychological gesture An archetypal gesture expressing a character's main desire.

purpose See *objective.*

relaxation The absence of physical tension that blocks movement, voice or feeling.

resonator The bony structures that vibrate and give tone to the voice.

resonance The tonal quality of the voice.

scene A unit of dramatic action that serves to advance the through-action of a play.

score The actor's record of beats and actions that create a role.

sense memory The process of recalling an experience through detailed attention to sensory data.

spine The purpose that drives the dramatic action of a play. See *super-objective.*

stage left The area of the stage to the left of an actor when facing the audience.

stage right The area of the stage to the right of an actor when facing the audience.

story The events in a drama.

style The manner of presenting reality on stage.

substitution The replacement of dramatic characters, events, and objects with meaningful people, events, or things from an actor's personal life.

subtext Thoughts and feelings that lie beneath the lines through which an actor creates the inner life of a character.

superobjective The main goal of a play or character that drives the dramatic action of the plot or the through-action of a character.

tactical action Action aimed at achieving an objective.

taking in The ability to let the actions and words of other characters affect you and provoke an emotional and physical response.

theme The main idea of a play.

through-line The series of actions that lead a character toward the fulfillment of the superobjective. Also called through-action or through-line of action.

upstage The area of a proscenium stage away from the audience.

vulnerability The ability to be touched by other characters and the imaginary circumstances.

warm-up A series of physical and vocal exercises that prepare the body to act.

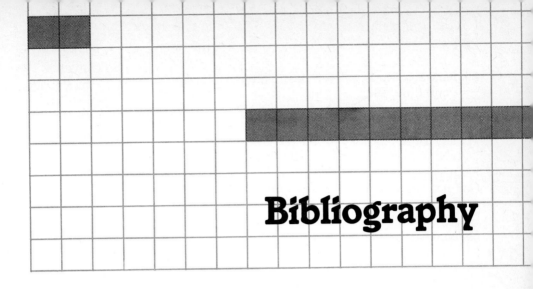

Bibliography

Alexander, F. Mathias. *The Resurrection of the Body*. Edited by Edward Maisel. New York: Dell, 1971.

———. *The Uses of the Self*. Long Beach: Centerline Press, 1984.

Aristotle. *On Poetry and Style*. Translated by G. M. A. Grube. Indianapolis: Liberal Arts Press, 1958.

Artaud, Antonin. *The Theatre and its Double*. Translated by Mary Carline Richards. New York: Grove Press, 1958.

Barker, Sarah. *The Alexander Technique*. New York: Bantam Books, 1981.

Barrault, Jean-Louis. *The Theatre of Jean-Louis Barrault*. Translated by Joseph Chiari. London: Barrie and Rockliff, 1961.

———. *Souvenirs pour demain*. Paris: Editions du Seuil, 1972.

Barton, Robert. *Acting On Stage and Off*. New York: Holt, Rinehart and Winston, 1989.

Benedetti, Robert. *The Actor at Work*. Englewood Cliffs, N.J.: Prentice Hall, 1986.

Berry, Cicely. *Voice and the Actor*. New York: Macmillan, 1973.

Boleslavsky, Richard. *Acting: The First Six Lessons*. New York: Theatre Arts Books, 1933.

Brook, Peter. *The Empty Space*. New York: Atheneum, 1984.

Chaikin, Joseph. *The Presence of the Actor*. New York: Atheneum, 1972.

Chekhov, Michael. *To the Actor*. New York: Harper and Row, 1953.

Clurman, Harold. *On Directing*. New York: Collier, 1974.

Cohen, Robert. *Acting Power*. Palo Alto: Mayfield Publishing, 1978.

———. *Acting Professionally*. Palo Alto: Mayfield Publishing, 1981.

Cole, Toby and Helen Chinoy, eds. *Actors on Acting*. New York: Crown Publishers, 1970.

Dullin, Charles. *Souvenirs et notes de travail d'un acteur*. Paris: Odette Lieutier, 1946.

Feldenkrais, Moshe. *Awareness Through Movement*. New York: Harper and Row, 1972.

————. *Body and Mature Behavior*. New York: International Universities Press, 1983.

Felner, Mira. *Apostles of Silence: The Modern French Mimes*. Cranbury, N. J.: Associated University Presses, 1985.

Fergusson, Francis. *The Idea of a Theater*. New York: Anchor, 1953.

Goffman, Erving. *The Presentation of Self in Everyday Life*. Garden City: Doubleday, 1959.

Goldman, Michael. *An Actor's Freedom*. New York: Viking, 1975.

Gorchakov, Nikolai M. *Stanislavski Directs*. New York: Funk and Wagnall's, 1954.

Grotowski, Jerzy. *Towards a Poor Theatre*. New York: Simon and Schuster, 1968.

Guthrie, Tyrone. *Tyrone Guthrie on Acting*. New York: Viking, 1971.

Hagan, Uta. *Respect for Acting*. New York: Macmillan, 1973.

Herrigel, Eugen. *Zen in the Art of Archery*. New York: Pantheon, 1953.

Hornby, Richard. *Script into Performance*. New York: Paragon House, 1987.

James, William. *Psychology: Briefer Course*. New York: Collier Books, 1962.

King, Nancy. *A Movement Approach to Actor Training*. Englewood Cliffs, N.J.: Prentice Hall, 1981.

————. *Theatre Movement*. New York: Drama Book Publishers, 1971.

Ladefoged, Peter. *A Course in Phonetics*. New York: Harcourt Brace Jovanovich, 1975.

Lessac, Arthur. *The Use and Training of the Human Voice*. New York: Drama Book Publishers, 1967.

Lewis, Robert. *Advice to the Players*. New York: Harper and Row, 1980.

————. *Method or Madness*. New York: Samuel French, 1958.

Linklater, Kristin. *Freeing the Natural Voice*. New York: Drama Book Publishers, 1976.

May, Rollo. *The Courage to Create*. New York: Bantam Books, 1985.

Meisner, Sanford. *On Acting*. New York: Vintage Books, 1987.

Mekler, Eva. *The New Generation of Acting Teachers*. New York: Viking Penguin, 1987.

Moore, Sonia. *The Stanislavski System*. New York: Penguin Books, 1965.

Munk, Erika, ed. *Stanislavski and America*. Greenwich: Fawcett Premier Books, 1967.

Olivier, Laurence. *Confessions of an Actor*. New York: Simon and Schuster, 1982.

————. *On Acting*. New York: Simon and Schuster, 1986.

Sabatine, Jean. *The Actor's Image: Movement Training for Stage and Screen*. Englewood Cliffs, N.J.: Prentice Hall, 1983.

Saint-Denis, Michel. *The Rediscovery of Style*. New York: Theatre Arts Books, 1960.

————. *Training for the Theatre*. New York: Theatre Arts Books, 1982.

Spolin, Viola. *Improvisation for the Theater*. Evanston: Northwestern University Press, 1970.

Stanislavski, Constantin. *An Actor Prepares*. Translated by Elizabeth Reynolds Hapgood. New York: Theatre Arts Books, 1936.

————. *Building a Character*. Translated by Elizabeth Reynolds Hapgood. New York: Theatre Arts Books, 1977.

————. *Creating a Role*. Translated by Elizabeth Reynolds Hapgood. New York: Theatre Arts Books, 1961.

————. *My Life in Art*. Translated by J. J. Robbins. New York: Theatre Arts Books, 1948.

————. *On Opera*. Translated by Elizabeth Reynolds Hapgood. New York: Theatre Arts Books, 1974.

Strassberg, Lee. *A Dream of Passion*. Boston: Little, Brown, 1987.

Todd, Mabel Elsworth. *The Thinking Body*. Brooklyn: Dance Horizons, 1959.

Willet, John. *The Theatre of Bertolt Brecht*. New York: New Directions, 1959.

Wilson, Edwin. *The Theater Experience*. 4th ed. New York: McGraw-Hill, 1988.

Young, Stark. *The Theatre*. 1927. Reprint, New York: Hill and Wang, 1958.

Index